Theories of Social Change

Theories of Social Change

A Critical Appraisal

RAYMOND BOUDON
Translated by J. C. Whitehouse

University of California Press
Berkeley and Los Angeles

First published in the United States by the University of California Press, 1986.

Original edition © Presses Universitaires de France, 1984. This English translation © Polity Press, 1986.

Library of Congress Cataloging in Publication Data

Boudon, Raymond
  Theories of social change.

  Translation of: La place du désordre.
  1. Social change.   I. Title.
  HM101.B66413   1986   303.4   86-40186
  ISBN 0-520-05759-7 (alk. paper)

Phototypeset by Dobbie Typesetting Service, Plymouth
Printed in Great Britain by
T. J. Press, Padstow

Contents

Foreword

Between 1950 and 1980 the social sciences – sociology, economics and political science – produced a considerable number of 'theories of social change'. Since they did not constitute a homogeneous unity, one of our first tasks is to establish and clarify their aims and indicate their major types.

The general impression prevailing in much current writing is that such theories have failed. Most of the predictions based on them have been proved false by reality. They have generated representations of social systems which are not only simplified – which is legitimate – but simplistic. And most of the macroscopic regularities which they put forward as generally valid now seem only locally so.

It is therefore quite understandable that they have ultimately given rise to scepticism. But this scepticism, though widespread, is far from unanimous, and theories of 'change', 'dependence', 'modernization' or 'development' are still put forward. The old law of the vicious circle of poverty, for example, has recently been brought out of its temporary obscurity, dusted off and polished up by Galbraith.[1] We also still believe – no doubt as a result of giving undue general validity to a proposition put forward by de Tocqueville and T. H. Marshall amongst others – that the evolution of societies implies a higher degree of participation in political life by the general run of citizens, but do not perceive that this development may well go hand in hand with greater despotism. At the same time, there are others who seek to prove, for instance, that social conflicts in 'post-industrial' societies are bound to bring into conflict very specific classes competing for control of the way history is to go. As a final example, we could consider the by no means negligible number of historians, sociologists

1

and economists who currently accept the false proposition that Third-World countries are underdeveloped because they are *dependent*.

So it may well be time to take a *critical* look at theories of social change. By this I mean that we should try to establish exactly what questions they are trying to answer and under what conditions such questions can be answered in a potentially valid way.

Karl Popper set himself very much the same kind of task as that contemplated here in his *The Poverty of Historicism*.[2] That book was a *critical* work in the rigorously Kantian sense of the word: Popper tried to show that certain propositions and theories relating to social change must be seen as scientific and others as metaphysical, that certain questions are formulated in such a way as to be unanswerable, while others admit of answers whose validity can be rigorously tested. Popper's debt to Kant is so clear in this work that it is even evident in the way he sets out his case. Like Kant before him, he develops his arguments with practically no recourse to examples of any kind.

There are two reasons why we should now take another look at the questions Popper raised. The first is that in the meantime a substantial corpus of theories concerning social change has appeared which, like those Popper criticized without naming them, are not susceptible to verifiable answers. The second is that a critical analysis of such theories makes it possible to refine and sharpen Popper's diagnosis and in particular to modify his famous distinction between metaphysical and scientific theories.

It may seem surprising to find a 'professional sociologist' interested in reflecting on matters that have more to do with the philosophy of the social sciences. I believe, however, that critical reflection is the path that has to be taken if there is to be any scientific progress. The sense of failure of theories of social change felt by many observers is a fact, and analysing it is more than merely speculative interest. Going beyond mere scepticism and trying to understand the reasons for that failure more clearly means being in a position to make more sense of what stands in the way of knowledge. Rather as investigating an accident gives a better understanding of traffic conditions, investigating failures in the scientific field can contribute to the progress of knowledge. Such investigations may be regarded as part of both the methodology and the philosophy of science. Moreover the *philosophical* questions I have raised in this book seem to me important not only from a philosophical and scientific, but also from a *political* point of view, since a good number of theories of social change, such as those of development or dependence, have had practical consequences precisely because they enjoy or have enjoyed scientific authority. For, even though strictly speaking they are not false, these theories claim a logical status they are not really entitled to and hence give rise to interpretations and beliefs that are not logically implied by them. That is one more reason for attempting to understand the criticism to which they have been subjected.

Finally, I should like to mention a more general reason. The various philosophies of science seldom concern themselves with the social sciences. Like physics or biology, however, the social sciences can throw some light on the way knowledge advances. The fact that the debates in the social sciences are more visible, the consensus more fragile and the questions they raise of a more 'public' nature is perhaps an advantage from the point of view of the philosophy of knowledge.

As will already be apparent, my aim here is in no way to draw up a balance sheet or an inventory of theories of social change, but simply to point out certain methodological and epistemological features.

The ideas I put forward here were first presented in a preliminary form in lectures at Mannheim (1979), Geneva (1979), London (Hobhouse Lecture, 1982, London School of Economics) and New York (Lazarsfield Lecture, 1983, Columbia University).

1

Theories of Social Change

Some years ago the historian of the social sciences, Robert Nisbet, brought out a book called *Social Change and History* which sparked off an old argument once more.[1] The sense of the title really hinges on the word 'and', which in fact means 'as opposed to' or 'versus', and calling the work *History versus Social Change* or *For History and against Social Change* would have given a clearer idea of what it was about. In summary, and hence in a simplified form, Nisbet's main thesis was that there can be no reflection on, theory of, or investigation into social change which is in any major way distinguishable from the intellectual activity we normally call history.

This thesis caused considerable controversy. As long as the social sciences have existed (institutionally speaking, of course, since intellectually speaking they have existed for a very long time and perhaps even since the very earliest ages), they have seen social exchange as one of their basic concerns, although, of course, it has had different names at different times. Today, we can no more imagine a textbook or treatise in the social sciences without a chapter on social change than a book on statistics without a chapter on the traditional distributions. The notion of social change has now come to mean, if not a speciality of the social sciences, at least an activity and an orientation of research and fundamental reflection. This activity, which has been seen as both legitimate and essential, has been very productive: we now have a whole range of results that can be described as theories of social change.

But Nisbet challenged its legitimacy, taking to task one or two outstanding people, Parsons in particular. Through them, however, he was really attacking a whole line of research. In his view, the theories of social change put forward by sociologists and political

5

scientists as well as economists or demographers (for there is no reason why Nisbet's criticisms should apply to one group rather than another) fall basically into two categories. The first category includes a whole range of false or, more generally, unacceptable theories. The second category includes a series of products which we can, if we are determined enough, describe as theories of social change, but which are not distinguishable from those processes of interest to historians. Theories of social change, indeed even the very notion of it, affirm the existence of a pattern of investigation and thinking that owes nothing to history. In Nisbet's view, this claim is without foundation. History exists as a legitimate discipline; theories of social change do not.

I do not want to spend too long on the arguments Nisbet adduced in support of his thesis at this point. We shall have occasion to come back to them and discuss them explicitly or implicitly at several stages of this book. His attitude did not fail to arouse protest, of course. In the leading American sociological journal, Lenski published an article on 'History and Social Change', turning Nisbet's title round.[2] Lenski reiterated one or two obvious points, namely that beyond the sound and fury of history and the complicated nature of change (as a singular noun) it was not hard to detect changes (in the plural) constantly moving in the same direction. Could one doubt that knowledge, population growth and urbanization had all developed and increased? In short, Lenski not only reaffirmed the legitimacy of the idea of social change, but tried to restore to its former status a notion – that of evolution – that had become a little time-worn over the years. From Comte to Durkheim and Spencer to Hobhouse, that idea had held an eminent place in the social sciences but had subsequently become seriously discredited.[3] In the early 1960s, the anthropologists Sahlins and Service nevertheless tried to give it a new lease of life by suggesting a distinction between two concepts of evolution, on the one hand *unilinear*, on the other *multilinear*.[4] Only the former, they maintained, needed to be scrapped. The view of human history as moving inexorably on to some kind of omega point was obviously untenable, as was also the idea that any particular society should follow the general course of history. Nor could one accept the idea that the various elements of evolution should all progress at the same rate. Technology could advance at a faster pace than scientific knowledge, and industrialization did not necessarily entail the democratic organization of political power. All this meant that a unilinear notion of evolution (which was by and large what the nineteenth century, using a less scientific and more popular linguistic register, called 'progress') was, according to Sahlins and Service, untenable.

The second kind of development, however, which they described as *multilinear*, was useful. There were many paths, and the goal was rather vague, but the destination was visible if blurred. Lenski adopted this theory for the purposes of his argument, using the undeniable fact that there are incontrovertibly such things as partial changes moving in a particular direction to defend the legitimacy of a theory of social change quite separate from history against the attack mounted on it by Nesbit. The declared aim of the theorists of social change, their nomological, or in Piaget's famous phrase their 'nomothetic' ambition,[5] was therefore not without basis, despite Nisbet's strictures.

Nisbet and Lenski are not names which spring immediately to mind when discussing the major theoretical arguments in the social sciences, despite the fact that both have written important books. Nisbet's *The Sociological Tradition* is one of the best histories of the social sciences currently available, even if some aspects of it are open to argument.[6] Lenski's *Power and Privilege* is considered to be a classic work on the theory and history of social stratification.[7] The former's reticence where any form of evolutionism is concerned is very evident in his book. For him, sociology is not, as it was for Comte, the ultimate and most complex of sciences, only possible at an advanced stage of historical evolution, but the result of a movement of thought and ideas which is itself linked to historical jolts. It came into being, in his view, at a time of romantic and traditionalist reaction to the French Revolution, which had been closely linked to the Enlightenment. The same rejection of evolutionism is apparent in both *Social Change and History* and *The Idea of Progress*, where progress is seen as an idea which comes and goes according to times and circumstances.[8]

On the other hand Lenski, in his *Power and Privilege*, staunchly defends the idea that the history of stratification moves in a certain direction. Thus it is not surprising to find him taking up arms against a book that sets out to attack not only evolutionism but the very notion of social change.

There thus seems no doubt that in the positions taken up by these two authors we can make out the presence of an abiding philosophical attitude or *Weltanschauung*, even though their respective conclusions for or against the idea of change and evolution are based on a precise train of argument. Does this mean that it is impossible to come down on one side or the other?

My main reason for introducing the discussion to which this book is intended to contribute by means of the Lenski–Nisbet debate is the fact that, as far as I am aware, that particular debate is the most recent manifestation of an ongoing argument. To put it more precisely, I have done so because it raises, in terms related to the present situation in the social sciences, the basic epistemological question as to whether there are regular patterns in social change. The same question had been repeatedly asked by others before Nisbet and Lenski, of course. By Schumpeter, for instance, when in his *History of Economic Analysis* he discusses the contribution of what he calls 'historical sociology', declaring quite explicitly that in his view the term is synonymous with a much older one, the philosophy of history. He does imply, however, that although 'historical sociology' might sound much better to his contemporaries, it still raises the same epistemological problems as 'the philosophy of history'. He does not deal with these explicitly, although the way he judges Condorcet severely and praises Montesquieu gives a fairly clear idea of where his preferences lie. His great merit is that he points out the fact that the same problems can appear in many guises.

Following Schumpeter's line of argument and discussion, we might wonder whether the idea of social change perhaps simply raises under a different heading the same problems as those presented by the once-flourishing notions of historical sociology and the philosophy of history. One observation might lead me to answer yes to this question. At the beginning of this century Georg Simmel,[10] discussing epistemological problems associated with the field of the 'philosophy of history' in his *The Problems of the Philosophy of History*, developed arguments of which some, albeit differently expressed, reappear in Nisbet's work. Whereas Simmel vigorously attacks Ranke's 'realism', however, Nisbet praises it and urges the social sciences to pay attention to it. (We shall return to this question in chapter 7.)

So perhaps the notion of social change is only a modern reincarnation of History with a capital H, and theories of social change no more than a resurrection of the philosophy of history. Did not Pareto declare that in social terms the prime condition for bringing an old idea back to life was to express it in such a new way that it was difficult to spot its ancestry?

I shall not return to the possible, and in my own view probable, relationship between Simmel's philosophy of history, Schumpeter's historical sociology and Nisbet's theories of social change. I shall restrict myself to theories of social change or, to put it in another and perhaps preferable way, to the analysis of social change in the contemporary social sciences, in particular sociology. I must stress, however, that the philosophical–and more specifically the epistemo-logical–questions that can be raised (and that Lenski and Nisbet do raise) with regard to the idea of social change and theories of it are very likely akin to those that Simmel raised at the turn of the century in connection with the philosophy of history.

A PROGRAMME: THEORIES OF SOCIAL CHANGE

By 'research programme' the philosopher of science Imre Nakatos meant the general mental pattern guiding the scientific subcom-munities in their research.[11] Cartesian metaphysics, that is, the mechanistic view of the universe as something like an enormous clock (and a system of vortices) is an example of such a programme. Classical economics, which ditinguishes between categories of economic agents according to their function, sees work as the basis of value and aims basically at analysing the phenomena of growth, is another. It is in contrast to the neo-classical programme, which sees no difference between various kinds of economic agents, makes utility the principle of value and sets itself the primary task of accounting for economic equilibrium. Similarly, theories of social change are, or rather imply, a programme (of a kind that Lenski advocates and Nisbet rejects).

Considered at its most extreme level of generality, this programme is based on the postulate that it is possible to make interesting, verifiable and *nomothetic* statements about social change: in other words, propositions not limited in validity to a specific place and time, but having a wider and more general bearing.

A definition of this kind is obviously too abstract to be of any use. It is as hard to define theories of social change in a sentence or two as it is to flesh out the programme of Cartesian metaphysics or classical economics in a few well-chosen words. It is more to the point and more useful, when we are trying to define something as abstract and complicated as a programme, to take a group of theories of social control and to see what the elements of this pseudo-sample have to tell us about the objectives they reveal and the principles they put into practice.

In my view, such an analysis would enable us to distinguish four or five main types of theories of social change. I say four or five, as one of the types, as we shall see, includes two variants. In every case, the objective of the programme is to bring out regular patterns or show their existence. The form and nature of these regular patterns, however, vary from type to type. A succinct description of these four or five types of theories, with supporting examples, will make it possible to describe the crudest features of the implicit programme common to theories of social change.

Type 1

The aim of certain of these theories is to point out and show the existence of more or less general and irreversible trends. It is supposed, for example, that the division of labour will become increasingly sophisticated, that modern societies will have ever larger bureaucracies, that relationships between individuals are doomed to become more and more impersonal, and so on. It is not hard to imagine any number of propositions of the same kind. These are nowadays widely called trends, but in earlier days, when Simmel was writing his *Problems* or even when Popper published his *Poverty of Historicism*, it was more usual to talk of the laws of history.[12] The growing influence of statistics in the social sciences has helped to bring about the present situation, in which a technical concept originally created to describe chronological series has dressed an old idea in new clothes. Statistically speaking, what is left when cycles of all lengths have been eliminated from a chronological series is a *trend*. When, for instance, seasonal, annual or longer fluctuations are removed from a graph showing the volume of imports, there remains a *trend* towards a fall, an increase or indeed a stable flow.

But it is one thing to observe empirically that imports are tending to rise or fall and another to suggest that, for example, one of the basic trends in modern societies is for impersonal relationships to increase markedly, or, in the language of Parsons, for universalist-type to replace personalist-type relationships. Showing trends in the field of the volume of imports is a matter of applying simple and relatively reliable procedures. The second proposition, on the other hand, is based on an intuitive interpretation of impressions resulting from ill-defined data that is difficult to verify. Between these two extreme examples, many intermediary ones can be envisaged. This observation entails an essential conclusion, which is that we must make a distinction between the technical precision of a concept (for example, the idea of a trend) and the accuracy of the data to which it is applied.

In this first type we should probably include statements affirming the existence of *stages* (which Comte called *états*) destined to appear in a certain order. Here, of course, the example that springs readily to mind is that of the law of the three stages. Although it is fashionable nowadays to reject statements of this kind, we should not forget that not so very long ago Rostow attempted to show that economic growth had to pass through a number of phases, the famous 'stages of growth'.[13] More recently, the theory of demographic transition put forward the idea that the demographic regime in modern societies would necessarily follow a three-stage process of transformation: first, a fall in the death-rate with no fall in the birth-rate, followed by a stable death-rate and a falling birth-rate leading to a stage of decelerated growth, and finally the stage of stable demographic growth.[14] In his book on class and class conflict, Dahrendorf maintained in the early 1960s that social conflict in industrial societies would less and less often be class conflicts.[15] With the help of social mobility and other 'factors' class conflicts would, Dahrendorf thought, inevitably become less important and give way to new types of conflicts involving the sharing of authority and influence. Some time later, G. Wright Mills was claiming that a phase of economic growth and increased social mobility would be followed by one in which social mobility would become stable and class conflicts would therefore make their appearance once more.[16] Political affiliations would also become more strongly class based. If we put Dahrendorf's and Mills's analyses together (and find it acceptable to combine their findings), we have a sort of law of the three stages leading back to square one after we reach the third stage. Other theories, which research of an 'archaeological' nature (in Michel Foucault's sense of the word) would probably trace back beyond Comte to Saint-Simon, stress the claims of *successive* groups to lead society. First the workers, then the technical experts. First the holders of capital, then the guardians of knowledge. In a like manner, there are those who think that whereas the conflicts in industrial societies set the workers against 'the functionaries of capital', those in post-industrial societies set the functionaries of the media (the employees of the quaternary sector, as Daniel Bell calls them) against the dominant classes originating in industrial society. That, according to Alain Touraine, is the meaning of the events of 1968, which were a foretaste of the conflicts of post-industrial society, reflecting the fundamental 'contradiction' between the importance of information and knowledge in such societies and the low level of power given to workers in the quaternary sector. We can see that it would be easy to go on producing further examples of the laws of succession. The law of the three stages may not convince many people nowadays, but that does not stop the search for the stages of change being a very popular activity.

Type 2

Theories of the second type take the form of what are generally known as *conditional laws*, or propositions of the type 'if A, then B', or, if cast in a probabilist form, 'if A, then (usually) B'. In the very first sentence of the foreword to his *L'Ancien Régime et la Révolution*, de Tocqueville says that his plan was not to write a *history* of the French Revolution, but a '*study*'.[17] Beneath the apparent modesty of the term we can see a project and an aim, namely, to put forward, on the basis of processes occurring at a given time in a given place, propositions of wider scope and validity. In modern terms, his ambition was not to suggest another interpretation of the French Revolution, but to make a contribution to the theory of social change. That ambition shows itself in complex and diverse ways, and I do not intend to look at the question very fully here. It is worth pointing out, however, that much of his project is partly centred on an attempt to re-establish conditional laws. One of the best known of these could properly be called de Tocqueville's law of political mobilization, which says in effect that it most frequently happens that people who have uncomplainingly borne the most wearisome laws will reject them violently as soon as their burden is lightened.[18] We have a statement in the form 'if A, then (usually) B'. There is no need to insist on the importance of the law, which is attractive precisely because of its paradoxical nature. Common sense tends to tell us that a real improvement in an individual's situation will very likely make him or her more contented and more disposed to respect laws, institutions and political power. But de Tocqueville suggests that liberalizing a political society may meet the wishes of most of the population or at least major sections of it, but may chiefly serve to make it easier to express discontent and opposition.

The formulation of conditional laws is undeniably an important part of the implicit research programme to which theories of social change are linked. The theory of political mobilization provides many examples, and these are listed, presented and discussed in a frequently quoted article by James Davies.[19] Certain writers maintain that political mobilization, or more exactly political violence, develops chiefly when a period of constantly improving conditions is suddenly followed by one when things stand still or get worse. In this case, the implicit or explicit hypothesis is that regular growth creates expectations which are suddenly left unfulfilled when recession follows. Others take the view that collective violence is likely to occur when there is a fairly sudden and universal improvement. It might well be that this improvement makes it easier to protest, as de Tocqueville envisaged. It could also give rise to expectations that the system is incapable of fulfilling, as Durkheim thought.[20] Yet others suggest that collective violence is merely a function of a worsening of living conditions, in which individuals adapt their expectations to what the situation can offer but are particularly sensitive and likely to react to any downturn in it. There are also those who stress that a deterioration in living conditions may well produce demoralizations and apathy rather than mobilization.[21] The question arising is therefore to what extent these laws are compatible or complementary, or, to use an expression of Feyerabend's, 'commensurable'.[22] That question, however, I shall leave to one side for the moment. I shall have the opportunity to return to it later.

The search for conditional laws does not of course only take place in the field of political mobilization. Indeed, it is a basic pattern in the theory of the 'social change' programme. A famous 'law' owing its origins to Parsons suggests, for example, that the effect of industrialization is to make the nuclear family of the couple and their children the normal or modal type.[23] This is seen as the result of a modification of the system of the division of labour and the processes by which social status is acquired by industrialization. Whereas in 'traditional' societies status is generally *ascribed*, in 'modern' ones it tends to be *achieved*. Thus, in many traditional societies, a peasant's son inherits a plot of land and works it, and his entire acquisition of skills takes place within the family milieu. An engineer's son on the other hand has to *acquire* his status, first by obtaining one of the qualifications the education system offers and then by looking for a job, which may be at a distance from his home. Parsons contends that when these partial mechanisms are taken together a convergent effect is produced, the extended family collapses and the nuclear family model develops. This analysis thus leads one to suppose the existence of a conditional law (i.e., when a process of industrialization occurs it tends to have as an effect the nuclearization of the family) whose validity, it is assumed, is not limited to a single field of application. Parsons may have drawn up his famous law on the basis of a study of a single society, that of North America, but the logical structure of his analysis implies that its area of validity is greater than that. Similarly, de Tocqueville's 'law' of political mobilization may have been the result of analysing a particular set of temporal and spatial phenomena, but by the logical nature of its reasoning it implies a desire for general applicability. What we might call its *area of validity* goes beyond the phenomena on which it is based.

The subprogramme which we could call 'the search for conditional laws' contains a basic variant that should be pointed out clearly at this stage. We can talk of 'structural' rather than 'conditional' laws when in statements of the type 'if A, then B' or 'if A, then (usually) B', element A describes not one single condition or variable (which, as in the case of 'industrialization', may be of a composite nature, i.e., the result of a combination of elementary variables) but a *system* of variables. The distinction between conditional and structural laws cannot always be completely rigorously described, but there are certainly intermediate cases between the two categories. Nevertheless, it is a useful one.

Let us consider an example. Neo-Marxist theories of social change are traditionally concerned to analyse the stability or instability of particular systems of conditions of production. Thus, they generally put forward the idea that a semi-feudal system tends to be stable. In a system of this kind, the tenant of the land is legally free to sell his or her labour but is usually constantly in debt to the owner, who is often reluctant to see innovations brought in that might increase the productivity of the land or of labour.[24] It is indeed likely that an increase in productivity would lead to an increase in the tenant farmer's income and perhaps to a reduction of his debt. The landlord may therefore be afraid that the increase in his income due to increased productivity would not make up for the fall in his profits from usury. From this it follows that in conditions of production of a semi-feudal type, technical innovation is very likely to be rejected. The corollary is that the system of forces and conditions of production in this more or less self-perpetuating system will almost certainly persist unless some *exogenous* event or factor comes into play.

For the moment, we are not concerned with whether this theory is credible or not, and can come back to this question later. What is important is that its conclusion is of the type 'if A, then B'. The difference between this and the examples we have looked at so far is that here A is not a *single* variable, but a *system* of variables or characteristics that can be summed up in the phrase 'conditions of production of a semi-feudal type'.

We have already seen that the programme consisting of a search for conditional (and structural) laws was not limited to problems or areas involving particular interests, but was indeed of a very widely applicable nature. We have examined illustrations from the field of political mobilization. The example we have just examined belongs to the Marxist tradition in its general pattern and to the sociology of development in the field it deals with. It could be said that much of that tradition is concerned with discovering the implications of the structure of the conditions and forces involved in production in the field of changes in social systems. It would be wrong, however, to see that concern as the whole of what Schumpeter calls 'historical sociology'. All theories of economic (and political) development, whatever underlying intellectual tradition, Marxist or non-Marxist, they are based on, consist of a search for the dynamic implications of 'structures'. Theories of development often try to answer a question in the following form: given that a social system is characterized, at point t, by a structure S_t, what will be the state of that system at $t + 1$? The theory briefly discussed above is indeed an answer to just such a question. It produces the conclusion that if at t the structure is semi-feudal, (possible) innovation will (usually) be rejected at $t + 1$; the structure will perpetuate itself, the forces and conditions involved in production will be identical at $t + 1$ with what they were at t. In the same way, Nurkse's theory of the vicious circle of poverty, which was much in evidence in the 1960s, asserts that in the absence of any external stimulus a poor country at t is very likely to remain poor at t + 1, since poverty implies a negligible savings and investment capacity and consequently an almost total inability to increase productivity. Since the latter cannot increase, poverty will necessarily persist. As with the case of the preceding example, we shall not discuss the credibility or validity of the theory at this point. All we need do here is point out that whatever patterns or intellectual traditions they are associated with, theories of economic (and also political) development generally take the form of a search for structural laws.

Incidentally, it is worth noting that the first two types of theory are not always independent of each other or, more precisely, that statements about *trends* are often based on more or less explicit *conditional laws*. Thus, the trend towards an irreversible spread of bureaucracy is generally asserted on the basis of conditional laws in the form of 'if A, then B', dealing with the consequences of industrialization (A).

Type 3

The first two types of theory are characterized by conclusions or diagnoses which could be described as *empirical* (although whether or not they have a proper empirical basis remains an open question) in so far as they refer to certain states or stages of society, maintaining, for example, that in a semi-feudal system innovation will very likely be rejected, that if industrialization begins, the extended family tends to give way to the nuclear family, that when mobility stops increasing, social conflicts usually tend to take on the characteristics of class conflicts, and so on. In contrast, the third type of theory deals with the *form* and not the *content* of change. One or two brief examples will suffice here.

In his *The Structure of Scientific Revolutions*, the philosopher and historian of science Thomas Kuhn suggests that scientific progress generally follows a three-phase process.[25] In the first phase, that of 'normal science', a range of more or less coherent intellectual patterns, a 'paradigm', serves as a frame of reference for the community of researchers attached to this or that discipline or this or that branch of scientific activity. After a time, difficulties, or to use Kuhn's term, 'anomalies', begin to appear. Observational data which do not seem readily interpretable within the dominant paradigm are amassed. It would be nearer the truth to say that they contradict the theory or theories formulated within the framework of the paradigm. But that does not mean that those theories or the paradigm they are based on are suddenly rejected, since it takes time to think out, refine and launch a new paradigm. It is also likely that some researchers will have an interest in keeping the old one afloat and will try to adapt existing theories to make them compatible with the new data and able to absorb the anomalies. In the meantime, however, there is a danger that the latter will mount up. In the end, the paradigm will collapse like a house of cards, and the beneficiaries will be the theory or theories that have had the time and the opportunity to consolidate their position. In place of the conventional linear image of scientific development, Kuhn puts a contrasting schema of normal science/revolution/(new) normal science reminiscent to some degree of the famous Hegelian triad and the Hegelian–Marxist idea in which 'contradiction' is essential for change.

Is Kuhn's three-phase picture of science more or less acceptable than the traditional linear representation? One may have some doubts, but that is not the question we are dealing with at the moment. What is important is the *formal* nature of Kuhn's conclusions. They do not tell us *what* will change, but *how*, in what form and in what way change will occur. The reference to the Hegelian and Marxian dialectic brings out clearly the fact that the search for the *forms* of change is by no means a new activity. Kuhn's picture also shows that despite the (temporary?) disfavour that dialectics seems to have fallen into, the task to which it claimed to respond is still in progress.

It should also be pointed out incidentally that, just as Kuhn's success is explained by the fact that he offers a contrasting discontinuist and conflictual view of scientific development to the 'traditional' continuist one, Hegel's success was largely due to the fact that he provided a similar alternative to the continuist view of change proposed by certain Enlightenment philosophers, Condorcet in particular.

Kuhn is not an isolated example. Working in quite a different field and on quite another matter, Crozier has, for example, defended the idea that in France change was bound to take the form of long periods in which social change is contained, followed by periods of crisis.[26] The analysis on which this conclusion is based is not unlike that of Kuhn, although it relies on cultural hypotheses that have no equivalent in the latter's work. In Crozier's view, the cultural habits of the French mean that when a 'problem' appears in an organization,

everyone tries to adapt to the situation individually without seeking
to discuss it with others. Indeed, it hardly is 'a problem' at first.
Similarly, Kuhn's 'anomalies' only become proper anomalies when
it is collectively decided that the attempts to absorb them have been
fruitless, just as the problems raised by the functioning of an
organization only become problems when they pile up and make
the situation 'explosive', when individual adjustments are no longer
practicable or the 'environment' of the organization is affected. The
important point, however, is that both Kuhn and Crozier are putting
forward theories dealing with the *form* of certain processes.

Whether change in this or that field is continuist, discontinuist,
linear, cyclical and so on is obviously a question as old as thinking
about change. In their desire for an empirical and modern image,
the social sciences generally refuse to accept the way these questions
have been formulated by the philosophy of history. What sociologist
studying organizations, what historian of science, what political
scientist would look at the Hegelian dialectic, for example? But even
if they quarrel with the way they are formulated, the social sciences
do not reject the *questions* that the philosophy of history raises. That
is why it is important to note the close relationship between
contradictions and anomalies, the Hegelian triad and Kuhn's three-
phase sequence.

Type 4

The fourth type of theory deals with the *causes* or *factors* of change.
Because of the existence of causal feedback, the notion of cause can
be very ambiguous when it is used in the analysis of social change.
This can be shown by one or two examples. Let us suppose that
the government takes measure A. This causes reaction B, which leads
the government to modify measure A and introduce measure A' in
its place. In this very ordinary example of causal feedback, it is quite
legitimate to attempt to trace the causes of A', provided that in this
case one does not see A' as a single factor, as the government and
the reaction it produced are conjointly and inevitably also causes
of it. In other cases, it is quite impossible to impute a cause. A
government might be convinced that a political problem can be solved
by a measure of a *technical* nature. This is tried, but no technical
measure produces the desired result. It gradually dawns on the
government that a social and not a technical solution is what is

required. What is the cause of the new policy? The idea contained in essence in the proposition that a social solution is needed? The breakdown of the previous paradigm? Ultimately, questions of that kind are meaningless. The new policy is in fact the result of a process characterized by a linked series of actions, reactions or retroactions rather than of a cause or even of a group of causes. It is the end point of the whole of the process, and one cannot impute causality to one or more of the elements of that process.

The foregoing observation gives us a glimpse of some of the epistemological questions we shall encounter again later. A proposition such as 'A is the cause of B' is of course valid and unambiguous in certain cases. I can say fairly safely, for example, that bad weather caused a poor harvest, which in turn caused prices to rise. In other cases, however, propositions of the type 'A is the cause of B' are fraught with ambiguity. From this danger of ambiguity there arises a problem of *demarcation*, namely that of defining the circumstances in which propositions of that type can be taken as unambiguous.

For the time being, I shall simply note that despite this problem of demarcation the search for the causes and factors of change has always been and still is one of the objectives of the programme covering theories of social change. Max Weber's *The Protestant Ethic and the Spirit of Capitalism* is undeniably a very important book, but it is perhaps not his most polished or fault-free work, even though it is his best known and perhaps even his most popular. The reason for its success does not lie in the truth of its theoretical content, which we now know to need extensive revision and correction, or in its complexity, but perhaps rather in the fact that it has an anti-materialist conclusion. If the theoretical element is true, it shows that values can bring about changes in the conditions of production, reversing the relationship that Marx claimed to have established between the two terms.

Today's 'professional' sociologist will no doubt deem it suitable at this point to move away if discussions of this kind are broached once more in his or her presence, no doubt dismissing them as purely philosophical problems. And yet in the social sciences a fair proportion of all discussion is about nothing else. In the 1960s and earlier quite a number of development theorists were already talking about the influence of *values* on development. In the 1960s and 1970s, the way social systems worked was analysed on the assumption that it hinged on *socialization*, which not only ensured that values were transmitted from one generation to the next but also that social 'structures' (that is, class relationships) were 'reproduced', or made permanent. In the same decades, theorists of political development were reflecting on the part played by values and the machinery of the socialization process in maintaining and changing political or social systems. McClelland's *The Achieving Society* is a well-known study in this field. Its main argument is that in a hard-working and innovatory society, its members tend to attach great importance or value to achievement. Achieving socially approved aims and self-actualization would, in McClelland's view, always be the dominant values in a society of that kind. McClelland's book, it must be admitted, now seems a little old-fashioned, and his notion of achievement brings to the reader's mind almost without fail the image of the young, go-getting and ever-successful executive of the 1950s. Nevertheless, the explanatory diagram he uses is, apart from its actual content, the one used over a great area of the social sciences today. It is based on the postulate that 'ultimately' any social process is the result of behaviour inspired by notions or values interiorized by individuals during their socialization.

Other sociologists of other traditions see change (or the lack of it) as the product of structures. It depends, of course, on what is meant by structures. There are a number of possible ways of seeing them. In a recent highly analytical book, Cohen tried to show that productive forces should be regarded as the *primum mobile* of Marx's theory of history.[29] Earlier, Lynn White had also proposed this hypothesis, seeing technical innovation as the basis of social change.[30] The latter also admitted that innovation had no chance of being accepted if the circumstances were wrong. A metal ploughshare, for example, which is heavy to pull and cuts deep into the earth, cannot replace the swing plough if dwellings are scattered and each peasant has only a single puny ox. Thus the *primum mobile* is seen by some writers to be the productive forces, by others the conditions of production, and yet by others as technical progress. The list is not, of course, exhaustive.

All these discussions, which I have so far had to describe in the most summary form, are responses to a classical question. Put in its briefest terms, it asks what is the nature of the area of the real within which the factors of change are to be sought. Is it a matter of structures or institutions?[31] Of ideas or myths? Of one set of structural variables or another? Of productive forces or the conditions of production? The question is not often put in such an abrupt and open way, but it is implicit in many of the discussions and debates that go on. It would be more exact to say that many theories of social change take it for granted that, in the range of variables that can in theory be considered when analysing social change, certain subranges seem by and large more relevant than others. One of the points we shall consider later is whether a question of that kind is meaningful.

For the convenience of the reader, the four types of project covered by the programme subsuming theories of social change are summarized in table 1. Although it has not so far been specifically stated, they are obviously to be seen as interdependent. A body of work such as that of Marx involves taking up a position not only on the question of the causes or the forms of change, but also involves

Table 1 The anatomy of a programme: four types of theories of change

	Definitions	Examples
Type 1	The search for trends	Parsons: the trend towards universalism Comte: the three stages Rostow: the stages of growth
Type 2	(a) Conditional laws	Parsons: industrialization→ nuclear family Dahrendorf: industrialization→disappearance of *class* conflicts
	(b) Structural laws	Nurkse: vicious circle of poverty Bhaduri: reproductive nature of semi-feudal relations of production
Type 3	The forms of change	Hegelian triad Kuhn: scientific revolutions
Type 4	The causes of change	Weber: the Protestant ethic McClelland: the achieving society

statements in the form of conditional or structural laws. Other writers have adopted a more modest programme, sometimes dealing only with the search for such laws, but even in such cases these laws imply a position with regard to questions of the fourth type.

I think that the grid in table 1 would be fairly useful for anyone embarking on a *history* of theories of change. That is not my intention, since the problems on which I wish to cast some light are epistemological, or more precisely *critical*, rather than historical in nature, although the two aspects are linked.

AN ILLUSION?

The least one can say about the programme of theories of social change as just defined is that in Kuhn's words it is riddled with *anomalies*. Many of the *trends* apparently discovered seem not to be confirmed by the facts, and many of the conditional laws proposed seem to be contradicted, as it were, by subsequent research. A case-study may lead to the statement 'if A, then B'; further research might suggest 'if A, then not – B'. The same thing is likely to happen with structural laws. In the case of the causes and factors of change (or possibly the lack of change) any answer is a long time coming.

We have been told that industrialization demanded a family reduced to the conjugal nucleus and to children and adolescents. There is obviously at least an element of truth in the theory. It is also evident that in an agrarian society the means of work and social position are often transmitted from father to son, whereas the status of a teacher or a doctor is *acquired*. The latter fact means that the individual becomes more autonomous with regard to the family he or she springs from. It is, however, one thing to perceive such distinctions and quite another to conclude from them that there is a conditional law to the effect that 'if A (industrialization), then B (the nuclear family)'. What indicates that this is a *non sequitur* is simply the fact that in *certain* societies, as in Japan, industrialization has occurred with, rather than against, the extended family and has tended to strengthen it, at least over a long period.

We have been told that poor countries are doomed to remain poor, that there can be no development without an increase in productivity, no increase in productivity without investment, no investment without savings, and hence no development without foreign aid.[32]

Once again, there is an element of truth in each of these propositions. Increased productivity does indeed provide increased wealth. Investment does indeed presuppose that certain economic agents will not be forced to consume their resources immediately. Thus the theory is made up of propositions which are perfectly reasonable in themselves but nonsensical together. If the theory were true, Japan would not have undergone development, at least in the way it actually has done.

We have been told that the working population would be increasingly employed in ever more enormous and bureaucratic organizations, and yet it appears that the distribution by size of French and Italian firms has hardly varied since the beginning of the century.[33] The theory that bureaucracy will *inevitably* expand is also based on propositions that are quite reasonable when taken individually but lead to very dubious conclusions when taken together. We have been told that modernization brings secularization, but also that the twenty-first century will see a growth in religion. In addition, Max Weber had already pointed out that the very rapid industrialization of nineteenth-century America brought about a revival rather than a decline of Protestantism. We have been told that revolutions are likely both when a period of growth is suddenly followed by a period of recession and when a period of stagnation is followed by one of growth. It has also been suggested that revolutions may have nothing to do with economic indicators.

It has been claimed that the acquisition and extension of legal rights is followed by the extension of political and then of social ones, in that order.[34] Unfortunately, however, we are now obliged to admit that social rights can also be extended to the detriment of political rights, a situation which de Tocqueville, it seems, had already glimpsed. It has been predicted that falling mortality rates would be followed by a general decline in birth-rates and a subsequent ceiling in demographic growth. We were to expect, it seemed, to see social conflicts and political choices becoming increasingly separate from class divisions. Subsequently, it was forecast that class conflicts would return. Neither of these predictions seems to have been definitively proved true.

In short, many and perhaps most of the conditional laws put forward by the social sciences seem to be of dubious validity, and others much more restricted in their scope than had been thought. The examples I have given are of course in no way a sample. They are, however, well-known instances, and each in its time has attracted attention and sometimes commanded support and aroused enthusiasm.

It would be only too easy to lengthen the list, and so I propose to talk about just one study, which in my view provides conclusions giving rise to some interesting questions.

In 1930, Robert and Helen Lynd published *Middletown*, the findings of their still famous survey.[35] It is a classic in that it represents an innovation at the methodological level. The title speaks volumes. Middletown was both a real town and one that for a number of reasons seemed to the Lynds to typify middle America and to offer an opportunity to understand American society as an entity on the basis of a study of one particular place. They therefore decided to observe everything possible, using many surveys and making use of various kinds of observations. A few years later, they went back to the field and carried out the whole process again, publishing their findings in *Middletown in Transition*.[36] Half a century after the Lynds' first study, Theodore Caplow and his fellow workers returned to Middletown and repeated (with one or two variations) the surveys carried out in the earlier studies. Caplow's aim was to check the conjectures of theorists of social change in a limited but *typical* context. It turned out that Middletown *had* changed over 50 years, but not in the ways forecast by the theorists. The implications of that conclusion are so important that it is worth quoting Caplow *in extenso*:[37]

Contary to what various theories of social change had led us to expect, we observed no convergent tendencies towards wider equality, secularization, bureaucratization or depersonalization. Rather than an overriding tendency towards equalization, the data revealed considerably greater educational equality, a marked increase in inequality of income and a barely perceptible increase in the equality of socio-professional status over the years 1921 to 1937. With regard to secularization, there was a considerable increase in attendance at church and religious occasions, in the number of churches and, both absolutely and *per capita*, in the proportion of household income set aside for supporting religious institutions, as well as a noteworthy increase in the power and prestige of the churches. On the other hand, there was a decrease in the popularity of bible-reading, greater doubt about dogma, shorter religious services, less interest in religious instruction, a fall in the rate of religious endogamy (but an increase in the number of marriages in church) and increased religious tolerance (but more political activity on the part of religious organizations). Instead of a straightforward trend to bureaucratization, the local labour force was spread over smaller units. Federal offices, however, of which there were none in 1924, were doing brisk business on every street corner in 1977. Rather than increased mobility, the data show a decrease in residential mobility for working-class people, little change with regard to others, reduced migration and a decline in job mobility during careers, but increased professional mobility from one generation to another. As for depersonalization, it was found that in Middletown family ties were closer in 1977 than in 1924, with less meeting in lodges and clubs and more in civic associations, and less knowledge of leading local figures. The only coherent trend shown by the findings was the incoherence of partial trends.

The only consistent feature apparent in the findings was a trend towards inconsistency.

THREE RESPONSES

Our first reaction to the long catalogue of errors in the preceding section and to Caplow's observations might well be to see them as irrelevant. Parsons's theory of a correlation between family structures and industrialization may well be wrong. So too may be de Tocqueville's theory of how revolutions start. It does not follow, however, that a finite list of wrong laws means that we cannot formulate true ones.

We could counter Caplow by saying that *Middletown* has no bearing on the matter in hand. It is true that there was no clear trend towards bureaucratization and that at the end of the 1970s the working population was scattered over a greater number of on average smaller units than in the early 1920s, but that may well have been the result of chance factors. The way socio-economic activities are structured in a particular town may change in one way, whereas the same pattern on another scale – nationally, for example – may change in another. Middletown certainly cannot be seen as an autonomous system. Nevertheless, the discrepancies between what was observed and what had been conjectured on the basis of theories of change were also observed at many levels and in other contexts.

In order to eliminate the problems raised by Caplow and deal with the observations in the preceding section, we should have to be able to present not only the list of vague and wrong statements that it is fairly easy to draw up, but also a list, however short, of propositions that seem undeniably true. It is not a foregone conclusion that *that* would be an easy job.

There have of course always been writers who have suggested that appearances are deceptive or that we should sort out what matters from what does not, and there still are and always will be such people. 'Appearances' indicate that democracy is not the inevitable form of political organization in developed societies. Perhaps we only need to wait and see. They also indicate that socialism does not necessarily entail an extension of individual rights. But perhaps we have never had *real* socialism to date. They also tell us that societies change haphazardly, when anyone with half an eye can easily see that although things *may* seem to change, underlying structures remain the same. Japan developed with virtually no contacts with the outside world, but perhaps Japan's case was atypical and that of England typical in this respect. There is nothing very surprising or noteworthy in the fact that it is easy to use every rhetorical skill to 'show' that a theory of social change is possible, even if it is hard to propound even a handful of its tenets. What *is* remarkable is just how widespread and enduring the belief is that a theory of social change is possible, although it is difficult to state its first proposition.

Our second attitude might be one of scepticism, which is the one adopted by Robert Nisbet in his book referred to at the beginning of this chapter. The idea of social change implies that we must seek out the regular features of that change, discover the laws by which social systems develop and isolate typical processes. In Nisbet's view, however, the theorists of social change tend to be day-dreamers. They like to think of change as being endogenous and necessary and of a state at $t + 1$ as being determinable by its 'structure' at t.

According to Nisbet, this 'endogenist' model can be seen both in Marx (the laws of development from a feudal to a capitalist system) and also in Parsons. More generally, it can be seen in the work of all those who talk about social change. Nisbet suggests that the idea of social change itself implies in practice an endogenist view which he sees as wrong. Naturally, he has no difficulty in showing that social change is not invariably endogenous: the collapse of the Inca empire was certainly less the result of decadence than of the Spanish conquest. But perhaps dismissing a whole body of writing in one sentence is rushing things a little. As we have seen, de Tocqueville declared that he did not intend to write a history of the French Revolution, but a *study*, a sociological study of social change, as we would say nowadays. Should we dismiss the distinction he made? Or should we see the *Ancien Régime* as a worthless book? Marx's *Capital* is not a work by a historian, but does that make it a tissue of errors? (The fact that it contains some more or less debatable assertions is another matter.)

A variant of the sceptical attitude is simply to maintain that failures in knowledge – in the field of social change as elsewhere – are due to the *complexity* of the world. The idea is both well-founded and dull, despite many attempts to give it some content and construct a theory of complexity, initially in the United States, since the 1970s.[38] It seems illusory, however, to attempt to explain the difficulties encountered in the pursuit of knowledge on the basis of a simple idea, even if it is the idea of complexity, for the idea of complexity is no more complex than the idea of a circle is round.

The third attitude can be described as 'relativist' or 'critical', using the latter word in its traditional Kantian sense. It consists of reflecting on the conditions in which the programme summarized in the expression 'theory of social change' would be possible. It is clear that many of the statements engendered by such a programme are null and void. Does this mean that the programme itself is meaningless and that theories of social change have nothing to tell us about the phenomenon they are supposed to be concerned with? Does it mean that their claim to be of general application, what Piaget calls their nomothetic ambition, is entirely without foundation? To put the question another way, is an acceptable, valid or legitimate statement necessarily time and context-bound? What remains of theories of change when many of the empirical statements they make are either proved wrong by the facts or made worthless by research? Why *are* many such statements worthless?

I do not intend to move on to any a priori analysis, since in my view any answer that includes all aspects of the question can only be based on the actual evidence.[39] Some of the enormous range of products that can be called analyses of social change are, as we have seen in a number of examples, incapable of standing up to close examination, but others certainly do not break down even under the most demanding form of what Popper calls rational criticism. The essential feature of such criticism is that it attempts to determine, or at least to identify and clarify, the reasons why a given theory will or will not stand up to close scrutiny and to draw conclusions of a general nature from such an enquiry.

Expressed in a summary form, the main idea that I shall defend in this book is that if we take the principles of what we might call the sociology of agencies seriously and give them their proper importance, even if they are often misunderstood and not accepted, then a number of consequences follow. These are:

1. It is dangerous to try to establish conditional relationships with regard to social change, for example, to attempt to determine the conditions in which collective violence is *generally* most likely to occur or socio-economic development to take place.
2. Similarly, in most cases there are risks in trying to draw dynamic consequences from 'structural' data. Thus, to revert to a question often asked in the Marxist tradition, the fact that a system is characterized by a particular 'structure' of the conditions of production does not usually have much to say about how it will develop.
3. In most cases there is no logical or sociological justification for seeking the *causes* of social change. This means that propositions of the type 'such and such a change is ultimately due to technical innovation (or cultural "mutation")' are largely meaningless.
4. Despite these reservations, social change can be the object of scientific analyses based on the principles of rational criticism as applied in the so-called exact sciences in particular. This observation is valid both at the level of societies, which is what chiefly concerns us here, and at the lower level of, for example, organizations.
5. Although it is dangerous to try to establish generally valid empirical propositions about social change, the idea of a theory of social change designates an activity that is not only meaningful but fundamental in any attempt to see the real meaning of the idea of a theory in this context.

2

Individual Action, Aggregation Effects and Social Change

A fundamental principle in action sociologies is that social change is to be analysed as the result of a set of individual actions. This type of sociology includes much of the classical German tradition (Weber and Simmel), much of the classical Italian tradition (Pareto and Mosca) and considerable sections of American sociology (Parsons and Merton). Their adherents can be seen as a branch growing from the same trunk. Another such branch is economics, of which both the classical and the neo-classical varieties share the principle that any economic phenomenon can only be analysed in terms of the elementary individual actions that go to make it up. These differing branches derive from eighteenth-century Scottish thought and the philosophy of the Enlightenment and can be seen as individual paradigms which, each in its own way and in terms of its own particular aims and principles, creates a more general paradigm, that of agencies. This paradigm is of considerable significance for the social sciences, and it is of crucial epistemological importance to try to establish how far it is compatible with the programme followed by theories of social change.

Max Weber was the first to see clearly that there was no reason why it should be confined to economics, where it had been widely accepted since Adam Smith's time, and that it was indeed applicable to absolutely all the social sciences. Its universal nature, probably one of the most important discoveries in the modern social sciences (though not always recognized as such) was shown by Weber both at the theoretical level, particularly in *Economy and Society*, and at the practical level in his various concrete analyses.

The paradigm can be summarized as follows. Let us assume the existence of any social or economic phenomenon M, for which an

29

explanation is sought. M is to be interpreted as a function $M(m_i)$ of a range of individual actions m_i, which themselves are, in conditions and a way to be made explicit, functions $m_i(S_i)$ of structure S_i of the situation including the social agents or actors. The function (in the mathematical sense) $m_i(S_i)$ must be able to be seen as having an *adaptational* function for the actor $_i$ in situation S_i. Weber would say that action m_i must be *comprehensible*. As for structure S_i, it is a function $S_i(M')$ of a range M' of defined data at a macrosocial level or at least at the level of the system in which phenomenon M occurs.

Explaining M_i means, in brief and in terms of the general paradigm, saying exactly what the terms of $M = M\{m[S(M')]\}$ are (we can express it more simply as $M = MmSM'$). Verbally, we can say that phenomenon M is a function of actions m, which are dependent on situation S of the actor, which situation is itself affected by macrosocial actions M'. This essential epistemological proposition holds good whatever the logical nature of M and remains valid in particular when M describes change or a lack of change, generally an item or range of items relating to the development of a system:

$$M_t,\ M_{t+1}\ \ldots\ M_{t+k}$$

The formula in which we have summed up the general paradigm guiding those sociologists studying action may seem commonplace. Let it suffice to say that it is not so in everyone's eyes, that it is indeed often disputed and that there is no shortage of alternatives.

For example, paradigms of a *positivistic* or *naturalistic* nature which maintain that the social sciences should be closely based on the natural sciences (or more exactly on the natural sciences as seen by the social sciences) are popular. Those who favour them argue that it 'follows' that the idea of action, which has no equivalent in nature, could not intervene in any would-be scientific analysis. Paradigms of this kind loom large in both the history of the social sciences and present-day practices. Thus a great many theories of political, economic or social change take the form of an analysis of concomitant variations between aggregated variables. Some of them are concerned, for instance, with a reflection on whether growth (an aggregated variable defined at the social rather than the individual level) depends on other aggregated variables such as the development of education. If the correlation is fairly high and remains stable when other variables are controlled, it seems likely that the second variable has a more or less considerable effect on the first. In this kind of analysis, there is never any question of individuals, their actions or relationships between actions and situations.

Other paradigms refuse to admit the principle that actions of the type $m_i(S_i)$ have any adaptational function. As a corollary, they reject the Weberian idea of comprehension. For Weber, to understand an individual action is to acquire sufficient means of obtaining information to understand the motives behind it. In his view, observers *understand* the action of an observed subject as soon as they can conclude that in the same situation it is quite probable that they too would act in the same way. This kind of comprehension is therefore not an immediate datum and does not imply that we can see right into what other people do. The opposite is normally the case, for observers generally have to make an effort to obtain information about the situation of the subject they are observing if they want to understand his or her motivation. Many people, however, refuse to accept that motivation can be something that can properly be subject to analysis, since it is difficult to grasp and the subject may either be unaware of it or have a wrong idea of it (cf. the Marxist idea of false consciousness). If we accept that such examples are indeed valid, perhaps we should keep any idea of motivation out of analysis. Many are willing to do so, and Marxists, followers of Durkheim and some behaviourists have all claimed to have rid themselves of that awkward notion. Their arguments have been varied, but they have all acted in the name of *science*.

So the question is clearly to what extent individual actions can *be* explained, if not on the basis of a motivation seen as not readily accessible to observation and perhaps 'false'. Whatever the positivists may prefer to believe, however, it is by no means certain that if we ignore the subjectivity of actors we make the task of explaining both their behaviour and the *social facts* arising from an aggregate of various sets of behaviour any easier.

Other paradigms stress what could be called an argument of scale, maintaining that it would not be possible to take explicit account of individual actions except in the study of small-scale processes. In practice, they say, it would not be feasible to do so once we are dealing with anything on a larger scale. A divorce could not be studied without taking the actions of the individuals concerned into consideration. Exactly the opposite is true of economic growth or political development, however, since neither could be analysed by attempting to study the actions and motivation of those involved in such processes. Nevertheless, we shall have occasion in subsequent chapters to consider many examples which demonstrate the fragility of such arguments and to note that it is not only possible but also advisable to use 'individualist' techniques to analyse macroscopic changes.

There are those too who argue against using this paradigm by stressing the notion that, properly speaking, the individual only exists in individualistic societies. Consequently, they maintain, the methodology expressed in the paradigm is only applicable in certain kinds of society. We shall see later, however, that such a methodology can be used with both 'traditional' and 'modern' societies.

So there is no shortage of arguments for questioning what I shall now call the Weberian paradigm of action. Some of them are technical in nature (for example, the difficulty of establishing the actor's motives) and others epistemological (for example, the argument that the notion of 'action' or 'motivation' is out of place in any discourse which claims to be *scientific*). The doubts that these paradigms raise shape alternative ones, some of which have been mentioned briefly. Such doubts are enduring enough to be the boundaries that mark off well-established traditions. To some extent it was because Durkeim considered the ideas of action and motivation to be inadmissible that he seems to have read Weber or Simmel with more hostility than attention. And perhaps Weber too did not give Marx the attention he deserved because he rightly saw a notion like that of false consciousness as being hard to square with the idea of comprehension.

THE WEBERIAN PARADIGM

There are very many examples that could be used as a concrete illustration of the Weberian paradigm. Because of their didactic value rather than their intrinsic interest, I shall choose examples from the analysis of the processes of social diffusion. Although they are of a specific nature, they provide a useful basis for the discussion of the principles underlying the Weberian paradigm and its relevance that will be undertaken in the last four sections of this chapter.

In this section, we shall start with a detailed examination of a classical study of the dissemination of new pharmaceutical products in medical circles. Subsequently, we shall see that the principles underlying the analysis can easily be extended to cover extremely diverse topics such as the diffusion of ideologies and, more generally, to any analysis that aims at explaining a process of social change.

The study of the dissemination of new pharmaceutical products carried out by Coleman and his colleagues gives an instance of baffling findings.[1] In the case of a population of hospital doctors, the diffusion process follows a characteristic pattern. Initially, it is very slow, with the number of doctors adopting the new product increasing at a very modest rate indeed. As time goes on, it speeds up and the number goes up more and more rapidly. It is at its fastest when roughly half those involved have been won over and thereafter slows down steadily and becomes very slow indeed when almost every doctor has adopted the new product. When the process is illustrated in the form of a Cartesian graph with time on the x axis and the cumulative number of 'converts' on the y axis, the process is expressed as a sigmoid (i.e., S-shaped) curve. Why should that be so? Why, at the aggregate or collective level, that of the population as a whole, should the process have an S-shaped characteristic *structure*? When we were using symbols in the previous chapter, that characteristic structure represented the aggregate phenomenon M that was to be explained. The explanation of M provided by Coleman, as we shall see, consists precisely of a clarification of the terms of $M = M\{m[S(M')]\}$, in short $M = MmSM'$.

Anyone can see, of course, that it is not immediately obvious. Why is there the sigmoid structure? The mystery deepens when we note that it is only characteristic of hospital doctors, and not of those working in their own practices. With the latter, there is initially a very rapid increase of those adopting the new product, and then the rate of increase falls steadily, getting slower and slower as more and more doctors fall into line and approaching zero when almost all of them have done so. If the process is represented graphically in the same way as for their hospital colleagues, we have an arc-shaped and not an S-shaped curve.[2] Thus there is a characteristic structure in both cases, but the structure of the process is different for each type of doctor. In Weberian terms, explaining that difference amounts to explaining how the actions we have called m_i, that is, adopting or not adopting the innovation, are affected by the difference in the structure of the situation S_i of each of the two populations.

If we are to make precise statements about the terms of $m(S)$ – how the decision depends on the structure of the situation – we have to undertake what might be called a phenomenological analysis of the reaction of a doctor faced with a new drug. Let us look first at the case of hospital doctors. Whether they will prescribe it or not is clearly a very important decision, since if they do they will be introducing into someone else's body a new substance with little-known effects. Since they have no personal experience of the drug, all they have to rely on is the publicity and handouts issued by the company producing it and possibly reports from independent organizations testing it for the health service, for example. Such information is no doubt useful, but doctors will probably consider it to be inadequate, given the intrinsic seriousness of the decisions they have to make. In such situations, either doctors have to make up their minds urgently whether to use a new drug instead of the one they are familiar with, or there is no such need. In the first case, they are likely to stick to their usual professional practice. There is in fact no problem, since the possible advantages of the new substance do not need to be considered for this particular patient, whereas the risks involved in giving it are clearly there, even if they are not precisely known. If, however, doctors are faced with a situation in which the new drug seems worth considering because it offers certain potential advantages, they will try to reduce their area of ignorance and hence seek further information. This means that they will turn to a source of information that they will probably feel to be more trustworthy than faceless administrative or drug company departments, namely their colleagues. These are the people they rub shoulders with every day, they know that they can trust Smith more than Jones, and they can approach them as equals.[3] So, before a doctor makes up his or her mind, he or she has a word with Smith. What he or she obviously wants to know is whether he has used the new product himself. If Smith has used it and thinks well of it, the odds are that there will be a new convert.

Seeing the situation through the eyes of an individual doctor enables us to pick out its salient features. At a given moment, he or she is very likely to be faced with cases in which (1) the new drug is of therapeutic interest but (2) entails unknown risks, in which (3) the immediately available data are inadequate because they come from anonymous sources but in which (4) his or her colleagues are an easily accessible source of virtually free information which he or she thinks (5) that he or she can easily evaluate in terms of its credibility, the question being of course (6) whether Smith has that information when he is consulted.

Obviously, there is nothing very original about describing it in those terms, and it is a means and not an end. It does enable us to clarify the $m(S)$ action/situation relationship, the object of the exercise being to elucidate $[Mm(S)]$, the sigmoid curve of the diffusion process. In order to do that, the behaviour of the individual actors must be 'aggregated'.

Sometimes, such an operation is a simple one. Here, it needs a moment's thought. Our doctor consults Smith. This will produce a new recruit if the latter has tried the new product and has a favourable opinion of it. At the beginning of the process, when the product has just been launched, Smith has no views on it. Our doctor thus has a 50 per cent chance of being converted by him. This holds not only for our doctor (let us call him or her i) but also for any other doctor in the same position (j, k and so on). Thus at any given time, conversion will be more frequent (1) the more doctors like i, j and k seek their colleagues' opinion, and (2) the more doctors there are like Smith who have adopted the new product.

Initially, there will be much seeking of opinion but few doctors able to give one, and conversions will proceed slowly. They will then increase at a faster rate until a turning-point is reached. What happens is that as more and more doctors are won over, the number of requests for information drops. Thus the maximum speed of the diffusion process is reached when those doctors able to give an opinion are as numerous as those likely to ask for one. Beyond that point, the process slows down. When virtually everyone has been won over, an opinion is rarely sought and the rate of conversion is therefore increasingly slow.[4]

To sum up: doctors are at first won over slowly and then increasingly rapidly until the number of those seeking advice roughly equals that of those able to give it. From that point, the number of converts grows increasingly slowly. When almost everyone has accepted the new product, the laggards come over at a slower and slower rate. If we 'aggregate' the whole series of behaviour patterns $M(S)$, we have the aggregated structure $M[m(S)]$, in this case the sigmoid curve showing the cumulative number of converts over a period of time. Reciprocally, the structure of situation S explains the sigmoid path of the curve that has been observed empirically.

In the fundamental formula describing the Weberian paradigm, the structure of situation S is presented as dependent on macrosociological data, or at least on defined data at the level of the social situation considered in the analysis: $S = S(M')$. That is certainly the case here, where the hospital structure creates the conditions in which doctors can have access to information that is to all intents and purposes disinterested and of a higher level of credibility than any from official sources, namely the opinion of colleagues. A further result of the hospital situation and the intercommunication networks it permits is that doctors can see themselves as in a position to affect the thinking of colleagues who are a degree or so higher up the ladder of professional standing.[5]

The situation of doctors in their own practices is *structurally* different. When the new drug comes on the market, they too may not need to use it at once. Like their hospital colleagues, they too are aware of the risks in doing so, and no doubt take a careful attitude towards information from impersonal sources. But, also like their hospital colleagues, they too might be faced with a clinical situation in which the new product could theoretically be the appropriate treatment if the risks, in the sense of the possible drawbacks, which are necessarily difficult to evaluate, do not outweigh the advantages. So far, there is no apparent difference between the two kinds of practitioners. However, as soon as doctors in their own practices try to get access to further information, a contrast becomes evident, for whilst the hospital doctor can make use of easily accessible sources of information, practitioners working on their own have none. They can, of course, turn to a colleague, but their network of professional relationships is very likely to be more limited than that as the hospital doctor. In addition, since they are not in daily contact with their colleagues, they will probably be less conversant with their ways of working, and it will consequently be harder for them to add the weight of any favourable first-hand observation of the way they carry out their professional duties. Last but not least, their position with regard to their colleagues is a *competitive* one. In short, it is not as easy for them to get information, it is also harder for them to assess its quality, and it is more expensive. It is therefore likely that they will rely more on official sources of information than their colleagues in hospital would. The structure of their situation (S) is different, and their behaviour $m(S)$ will very probably be different.

What follows from this at the 'aggregated' level is that initially the individual doctor will hesitate to use a product he or she does not know much about. As time passes, the body of impersonal information grows, articles on the effects, quality and drawbacks of the new product are published, and a collective opinion tends to form. If it offers real therapeutic advantages, the increase in the number of converts will at any given moment be proportionate to the total number of those *not yet won over*. This contrasts with the case of hospital doctors, for there, because of interpersonal influence made possible by the hospital milieu, that increase is proportionate to both the number of converts and the number of those not yet won over. With doctors working on their own, interpersonal influence is much less significant. The number of those able to give an opinion based on personal knowledge is irrelevant here, since they are rarely asked for one. That explains why, at any given moment, the number of new converts among such doctors will only increase proportionately to the number of those still unconverted.

Once we have conducted that analysis, we can determine the structure M. Since the rate of increase depends at any time on the number of converts there are, and since that number can only decrease, the rate slackens off as more doctors accept the product. Hence the arc-shaped curve in the Cartesian diagram described earlier. Unlike that for hospital doctors, which initially accelerates and then decelerates in the second part of its path, the curve showing the second process is characterized by constant deceleration.

These two specific situations have features in common (uncertainty, the seriousness of the clinical circumstances), but are also quite different in some ways (information which for one group is accessible, free and reliable and for the other hard to come by, expensive and unreliable. As a consequence, interpersonal influence plays a major part in the first group and a minor one in the second. Hence the two differently structured curves.

As for the way the *explanation* is structured, it certainly takes the expected form. S(M'), the structure of the situation, clearly depends on the aggregated variables comprising M', with both the hospital milieu and the circumstances of the doctor working alone affecting their respective opportunities for access to information. Since that difference exists, *m*(S) is not the same in both cases. In one group, there is reliance on a network that can be activated, and in the other recourse to information from impersonal sources. The difference in *m* itself brings about a difference at the level of the structure, defined here as the function describing the number of converts in terms of time. In its entirety, the analysis is M = M*m*SM' in form.

The foregoing example means that a certain number of interesting epistemological conclusions can be demonstrated. The analysis includes a 'phenomenological' element consisting of a simplified description of the reactions of a doctor faced with a new drug, his or her subjectivity being reconstructed on the basis of the data of the situation. That presupposes that the observer or analyst, although not in the same situation as the doctor, is nevertheless capable of imagining the latter's state of mind if he or she has an elementary understanding of a doctor's 'role' and the conditions in which it is carried out. Moreover, there is nothing to prevent empirical verification of the reconstruction of *m*(S). A fairly straightforward survey – which was indeed carried out by the authors of the study – would make it possible to check that the *m*(S) hypotheses are not pure fiction and, more specifically, that they are accepted by the persons involved themselves. We should also note, however, that to a certain extent the analysis can be carried out a priori. This implies that if he or she has enough information about the subject's situation, the observer can, up to a point, anticipate his or her reactions or, in the sense that Weber gave the expression, *comprehend* them once he or she has observed them. Elaborating *m*(S) is thus the result of information about the properties of S and the application of a priori *psychology*. It may be possible to let the persons involved assess *m*(S), but in any case constructing it implies a relationship of comprehension between observer and subject.

The second point that needs stressing is that *m*(S), the 'phenomenological' description, is an indispensable element of a description of the structure M which, in the example quoted, has a mathematical form. Far from being completely contrasting, phenomenology and quantitative analysis can be seen as organically linked. It is impossible to *explain* the sigmoid structure of the first curve without *understanding* what goes on in the doctor's mind when he or she first encounters the new product. This means that *explanation* (of the structure) and *comprehension* (of the actions of the subjects under observation) are quite inseparable aspects of the analysis. This proposition is also true in general terms, for whatever form M may take, be it mathematical, statistical or factual, a phenomenological element – M(*m*) – is needed if it is to be explained.

We can now also emphasize a third point: *verifying* the analysis can – and can usefully – take place at two levels. One is that of *m*, the level of comprehension, where the object is to find out whether the psychological mechanisms postulated by the observer appraised of the main data of situation S correspond to reality. The second, that of M, is where the object is to check whether the consequences at the aggregated level of microsociological hypotheses *m* are indeed in conformity with the aggregated data as observed empirically.[6]

It is not hard to show that the Weberian model $M = MmSM'$ is universally applicable, and more specifically that it describes the structure of any M phenomenon, whatever the logical nature of M might be. In the analysis we have just looked at, M, the aggregated phenomenon to be explained, is a 'law' in the statistical sense of the term, that is a mathematical function of known form, expressed graphically by a well-determined curve. All I need do here is remind the reader of one or two examples that I have discussed elsewhere.[7] In a classical study, Sombart asked at the watershed of the present century why there was no socialism in the United States.[8] In that work, the question M hinges on a unique case: why the United States, alone amongst industrialized nations with a parliamentary system, has never had socialist movements of any importance. Sombart's answer is based on the fact that the United States is a frontier country in terms of M'. The consequence of this is that individuals dissatisfied with their lot can (or think they can) seek their fortune elsewhere. What Hirschman calls the exit strategy is open to them. The structural datum S(M') is of capital importance: as a result of S, the individual sees no real personal advantage in joining protest movements essentially aimed at benefiting social categories rather than the individual. Indeed, such a social strategy is chancy and its effects slow to manifest themselves. This means therefore that he or she is more likely to choose the individual exit rather than the collective protest strategy: *m*(S). Once aggregated, *m*(S) behaviour patterns entail the consequence that, as individuals are less attracted by the collective protest strategy than by a strategy of individual defection, the potential pool of recruits for movements making use of the former will be restricted. Socialism, however, Sombart would have us believe, is essentially an ideology that makes it possible to endow such movements with a pseudo-objective basis. It can only attract a body of adherents who have something to gain by following it. Since the pool of such adherents is tiny, socialism has a very

restricted number of people interested in it: M(*m*). We are not
concerned for the moment with whether the theory is credible or
not; all that needs stressing is that the structure of the explanation
it offers is indeed of the form M = M*m*SM'.

Sombart's theory deals with the *raison d'être* of a specific single
phenomenon. In other words, in it M is in the form of one particular
datum, namely the low level of influence of socialism in the United
States at the end of the nineteenth century. In what are called
comparative analyses, M is concerned with *differences*. Thus de
Tocqueville, in his *Ancien Régime*, reflects on why there should be a
whole range of differences between England and France at the end of
the eighteenth and during the first half of the nineteenth centuries.[9]
Why was French agriculture underdeveloped in comparison with
British agriculture at the end of the eighteenth century (M)? Because
the centralized administration in France (M') involved a range of
consequences and brought about a situation in which the conditions
(S) certain categories of actors operated in were different in that
country from those across the Channel. The French landowner, for
example, who took up residence in a town and benefited from the
privileges the bourgeois had won against the stranglehold of central
authority, had the advantage of escaping tallage: *m*(S). In addition,
centralization meant that there were many royal offices and that
service to the state was prestigious, more so than in England at least:
S(M'). Consequently, French landowners had more reason than their
English counterparts to covet such offices: *m*(S). The result at the
aggregated level was that French landowners were more frequently
absentees than English ones. They installed tenants who, since the
land did not belong to them, were not very interested in techniques
for making it more productive, and had neither the motivation nor
the means for investment. As for the landowners, their minds were
elsewhere. Despite the physiocrats and the enthusiasm their doctrines
aroused in the *salons* of the times, agricultural methods followed
traditional patterns, and the stagnation in French agriculture was
in marked contrast to the modernization taking place in England:
M(*m*). Given the existing structures, the actors had rarely both the
motivation and the ability to modernize techniques. The physiocrats charmed ministers, *intendants* and intellectuals while the state
charmed the landowners and drew them away from their estates.

Sombart's and de Tocqueville's 'qualitative' analyses are both
abstract in structure and in that respect indistinguishable from the

'quantitative' and mathematical kind of analysis of the diffusion process that our discussion started with. In both cases, the structure permits of an easy return to what I have called the Weberian model.

M, the aggregated or macrosociological datum which serves as the starting-point of the analysis, can thus be of any kind. Sometimes, as in the first example, M is a *mathematical or statistical structure*. At other times, as in the second, it is a *single phenomenon*. In other cases, it is a *difference* (as between a backward agricultural system in one place and a modern one in another). Yet again, it may be a *statement* about a range of diachronic data, as when we reflect on why a given country is economically stagnant, which comes to the same thing as analysing why between t, t+1 . . . t+k, there is a slight variation in this or that datum or set of data such as the GNP, the number of industrial concerns and so on. Sometimes, M is both diachronic and comparative in nature, as when we ask why Japan underwent rapid development in the nineteenth century despite its isolation.

These examples show clearly that M, the aggregated or macrosociological datum under analysis, can assume more or less complex forms (although complexity is of course difficult to measure). However complex M may be, the Weberian model expressed in summary form as $M = MmSM'$ can be detected in most of the major sociological studies. It is, of course, essentially a *thesis*, and its interest can be suggested but not demonstrated, since to do so would entail examining all the components of a very large and undefined corpus of studies. The few examples given here do, however, show that the model is relevant for studies of a very varied type and style and that M can take very different forms. In particular, it can be a statement or range of statements about time-indexed data (m_t), and when that is the case, we are dealing with social change. There is no reason why the Weberian paradigm should not be as useful here as it is elsewhere, as indeed the examples above have shown. De Tocqueville deals with the *static* nature of French agriculture, Sombart with the non-diffusion of socialism in the United States in the nineteenth century, the first study of the diffusion of an innovation, and these all entail linking with time.

This means, therefore, that from our point of view a basic question is whether the Weberian paradigm and the programme of theories of social change are compatible.

We should remember that in our reflections so far, M has been defined in very broad terms and seen as any topic of interest to sociologists, demographers and economists. By topic, we mean here any combination of observed phenomena not immediately explicable to the observer. The form generally taken by questions in the social sciences is that of 'why M?' Why is a given process characterized by a sigmoid curve? Why did French agriculture not develop when English agriculture *was* developing? Why was there no socialism in the United States in the nineteenth century? why did Japan develop at a stage in its history when it had no contacts with the outside world? All these questions and, in my view, in a general way all questions in the social sciences take the form of 'why M?' with M being a combination of observations that arouses curiosity. That indefinite range of questions is the *object* of that field of investigation. I believe it is wrong to try, as we sometimes do, to mark out territories for sociology, economics or demography in the real world, as if we were geographers. It is true, of course, that by tradition each of those disciplines concerns itself with one type of phenomena rather than another, but the boundaries between them are far from firm. The family is just as important to sociologists as it is to demographers, and both sociologists and economists are interested in crime and divorce. What is *specific* to each discipline is rather to be found in certain habitual ways of thinking. Nevertheless, 'why M?' is a common concern. That is why it is not always easy to follow certain discussions about the object of sociology and how it is to be constructed. It is fairly clear that this object is not drawn from the real world like a bucket of water from a well, because the object of knowledge is always to answer a question, and there are no questions without subjects to ask them. Since they *are* questions, the objects of the social sciences are necessarily constructs and, as Popper would say, belong to the 'third world'.[10] If that is so, it is far from easy to see the rules and norms governing the way in which they are constructed. This is because de Tocqueville's *answer* (which not anyone could have provided) to the question of the underdevelopment of French agriculture shows that the question asked – a simple observation of a readily ascertainable fact – was interesting.

The fact that in the Weberian model M can take any form and be for example an event, a single datum, a series of differences, a distribution or a range of univariate or multivariate distribution or anything else is of considerable epistemological importance. Here, it is essential to note the contrast between, for example, Weber and Durkheim. Whereas the latter thought that sociology could not lay claim to any sort of general validity if it did not set iself the task of seeking empirically regular patterns in either trends or relationships, the Weberian model sees such patterns – where they can be observed – as one type of objects amongst others. In other words, this model implies a refusal to define the social sciences as nomological, a definition which it sees as arbitrarily limiting.

Having shown (or at least suggested by the examples given so far, which are to be filled out by the remainder of this work) that the Weberian model could be considered as being universally valid, we shall now look at both the principles involved in it and the misunderstandings it has often given rise to.

THE PSYCHOLOGY OF THE SOCIAL SCIENCES

Comte once decreed that psychology, like probability studies, was an 'aberration' that could have no claim to scientific standing. As is the case with most wild generalizations, there is a grain of truth here, for explaining even the most ordinary kind of individual behaviour is an infinitely complicated undertaking. Even the subtlest introspection can hardly account for artistic or gastronomic tastes. On the other hand, it is not too hard to establish correlations (even if they are most often fairly weak ones) between tastes, or any other psychological variable, and *sociological* variables such as social class, area of residence, age or religion. It is very easy to jump to the conclusion that psychological phenomena are, scientifically speaking, only comprehensible or interesting in so far as they are subject to 'social determination'. The questionable juxtaposition of these two truisms was the starting-point for every sociological perspective, in the first place Comte's and subsequently Durkheim's. If motivation is unfathomable and behaviour varies in a simple way according to the social characteristics of agents, does this not mean that the former should be ignored and the latter restricted to the study of co-variations between social characteristics and behaviour? A conclusion of this kind is clearly incompatible with the Weberian model, which presupposes that the subjectivity of the actors will be reconstructed:

$m(S)$. How can such a reconstruction be reconciled with the complexity of motivation?

By definition, the social sciences are never concerned with explaining individual behaviour patterns in all their complexity. As such, the individual is not their object. Economists do not claim to be able to decide why Mr X likes a particular product, which is normally a very difficult question. On the other hand, if they note that whenever the price of product P goes up slightly he buys product Q instead, they conclude that Mr X's preference for P is not very marked. If Mrs Y buys Q, an equivalent of product P, whenever P costs twice as much as Q, they conclude that Mrs Y's preference for P is twice as marked as that of Mr X. Such propositions are important statements about the *subjective* states X and Y experience, but do not set out to explain why X has a slight preference for P. Similarly, the statement that X is running because he has seen the bus at the street corner and does not want to miss it tells us something about why he behaves in such a way, but cannot be seen as a complete explanation. Does he want to catch the bus because he is late or because he hates hanging about? If the latter is the case, does it show that he is impatient by nature? And so on. Giving a 'psychological' explanation even of such a commonplace way of behaving is a very complicated undertaking. Fortunately, neither sociologists, economists nor demographers are in practice ever called upon to produce psychological explanations in the sense I have used the expression here. Similarly, when de Tocqueville says that in the eighteenth century the landed proprietors were very aware of the tax exemptions enjoyed by the urban middle classes, he is not offering a 'psychological' analysis of their behaviour, but simply providing a valid microsociological explanation of an observed macrosociological phenomenon. Again, if I see a crowd hurrying towards the Parc des Princes, I conclude that they are on the way to a match. An observation of that kind is no doubt concerned with the subjective state of mind of the individuals making up the crowd, but it cannot be seen as a statement about their 'psychology'. It would be more accurate to describe it as a *macrosociological* statement in the sense that it deals first with what is happening in the mind of each individual and secondly it explains the *aggregated* phenomenon (the hurrying crowd) that I am trying to account for.

If we make no distinction between 'psychological' and 'macrosociological' statements, we run the risk of getting hopelessly confused, since the former highlight a relationship between observed behaviour and personality that is normally of no interest to the latter.

Since microsociological statements *m* are determined by the nature of the question M, there can be no *general* microsociological model. To put it clearly, there is no generally valid model of sociological or economic man. Negating this proposition would contradict the proposition that *m* is determined by M. In other words, *m* statements are not drawn from a simplified kind of psychology specially for sociologists or economists. Thus, the model of the calculating and reasoning man sometimes offers a useful summary of the 'psychology' used by economists and is clearly much more helpful than sociologists often think. But that does not mean that it is of general validity. Similarly, the 'cognitive' model that certain people set up in opposition to the 'utilitarian' model favoured by economists is sometimes of value.[11] It would be hard to deny, for example, that certain kinds of behaviour are meaningless if we do not see that the subject carries within him or herself certain representations. Sometimes, however, that particular model simply cannot be used. It is obviously absurd to try to explain religious behaviour in terms of a 'utilitarian' model, but it is just as absurd not to see that certain kinds of behaviour are explicable in terms of interest. Discussing the comparative validity of various models – utilitarian, cognitive, *homo economicus* and *homo sociologicus* – is thus about as pertinent as a general discussion of the comparative usefulness of pliers and pincers. There is only one yardstick for judging the value of a microsociological model: does it enable us to explain M? No doubt it is useful to point out to sociologists that in their investigations the *homo economicus* model is sometimes occasionally more useful than they think, and that rejecting it is partly metaphysical in origin, since it is pretty heart-breaking to picture man as an English grocer.[12] But it would be quite wrong to suggest that this or any other model is universally valid. The reason why it would be wrong is that it would contradict the fact that the validity of a microsociological model depends on its ability (which can be assessed in terms of certain criteria) to reply to a question M, and that the microsociological model *m* is a function of the nature of M. It is obviously absurd to accuse de Tocqueville of having a utilitarian 'view' of the world simply because he puts forward the hypothesis that some taxpayers are aware of the possible ways of avoiding taxation.

THE NOTION OF RATIONALITY

It is very often possible to put forward with a high degree of certainty
the hypothesis that behaviour is explicable because a subject is
pursuing an aim and consequently using a given means. Does that
mean that any behaviour will fit into the 'ends and means' pattern
or, to put the question more exactly, that it *can* be explained in such
a way?

There are certainly times when the classical rational model is
applicable. A subject sets him or herself an aim and is in a position
to examine the whole range of means he or she can use to achieve
it and to select the most advantageous or at least the preferable one.
In most cases, however, rationality must be seen as 'limited'.[13]
When it *is* limited, drawing up a full and complete list of the means
available is impossible and indeed too costly.[14] It is 'irrational' to
spend too long looking for information that is difficult to find, and
consequently the exploration of possible means will very likely stop
short at a given threshold, which itself is incapable of rigorous
definition. This is of course due to the fact that although it could
in theory be determined by a comparative assessment of the value
of the information still untraced and the cost of acquiring it, it is
in most cases very difficult to establish the value of this, since by
hypothesis the nature of the information is unknown. In practice,
therefore, the threshold is established more or less arbitrarily as a
result of impulse, intuition or weariness.

Although it is not hard to imagine situations in which action or
decisions are called for and a traditionally rational decision can be
made, there are, it follows, others in which the boundary between
rationality and irrationality tends to become blurred.

These observations also apply to situations with a strategic
dimension where, depending on the structure of the situation,
rationality may be either definite or indefinite. In the case of a
co-operative game involving two players, there is always a *dominant*
strategy that it is rational for both to play, since this idea is implicit
in the notion of co-operation. There are, however, situations in which
each of those involved has a *dominant* strategy, that is, in which it
is of advantage to each to adopt that particular strategy whatever
the others decide and by doing so bring about a rather unfavourable
result.[15] The arms race is a case in point: it is better for both sides

to arm than not to arm as long as neither can be sure that the other is determined to disarm. The result, however, is astronomical expenditure that could be avoided if both sides disarmed. In a case of that type, the notion of rationality is an ill-defined one, for by behaving 'rationally' both help to produce a less favourable result than if they behaved 'irrationally'.

Pareto, whose famous distinction between logical and non-logical action is well known, was clearly aware that such ambiguous examples exist. For him, any action which was based on logical considerations but produced results different from those aimed at was not logical.[16] If businessman A is in a competitive market and reduces his prices to attract customers from businessman B and the structure of the situation induces B to do the same, A's stratagem has failed. All that the two competitors bring about is a situation in which the only winner is the consumer. A could of course see that this would be how B would react, but nevertheless was obliged to reduce his price, for if he did not, B would have been in a position to entice his customers away from him. What A did was rational in that it afforded him some protection from the possibility of aggressive competition by B, but also irrational in that he lost profits. An *agreement* between the two would solve all the problems, but that would only be a practical proposition if the two concerns shared the market between them or with very few others. Otherwise, such an agreement might well be prohibitively expensive. The *structure of the situation* in which each is involved thus varies according to the number of protagonists, as Pareto indeed stresses.[17] If there are not many of them, an agreement is possible, and everyone can act rationally or 'logically', but if there are several they are all trapped.

This means that the idea of rationality is only definite in *certain* situations. In other words, whether or not it can be given a precise meaning is a function of the structure of the situation under review, as Pareto clearly saw and neatly expressed. These observations will suffice, it seems to me, to invalidate the summary and common (and perhaps common because it is summary) interpretation of the notion of 'non-logical action'.[18] The fact that Pareto makes much of non-logical acts certainly does not mean that his work can be simplistically seen as exemplifying the popular 'metaphysical' view of human behaviour as guided by either blind instincts (man as a beast) or by unbridled and free-floating imagination (man as an angel). To see just how great a misunderstanding that would be, we need of course only compare Pareto's typology of action with that of Weber. Certain types of action that Pareto classifies as 'non-logical' are seen as 'rational' by Weber (sometimes with reference to values, but also with reference to aims).

Sometimes the idea of rationality is countered by the observation that human behaviour is on occasion guided by more or less solidly based *representations*. An engineer building a bridge takes into consideration certain scientifically based 'representations' about the effects of gravity. A politician who decides to take a certain line also has certain 'representations', even if they are for the most part less solidly based than the engineer's and may be of the nature of 'myths'. Does this mean that the behaviour of social agents must always be seen as 'irrational'? We must be clear about the words we are using here. If we mean that they are always in a state of hallucination and delirium, the proposition is pointless and dubious. If we mean that *in certain situations*, and in particular those characterized by a high degree of uncertainty, they have recourse to more or less solidly based representations, we can no doubt describe their behaviour as *irrational*. We can, however, also describe it as *rational*, provided that we make it clear that rationality is limited by the uncertain nature of the situation and thus move a certain distance away from the *classical* notion of rationality.

Let us suppose that I have to vote for a candidate in the presidential elections. I have heard what they have all promised. I do not know them personally and cannot say whether those promises will be kept or to what extent they *can* be kept. Nor do I know whether if they are kept they will have undesirable consequences. What do I do? I can abstain, and there are arguments for doing so, since one vote hardly carries any weight.[19] Vote for the one who seems to me to be the most sincere? The one whose principles come closest to my own? The one who seems determined to defend the interests of someone of my kind? Why not? All these responses are equally rational.[20] Or, more precisely, it is hard to put them into any kind of hierarchy of rationality or to imagine a different response that would indubitably be more rational than any of them. *Given the structure of the situation*, all such ways of behaving can therefore be described as rational, if we use the term in a broad sense.

Faced with the problem of making a choice, the actor tries to base his decision on reasons which, although they are not and cannot be as rigorous as the laws of gravity, nevertheless seem to him to be plausible. The action will be grounded in reasons which are more or less decisive or constraining according to the situation. In certain situations, however, one cannot imagine there being *clinching* reasons. Nevertheless, in such cases action which is not based on compelling reasons cannot be described as irrational. What *would* be irrational would be the failure to see that the situation was such that there was no hope of finding compelling reasons to choose one course of action rather than another. That point has a certain practical importance. Thus, when there is a low degree of correlation between social attributes and behaviour, it is often because that behaviour is a response to situations in which choice cannot be based on decisive reasons. The low correlation is a meaningful signal rather than random noise, and information about the structure of the situation rather than entropy.

And yet cannot those actions which seem to arise because the social actor is simply following tradition (cf. Weber's 'traditional actions') be described as irrational?[21] Are there not cases of '(irrational) resistance to change', to use an appallingly prejudice-ridden and authoritarian expression?

Very often, however, when an observer is surprised by the way in which an actor is faithful to or *submits* to a tradition, it is really that surprise which is worth examining. The Western observer, coming from a society in which a restricted family is the rule and the norm, is sometimes astonished to find that peasant families in the Third World still produce many offspring. There can be no doubt that the population explosion has effects that are collectively disastrous or that it helps to keep peasants in a state of destitution. It seems certain that in the developed countries of Europe and America a restriction on the size of the family offers advantages for the individual and, other things being equal, gives him or her a higher standard of living. It does not, however, follow from these two propositions that a birth-rate always reflects a compulsive submission to tradition.

We can illustrate this point by one or two simple examples. In certain parts of India, irrigation has meant that the peasants can start to grow sugar cane, which provides a higher income than traditional crops.[22] In order to avoid over-production, the department buying the cane fixes by contract the amount it will buy from each farmer, who will therefore obviously benefit from quickly setting up one or preferably two of his sons on a separate patch of land. As agricultural incomes are always low, the family will be in a better position if one, or preferably two, of their other sons have a job in a nearby town. Their wages will probably be fairly low, but will nevertheless help to supplement the income from the farm. In return, those sons will receive advantages in kind from the family in the country and will be able to rely on services that will make up for their low wages. With four sons – and hence an average of *eight* children – the family is therefore *from its own point of view* better adapted to the situation than it would be with two. That is why anti-natalist propaganda is not always totally effective in this context.[23] The structure of the situation reinforces the traditional model of the large family. There are, of course, effects which are collectively and *consequently* individually negative as a result of this, but in this situation it is obviously not in the individual's interest to adopt the model of the restricted family.[24] An observer diagnosing 'resistance to change' or 'irrational' fidelity to traditions is therefore simply displaying his or her own ignorance.

Similarly, educational sociologists (who owe their social position to their educational qualifications) often imagine that children from the underprivileged classes have limited educational aspirations as a result of an ('irrational') fidelity to a subculture or a class ethos.[25] But such behaviour is irrational only in terms of the *observer's* situation, when it is obvious that 'rationality' or 'irrationality' can only be determined in relation to the *actor's* behaviour. The only exception to this is when both are indistinguishable, which is not the case unless we deny the existence of social classes.

In the foregoing examples, seeing behaviour as irrational implies that the observer has an egocentric or society-centred attitude and thinks that he or she sees more clearly than the actors themselves how the latter should act in their own best interests. They do not do this, and are therefore irrational. But it is hard to see how actors could in fact be so blind to their own advantage.[26] It may occasionally happen, but how can all Indian peasants or members of a particular social class fail to see what is beneficial for them? We can of course resort to sophistry and talk about the effects of 'alienation', 'the weight of tradition', 'resistance to change' or 'false consciousness'. However, it would probably be a great deal simpler to avoid such roundabout and peripheral explanations and confused ideas and admit that even a qualified observer can be prejudiced, less well informed than he might be about the actor's situation and, indeed, *wrong*. When traditions are accepted by the actor, it is generally because he or she sees them as meaningful, adaptatively effective and in a word *rational* in the widest sense of the term or indeed *comprehensible* in the Weberian sense.

The microsociological point $m(S)$ in a sociological analysis can be briefly said to consist in bringing out the adaptative nature of a pattern of behaviour with reference to a situation. An analysis presupposes that an observer will try not to see him or herself as the centre of things and not to be caught up in them, and this implies that he or she will try to keep informed about the constituent elements of situation S and treat it as an external object. Only by acting in this way will he or she be able to 'understand' the actor's behaviour.

As can be seen, *understanding* in the Weberian sense (which I think I have restored here) implies the ability of the observer *to put him or herself in the actor's place*, but does not in any way imply that the actor's subjectivity is immediately transparent. Being able to put oneself in someone else's place indicates a relationship, that of empathy, that can exist between any two people however great the spatial or temporal distance between them. It is a relationship which does not exist, or at least not to the same degree, between a human being and a budgerigar, and is enough to give a meaning to the notion of human nature. It is, however, something that is produced, if at all, not from some fusion of separate consciousness, but from a deliberate *distancing* process.

Indeed, the Weberian notion of comprehension designates a procedure which is very close to what textbooks of logic call 'ampliative induction' and which consists of reconstituting motives not directly accessible by cross-checking facts.

THE NOTION OF INDIVIDUALISM

This notion is also the source of much confusion. Weber is totally explicit; sociology too, he said, owes it to itself to adopt strictly *individualistic* methods.[27] Where any M phenomenon is the result of the aggregation of behaviour and can only be explained if the behaviour itself is understood, the observer needs to be able to put him or herself in the actor's place. This statement, however, only makes sense when it is a question of *individual* actors, and indeed mental states can only be attributed to individuals. Concepts such as *will, consciousness* or *psychology* can only be applied to non-individual 'subjects' *metaphorically*. An idea such as class consciousness is perfectly legitimate if used of individuals, that is, if it is seen as describing the feeling (varying in intensity) that an individual has of belonging to a class. The idea of a 'collective consciousness' is much more doubtful. As for an expression like 'crowd psychology', it has all sorts of unhelpful metaphysical overtones, which are also based on a dubious rhetoric. In a crowd, the individual is dissolved, which means that the subject of collective behaviour can only be the collective itself.

There is little doubt that an individual in a crowd is under the immediate control of other people and that his or her autonomy is temporarily limited. Being in a crowd and being in a drawing-room are certainly two different situations, and the same individual is likely to behave differently in each. Should we then conclude that in the former observers lose not only their autonomy, but also their individuality and their subjectivity, and that 'consequently' that subjectivity is transferred to the superior authority, 'the crowd'? Like other ideas (resistance to change, weight of tradition, and so on) that of *crowd psychology* is the creation of the illusions, anxieties and moods of the observer. Such ideas say more about his or her subjectivity than about the object he or she claims to be observing. A platoon of soldiers is said to be moving like 'a single man', so each soldier has handed over his ability to make decisions, his autonomy and hence his individuality to the group. They are all under hypnosis, which curiously enough will only come to an end when they are ordered to fall out.[28]

We are not, of course, denying the existence of phenomena such as influence, authority or charisma. Such phenomena, however, cannot be seen as indicating that the social actor is passive or fundamentally inclined to be manipulated. Indeed, influence (for example) is only meaningful if the actor is perceived as a subject capable of forming intentions: the doctors in our earlier example *accept* their colleagues' influence because they know that they can provide them with invaluable information when they are faced with a situation in which they have to make a decision. Except in extreme cases, therefore, influence and authority are phenomena fairly unrelated to suggestion or hypnotism. Similarly, the observer who cannot wait to see Indian peasants limit the size of their families or children from the underprivileged sections of society widen their educational ambitions will suggest that their consciousness has been *adversely affected* by the *weight of tradition* or their *class ethos*. But we need only scratch the surface of these collective concepts (*Kollektivbegriffe*, as Weber calls them)[29] to see clearly that they are based on the society-centred illusions of the observer.

It is worth making an important point in passing here. The incomprehension that is often the reaction to the idea of methodological individualism is largely due to the exaggerated consequences sometimes drawn from the classical idea of *Gemeinschaft*, or community. In distinguishing between *Gemeinschaft* and *Gesellschaft*, Tönnies was trying to focus attention on the obvious fact that interdependence between individuals is more marked in certain types of social context.[30] People are more subject to the attention and scrutiny of those around them in a small provincial town than in a capital. This idea was taken up by Durkheim and later by Redfield and others,[31] and in sociology textbooks it has gradually taken over the place of Pythagoras' theorem in textbooks of elementary geometry. Tönnies's obvious fact, however, has given rise to tiresome corollaries, amongst which is the view that in a *Gemeinschaft* individuality dissolves, the individual as such does not exist and is simply a focus of the collective will. The proof of this is the unanimity and consensus reigning in village *communities*. The individual is thus seen not as an immediate datum, but as a concept linked to a particular form of society, the *Gesellschaft*, which contrasts at every point with the *Gemeinschaft*. This means that individualism is an ideology, the characteristic ideology of the *Gesellschaft*.

Intellectually, these corollaries are all equally unsatisfactory. An individual may be closely scrutinized in a small provincial town, but that does not mean that his or her individuality is dissolved. Nor does the fact that in a particular village in Asia all decisions are unanimous necessarily mean that there is a consensus. It can indeed be a sign of distrust, which is a consequence of interdependence.

To realize that there is nothing paradoxical about this way of looking at things, we need only reflect on the meaning of the rule that all decisions must be unanimous. What it really implies is that it is agreed that each and every individual has the right of veto and in exchange recognizes that each and every other also has it. The right of veto, of course, *maximizes* rather than minimizes the importance of the individual in community decision-making, since it gives him or her the right to stop a decision desired by everyone else. Thus, insisting on unanimous decisions does not necessarily show that there is a consensus, as is also indicated by the fact that unanimity is only achieved as a result of long 'palavers'.

What a rigorous adherence to common values *does* show is not some abolition of individuality, but the effectiveness of social control and the high level of interdependence amongst members of the group. In the same way, traditionalism and a low level of innovation in village communities of the classical kind is not necessarily a sign that their members are compulsively addicted to a collective model. What we should rather see in them in most cases is the result of a very high level of mutual dependence amongst individuals. In highly interdependent systems, any innovation is likely to entail external effects, consequences, that is, that might adversely affect other people. Thus, as has been observed in the case of Vietnamese villages in particular, an increase in the harvest yields in one person's fields can bring about a fall in what another can obtain by gleaning.[32] Hence – and this takes us back to the earlier point – the universal advantage of a system of collective decision-making with a built-in right of veto.[33]

The corollaries to the distinction Tönnies made are both doubtful and redoubtable, because they tend to make us see a *Gemeinschaft* as one and the same thing as the warm, harmonious community of the romantic tradition. It is one thing to see that the degree of interdependence and the rigour of social control vary as between the two forms of society, but to see individuals as suppressed in the warmth of the *Gemeinschaft* and existing as individuals only in the *Gesellschaft* is quite another. The first proposition puts forward distinctions that are acceptable, clear and evident, and it has a cognitive value. The second imposes a Utopian view on real societies and inhibits rather than serves knowledge.

Whatever social form may be the object of our interest, it is therefore advantageous to relegate Weber's *Kollektivbegriffe* to a secondary place and refer the aggregate phenomena we are trying to explain to the *individual* behaviour that makes them up. This proposition is valid whether it is a question of analysing the system of collective decisions in force in the 'Asian villages' so beloved of the Marxist tradition, the underdeveloped state of agriculture in the France of pre-revolutionary days, social mobility in industrial societies, or any other topic.

Furthermore, whatever the spatial or temporal gap between observers and actors, the former will always be able to *understand* the latter, provided that they have at their disposal sufficient information about the *conditions* which are characteristic of their social environment. *Comprehension*, it is well worth repeating, does not mean trying to experience feelings similar to those of the actor, for an attempt of this kind is certainly doomed to failure from the start and is in any case not susceptible to verification. In the sense in which Weber used it, it means establishing the kind of relationships between the actors' situation and their motivation and action which enable the observer to conclude that in the same situation he or she would probably have acted in a like manner being able to persuade his or her reader to feel the same.

We can *understand* that villagers, who count on what they can gain from gleaning to supplement their resources, are anxious to avoid the external effects that their neighbour's proposed action would entail for them, and consequently feel perfectly justified in using the right of veto. We understand the behaviour of such people, *distant* from us in terms of both geography and culture, just as well as we understand that of the local doctor who is aware of the risks involved in using a new drug and tries to get information from those of his or her colleagues in whom he or she has confidence. The fact that one belongs to a *Gemeinschaft* and the other to a *Gesellschaft* does not *in any way* affect the ability of the observer to understand. The most the observer has to do is make sure that he or she does not project elements that are specific to his or her own situation on to what he or she is observing. This, of course, is even more important in the first of the two examples above than in the second.

These principles, which were clearly indicated by the classical German sociological tradition (Weber and Simmel, for example) are generally referred to as 'methodological individualism'. As we have seen, they neither presuppose nor rule out any particular 'microsociological model'. Depending on the circumstances, the appropriate model might be of the 'utilitarian', 'cognitive', or 'strategic' type, or indeed of others. All they recommend is that we should seek what the subjects' actions *mean to them in their own particular situation* or, in other words, the *adaptative value* of such actions. Nor do they imply any atomistic approach, since they in no way rule out the phenomena of relationships (such as influence and authority) and indeed stress that we need to understand an actor's behaviour with reference to a situation, which itself has been partly determined by macroscopic variables.

THE AGGREGATION OF INDIVIDUAL BEHAVIOUR

When a group of individuals carry out an action m, the result is an aggregation effect M. We still talk – in the same sense – of emergent, composition and – if the effect has a collectively or individually negative value – of perverse effects. In the system of symbols we used earlier, M represents the aggregation *effect* and M() designates the *operation* of aggregation.

Sometimes, the effects of the aggregation of individual actions or behaviour can be perceived intuitively, as when for one reason or another everyone is led to believe that the price of a product is about to go up. This leads to increased demand and, according to circumstances, either a shortage of the product or a price rise. These phenomena are aggregation effects, and it is not particularly hard to see what shapes them. The behaviour of the landowners that de Tocqueville describes also gives rise to an aggregation effect of some historical significance, namely the relative underdevelopment of agriculture in France at the end of the eighteenth century. All these results, which no one, of course, sought as such, arise nevertheless from no other 'force' than the wish of each individual to achieve certain aims.

Often, it is impossible to determine aggregation effects intuitively. Or, more precisely, determining M on a basis of knowledge m presupposes that we will make a conscious and determined effort to amass the relevant knowledge or conduct an appropriate analysis. The analysis of the diffusion process mentioned earlier is a case in point. It is not immediately clear that, when all the doctors have been led to seek information from their colleagues before adopting a new pharmaceutical product, the process will eventually have to take the form of an S-shaped curve. Vice versa, when a diffusion process is S-shaped, it is not immediately evident that the *macrosociological* phenomenon in question is a *microsciological* phenomenon involving interpersonal influence. We cannot intuitively establish an immediate link between the 'S-shaped curve' and the microsociological mechanism involving influence.

To conclude this chapter, I shall simply mention one or two further examples of non-intuitive aggregation effects. Since there is an indefinite number of them and it is both difficult and pointless to try to classify them, they will be presented more or less randomly, and since a great many aggregation effects will be analysed in detail later, they will only be dealt with briefly at this point.

1. If producers tend to expect their product to attract a relative price comparable to that obtaining in the previous accounting period, this will bring about a cyclic development in prices.[34]
2. If every individual wants to belong to an environment in which *half* his or her neighbours belong to the same category as him or herself, the result will be that *almost all* of them will do so. An aggregation of moderate individual demands (i.e., not to belong to a minority) gives rise to a segregation effect that goes far beyond such demands and produces a caricature of them.[35]
3. If opportunities for everyone are objectively increased, it is possible that the result will be an increase in collective discontent, since in certain cases and in terms of certain hypotheses, each individual will have been led to expect more than he or she can obtain.[36]
4. Individual preference may be non-contradictory, or more exactly, transitive (if I prefer A to B and B to C, then I also prefer A to C) without collective preference being so.[37]
5. Social inheritance between generations is increasingly marked as inequalities of educational level in terms of social origin and inequalities of social position in terms of educational level increase. Despite this, the educational level of the lower social categories can approach that of the higher ones without any attenuation of social inheritance occurring as a result.[38]
6. Educational level may have great influence on social position but none on social mobility. My social status may be very closely linked to my educational level, but that does not mean that there is any sort of relationship, at the aggregate level, between an individual's educational level and the likelihood of upward, downward or nil social mobility in relation to his or her own family.[39]
7. If a contagious disease disappears, individuals will be tempted to avoid unpleasant vaccinations. The disease will consequently tend to reappear, and once again to disappear as people resort

to vaccination once more. The cyclical nature of the return of the disease is not desired by anyone, but follows from the *understandable* attitude of all individuals to the illness and the remedy for it.

8. An example of a case in which supply and demand never coincide: at *t*, there is a shortage of doctors. The public at large becomes aware that this is so, and there is a rush of young people to gain admittance to the medical schools. The shortage persists the following year, since the eager students have not yet come back on to the labour market, and the popularity of medical studies is maintained. At the end of the cycle, there are too many doctors.

9. An example of a spiralling aggregation effect: as things are getting worse in a particular type of school, a particular region, a particular firm or a particular political party, those individuals who demand most from them leave and turn to other schools, regions, firms or parties. Since those left behind are less likely to take steps to improve the way things are going, there is further deterioration, a new exodus and more deterioration.[40]

10. Intellectual conformity as an aggregation effect. The intellectual producer, who normally – by virtue of his role – seeks influence and prestige, benefits from being discussed. Trotting out received ideas and rubbing up this or that section of the 'thinking public' is therefore a good stratagem, provided that the *form* of his work proves that he is being sufficiently original.[41]

11. If we examine the wages of a sample of individuals at a given point, they often seem to increase up to a certain age and then to fall. This aggregate finding is not incompatible with the fact that in the population examined wages increase at a regular rate throughout their working lives.[42]

The way in which aggregation effects of the type $M = M(m)$ shape things is thus not always straightforward, and a more or less lengthy training is necessary if we are to understand it. It is no more 'natural' to the human mind than handling the differential calculus and, like that discipline, has to be learned. The best method of doing so is probably to read authors like the Scottish moralists, the German dialecticians and certain modern economists, political scientists and sociologists who are aware of the basic notion of the *aggregation* of individual actions, whatever the way in which they describe it ('dialectics', 'unanticipated consequences' and so on).

The opposite process, which can be called *separation*, consists of searching for the microsociological model responsible for the effect M. Since it is symmetrical with and complementary to the operation we have just described, it runs the same risk of *tautology*, for the temptation to *transpose*, that is, to model macrosociological data on a microsociological level, to assume that a given M phenomenon occurs because individuals behave in such a way as to bring it about, is always present. Such things do sometimes happen, but when they do we hardly need the services of the social sciences. Sometimes, when actors give no clear indication of their desire to bring about M, it is assumed that that desire is *unconscious*. But why should their unconscious minds desire a result that their conscious minds are not aware of? Certain ideas in the social sciences – those of *resistance to change, the weight of tradition, the interiorization of values* and *habitus* – could provide a convenient answer, but it is usually tautologous.[43] Indeed, to say that the persistence of this or that macroscopic characteristic is attributable to the fact that individuals are impelled to resist change is no explanation. In chapter 5, we shall examine in detail this problem of *transposition*, using as our starting-point the discussion of Weber's theory of the development of capitalism.

Once we reach the point where social change must be seen as produced by the aggregation of individual actions – and what else could bring it about? – what is left of the programme defined by the theories of social change? This will form the subject of detailed discussion in the following chapters.

The principles of the sociology of action mentioned above are generally accepted where small groups and organizations are concerned.[44] In such cases it is normally accepted without much question that the 'system' can only be analysed on the basis of an individualistic methodology. (This does not, however, apply to the neo-Marxists, who keep a holistic perspective even when dealing with organizations.) On the other hand, where changes at more complex levels than that of organizations are involved, those principles are still often seen as being either useless, inefficient or even dangerous. For our part, we shall continue to interest ourselves exclusively in *macroscopic* change here, that is in change that tends to affect not a given organization but society as a whole. At this level too, at least in the thesis to be proposed and defended here, an individualistic type of methodology is to be recommended.

As a conclusion to this chapter, I should like to introduce an observation that I shall not be able to follow through in the framework in which we are operating. As I have already reminded the reader, Nisbet puts forward in his *The Sociological Tradition* the idea that sociology developed in the fertile soil of the romantic reaction to the philosophy of the Enlightenment. That thesis, however, is only readily applicable to the *French* sociological tradition typified by Comte and Durkheim. In the case of Germany (with Weber and Simmel) or of America (with Parsons and Merton) or to that part of the French tradition that escaped the influence of Comte (exemplified by de Tocqueville), one can detect a constant reference to the individualistic method produced by the Englightenment. It is also important to realize that when types of the sociology of action move away from the economy, discussion is not concerned with the principle of individualism. What it *is* concerned with is on the one hand the part played by *interests* in an explanation of behaviour and on the other the notion of the rationality of action, the meaning of which they widen. They do not underestimate the part played by behaviour, but they do relativize its importance in relation to the economic tradition. The examples I shall consider in detail later will, I believe, offer sufficient illustration of this twofold development in the sociology of action as it manifests itself in the practice of research.

3

The Laws Governing Change: the Nomological Bias

In his *The Poverty of Historicism*, Karl Popper contrasts conditional laws ('if A, then B') with laws of succession ('A, then B, then C'). In his view, only the former are scientific. Physicists, in fact, always conclude with statements of the type 'in such-and-such conditions, such-and-such an event will occur', or 'if such-and-such an event or phenomenon occurs, such-and-such another event or phenomenon will follow'. They never, on the other hand, maintain that if event A occurs, it will be followed by B and then C. This may be true of physicists, but what about astronomers? Do they not formulate 'laws of succession' when speaking about the future of stars or the different phases they are supposed to go through? And what of the biologists? No one argues with their right to formulate laws about the development of living systems. We also recognize the right of the psychologist (as with Piaget's work, for example) to formulate the laws of mental development. This means that we cannot *absolutely* deny the scientific nature of laws of succession, although it is quite legitimate to express serious doubts about the possibility of formulating such laws where social systems are concerned.

A further problem arising from Popper's distinction lies in the fact that in the social sciences laws of succession are often the implicit or explicit consequence of conditional laws. If we are willing to admit that conditional laws are valid and well founded, does it not follow that laws of succession may also be? Thus, when Parsons puts forward the idea that the modern family is of the nuclear type, he is formulating a law of evolution. That law, however, is based on a conditional law that could be formulated as follows: the modernization of socio-professional structures has a corrosive effect on the traditional model of the extended family. Similarly, Rostow's law

61

of the stages of growth rests on causal laws – that, for example, when a powerful industrial sector develops, it sets up systems of chain reactions that set a cumulative process in motion. Likewise, Mendras recently announced 'the end of the peasantry', the end of a peasant subculture hitherto strikingly different from urban industrial culture.[1] The phrase he used certainly designates a 'trend' or a law of succession, but that law is based on a range of conditional relationships. Technical innovation produces a debt-ridden peasantry and hence means that they will be dependent on the financial market; an increase in the proportion of the agricultural product offered on the market means that the peasants' standard of living will be more directly affected by agricultural prices. The result is that peasants are encouraged to organize and to take militant action to bring pressure to bear on the authorities, since they partly control the availability of credit and agricultural prices. The outcome of this series of events is that peasants are induced to calculate, to borrow, to modernize the way they run their farm, to be militant, to take an interest in 'political life' and hence to abandon their former isolation and all those characteristics that once marked them off from the rest of society.

This means that we cannot adopt Popper's distinction between conditional laws and laws of succession too rigidly. The latter are often based on the former. Let us suppose that we are certain that 'if A, then B' holds good and that A is bound to occur. In such a case, a law of succession ('A then B') will automatically follow from the conditional law 'if A, then B'. Consequently, we need to look very closely at the conditions in which conditional laws are valid in the field of the social sciences. As has already been said, Popper maintains that searching out such laws is as legitimate in the social as it is in the natural sciences and suggests that it is the main and indeed the only possible aim of any theory of social change. Are we not faced with a bias here, a nomological bias which sees the inevitable aim of scientific knowledge as being the production of universally valid empirical statements? This chapter is devoted to a discussion of that proposition.

CONDITIONAL LAWS IN GENERAL

When two elements, A and B, are linked by a conditional law 'if A then B', element A induces the actors involved to behave in such a way as to produce B by aggregation. In terms of the symbols we used in the last chapter, the conditional law is observable if B = Mm S(M',A): the situation of the actors (of certain ones) depends on the macrosocial variables M', but is also affected by A, with the result that the microscopic behaviour patterns m depend on A; as regards B, it is the result of those behaviour patterns. Since the structure of situation S depends on A, B itself also depends on A, and this can still be expressed briefly by the proposition 'if A, then B'.

Nevertheless, it must be pointed out at once that A is generally neither the necessary nor the sufficient condition for B. The formulation we have just used has the advantage of showing that B accompanies A provided that the chain of relationships linking them is also present. It is, however, quite easy to imagine circumstances in which the situation of the actor would not be affected by the presence of A. We can also envisage the situation of the actor being affected by A, but, for one reason or another, his behaviour remaining unaffected by it. In both those cases, A occurs but not B. On the other hand, there is noting to show that other phenomena than A cannot bring about B. A is therefore not the necessary condition for B.

A simple example will enable us to assess the consequences of what has just been said. Let us suppose that we are inclined to formulate a conditional law as follows: when the price of product P goes up (A), demand for it falls (B). It is not hard to imagine ideal situations that would confirm the relationship. Let us suppose that product P meets a need, that on average each individual consumes p units of P per unit of time, and that on the market there is a product Q with exactly the same virtues as P. Let us also suppose that Q is as well known as P, that is, that everyone is just as well informed about not only its existence but also its qualities. Further, let us suppose that both products have the same 'image', in the sense that there is no difference between them as far as their secondary characteristics rather than their fitness for purpose are concerned, that is, that there are no non-essential differences (such as one being a home and one a foreign product) that might affect purchasing behaviour. If all these conditions (which we shall call K) are met, the 'if A, then B' relationship will hold good, and an increase in the price of P will cause a fall in demand. We can even postulate that if the conditions K are fully met, we shall be virtually certain to observe the relationship, and at a pinch this virtual certainty is enough to enable us to dispense with testing it.

But this certainty comes from the fact that the set of conditions K creates a situation which, although not fictitious, is certainly *ideal* and of such a kind that each individual actor is supposed to have to make a choice between two products, P and Q, identical in *use*, *visibility* and *image* and differing only in the fact that – once the price of P goes up – between t and t+1 the quantity of P that the actor can buy for a given sum of money decreases, while for the same price he can buy an increasing quantity of Q. This means that he finds himself in an ideal situation in which he can either reduce his purchasing power or keep it constant. In such a position, the response $m(A)$ is hardly in doubt. He will clearly not cut his purchasing power if he can avoid it. For its part, the aggregation effect will simply be a matter of *adding up*, for everyone in that situation will act in the same way. The result will be that Q will benefit from the falling demand for P. In the last analysis, the macroscopic 'law' is virtually certain because it rests on what is evident at the microscopic level, and what gives rise to this is the fact that K creates an *ideal* situation in which the terms of the alternative as the actor sees them are defined with perfect clarity and their relative value is normally not in doubt.

It is therefore only in very limited K conditions that we can be virtually certain of seeing the 'if A, then B' relationship. Let us see what happens when one or more of the conditions of K are not met. The price of P goes up and that of Q remains stable. P and Q have exactly the same fitness for purpose, but Q is a new product and hence less well known. Some consumers are not even aware of its existence, and those who are have not tried it themselves or heard people they know talking about it. In a case of that kind, the increase in the price of P may well have no effect on demand, even if objectively Q is an advantageous buy. After a time, when consumers are better informed, there will probably be some transfer to Q, but it is difficult to say in advance how long that will take, for this process certainly varies greatly, depending as it does on the type of product, the nature of the clientele in question, and many other factors. Here, one can scarcely foresee what the empirical results are likely to be. Depending on when observations are made and many other factors, the rise in the price of P may or may not affect demand. If the interval is long enough, the producer of Q may also be forced to put up his price for quite different reasons, with the result that the effect of a rise in price of P on demand may never occur.

Alternatively, let us suppose that P is in a monopoly situation (and in that case, another K condition would not be met, since Q would not exist). What is likely to happen? Obviously, there can be no a priori answer to such a question. If P meets a naturally or socially compelling need, demand will not be affected by a price increase. The customer will have to spend more to obtain the quantity p of product P, but he will prefer to reduce his consumption of other products. If P does *not* meet such a 'need', an increase in its price might entail a restructuring of consumption in favour of R, S and so on.

Trite as they may be, these observations lead to some important epistemological conclusions. In the first place, certain sets of K conditions give rise to structure situations that are both unambiguous and *decisive*, in which there is scarcely any doubt about what the actor will do. An a priori analysis enables us to state with virtual certainty that in circumstances K, if A, then B. There are, however, other sets of K conditions in which an a priori conclusion of this type is impossible. If, for example, P and Q are competing products and Q is new and unknown, an increase in the price of P will mean that the actor is faced with a *non-decisive* situation. Consequently, in such conditions the effect of an increase in the price on demand is not a theoretical matter that can be dealt with by an a priori analysis, but an empirical one for which an a posteriori observation is the only possible method.

We naturally tend, however, to pay particular attention to sets of circumstances that create unambiguous and decisive situations of the kind that enable us to make an a priori forecast of how the actor will behave that is almost certain to be correct. But the fact that these types of circumstances are theoretically interesting does not mean that *empirically* they are the most frequently occurring, since there is no reason why theoretical interest and empirical frequency should be connected in any way.[2]

So the situation of the sociologist, economist or demographer is very different from that of the physicist. The laws that they formulate hold good in certain limited areas. In the social sciences, the boundary of those areas is almost always vague, and it is in fact impossible to describe all the sets of circumstances such as K in any exhaustive way. Some, but only some, of them can be easily identified, and they are the ones which have the characteristic of creating an ideal situation S which is decisive and unambiguous from the point of view of the actor. This means that $m(S)$, the microscopic behaviour, can easily be determined. Once a set of conditions K' no longer has this feature, $m(S)$ is uncertain, and then there will be either a situation in which A is fittingly followed by B or one in which it is unfittingly followed by not-B.

The limited areas in which laws hold good, the vagueness of the boundaries of those areas and the difficulty of determining what the real circumstances of a concrete situation might be are the three factors that play a part in giving the notion of constitutional law a different epistemological status in the natural and the social sciences. Objects heavier than air may not always fall to the ground – as witness aeroplanes, rockets and leaves carried along by the wind – but the physicist can give a very accurate description of the conditions in which the law of falling bodies applies or does not apply. On the other hand, for the sociologist the boundaries can only be drawn with that kind of precision in extreme cases.

Regularities of the 'if A, then B' type can only be the result of the aggregation of microscopic actions. Since they *are* the effects of aggregation, they can only be valid in certain limited areas, for they depend on sets of circumstances K. Attempting to make them generally valid, therefore, means supposing that they have their basis in a transcendental order, whatever name we give it. Some of these names have been 'society' (Durkheim), 'humanity' (Comte), 'history' (Marx), 'spirit' (Hegel), and 'modernization', 'structures', 'evolution', 'development' and so on.

That is why there is still a correlation between the naturalist view of social change and the refusal of individualist methodology. Durkheim, who was steeped in Comtian positivism and influenced by the naturalism of 'social physics', insistently tried to show that sociology *could* not only pay no attention to the motives of social actors but indeed *ought not* to take individuals and their subjectivity into account if it wanted to treat its subject-matter scientifically. In this connection, Marx's case is more complex. He had long been a student of English political economy and was well aware of the value of individualist methodology. At the same time, however, he introduced notions, like those of false consciousness and alienation, that were incompatible with it. The fact that he abandoned the notion of alienation after his 1844 manuscripts no doubt shows that he was aware of the clash between that notion and the methodological individualism he employed when writing *Capital*. These problems of the history of the social sciences can be found elsewhere, and for the moment we shall simply note that methodological individualism entails the particular consequence that it is impossible to establish conditional laws of the 'if A, then B' type that are generally valid once they are seen as aggregation effects.

Local regularities, of course, are commonly noted. In the period studied by Durkheim, for example, suicide seemed to be increasing in the countries for which he had statistics. But even if we assume that the increase was not a statistical artefact arising, for example, from the fact that certain processes such as urbanization make it easier to keep statistical records of suicide, we must also bear in mind that, as Halbwachs pointed out in his *The Causes of Suicide* as early as 1930, the regularities established by Durkheim were very largely overthrown in the subsequent period, despite the fact that his laws implicitly 'excluded' such a possibility.

MODELS AND LAWS

At this point, it would be helpful to introduce a further theme that will receive more detailed treatment in chapter 7. Like the topic we have just examined, it too has to do with the epistemology and history of the social sciences. We have already seen that certain sets of circumstances, like K in our example, have the property of creating situations in which it is possible to come to a priori conclusions about $m(S)$ and $[Mm(S)]$. In modern jargon, we would say that in such cases we have created a *model*. The whole range of models proposed by sociologists makes up what has traditionally been called *sociological* or *economic theory*.[3] It is, however, understood that a model, in so far as it is based on *ideal* circumstances, can only be applied to a limited number of real situations and also that it can only be seen as an approximation. The second of these two points scarcely creates any difficulty, since any law, even in the natural sciences, always *is* an approximation. The first, however, shows just how far a *model* is from being a *law*, considered epistemologically. A law applies to all cases, a model to *ideal*, that is, to *particular* cases. Thus K, as seen in the foregoing example, can only be seen as a suitable approximation of reality in certain cases.

Simmel – to raise in passing a point that we shall return to in chapter 7 – was perhaps one of the writers who saw this distinction most clearly.[4] When he defends the importance of formal sociology (a notion which is often quite misunderstood), what he is really saying is that the theoretical activity of the sociologist and the economist is chiefly a matter of working out idealized models rather than laws. When he takes up a deliberately nominalist position in his writings on formal sociology, he is trying to counter the realism of those claiming to have discovered the laws that social systems are supposed to obey.

All that has just been said about causal laws would apply equally to mathematical or statistical laws. We saw in chapter 2 that *certain* diffusion processes develop according to a so-called logistical law, with the number of converts to the new product increasing very slowly at first, and then increasingly rapidly until roughly half of the potential converts have been won over. Thereafter, the process slows down and tends to zero speed when *almost all* the individuals concerned have been converted. The characteristic curve of the process is S-shaped. Here we are talking about a *model* in the sense in which diffusion processes *rarely* have this characteristic feature, even in a rough-and-ready way. The logistical model presupposes very restrictive circumstances: they must be such, for example, that the individuals likely to convert each other have equal chances of meeting or consulting together. That condition may be very far from being met if, for example, the population likely to be won over to some technical innovation is a rural one. In such a case, it is impossible to suppose even in the most approximate terms that every individual concerned is just as likely to meet and consult every other one. Geographical obstacles may mean that there are virtual isolates where internal communication is much more frequent than communication with other such groups. Nor can we assume that every individual would benefit from the innovation to the same degree. Some may be tenant farmers, others may own their own land. The older ones may have no descendants likely to take over the farm and may therefore see no advantage in getting into debt for the sake of an investment whose benefits they will not live to see. We can, therefore, see that the logistical model applies to some, but not to all, diffusion processes. It does not apply to those where no mechanisms of interpersonal influence are brought into play, and within the range of processes where that factor *is* involved, it does not apply to those where circumstances are relatively restrictive. That is why it is a *model* and not a *law*. It is *typical* of certain diffusion processes; namely, those in which *influence* is operative. However, it only describes faithfully the simplest real processes belonging to this class. We can of course remove some of the restrictive conditions it is based on. It would be possible, for example, to develop a variant of the model in which the likelihood of individuals meeting each other is a function of the distance between them and to introduce hypotheses or conditions relating to the distribution of these distances. That gives a wider view of the model, of which the classical logistical model then becomes one particular case. But generalization very soon reaches a point beyond which it cannot go, and this means that, even in its most general form, the model will only apply to a limited part of the subclass of real diffusion processes in which interpersonal influence comes into play.

By replacing the notion of *laws* with that of *models*, we have therefore crossed a yawning epistemological gap. Tarde thought that there were *laws* of imitation capable of accounting for every social process.[5] We now know that not every social process is a diffusion process, that not every diffusion process involves 'imitation' (i.e., 'influence') mechanisms, and that diffusion processes that do involve mechanisms of interpersonal influence are not expressed by a law of determinate form. In the place of Tarde's unified and reassuring vision of the future shape of society governed by the laws of imitation in the same way as the movements of the universe are governed by the laws of celestial mechanics, we must put a less comfortable one, in which there emerges from the whole varied range of social processes an archipelago, small in total area, of processes simple and idealized in structure that obey the restrictive conditions of *models*.

Tarde is hardly a fashionable figure today, but his relegation to limbo or oblivion is not the result of his belief that it was possible to formulate laws about change in societies, since the search for such laws, whether they be laws of succession, conditional, structural, or statistical and mathematical, is still one of the most sought-after and explicit aims of the social sciences. Durkheim, his *frère ennemi*, did not suffer the same fate. Of course, although he differed from Tarde in many ways, his views on the point at issue here were identical. Both set out to discover *laws* which in their mind were not fundamentally different from the laws of nature.

There are two fields of investigation – political mobilization and socio-economic development – that can be used as examples to illustrate the nomological ambitions contained in the social sciences. They will also show us just how fragile those ambitions are.

THE LAWS OF MOBILIZATION

There is no area of investigation in the social sciences in which the desire to establish causal laws has not been manifest. To take an example: is it not 'obvious' that collective violence will occur more frequently when collective discontent is most marked?

To show whether or not it really is 'obvious', Snyder and Tilly undertook a study covering 130 years of French history, the period 1830–1960.[6] To measure the annual level of collective violence, they first established two criteria of assessment, one based on the number of social disturbances during the period in question, the other on the number of participants involved in them. By 'disturbance', the authors understood 'continuous interactions involving at least one group of fifty or more persons in the course of which someone seized or damaged persons or objects over resistance'. The estimated number of such disturbances and participants was based on a day-by-day analysis of two national daily newspapers. They established that there was a close link between the two: the number of participants was at its highest when the number of disturbances was greatest. There is nothing surprising in that. Nevertheless, collective violence varied in magnitude from one year to the next, and the two curves are very jagged.

It is very hard to know whether or to what extent collective violence is a function of discontent. Since it is difficult to measure the latter, Snyder and Tilly used two 'objective' variables, supposing – plausibly enough, it might seem – that they would measure hardship and hence could be expected to be closely linked to the degree of collective discontent. These were an index of food prices, of manufactured goods and of industrial production. The problem was then that of analysing the available data to show any effects that each of the three variables might have had on collective violence as measured by either of the two methods described above. Their hypothesis – which I shall call here H1 – was that an *increase* in the price of food products or manufactured goods or a *decrease* in industrial production from one year to the next would be reflected in an increase in the number of disturbances or the number of persons involved in them.

The interest of the study lies in the fact that it produced an entirely negative result. There was *no variation* in collective violence over the period and in the context chosen as the level of hardship rose or fell. If we posit hardship as the cause of discontent, this means that in the time-span under consideration collective violence did not vary as discontent increased or decreased.

These findings perhaps surprised Snyder and Tilly, who wondered whether they were the result of doubtful hypotheses. The effects of rises in the price of foodstuffs on living conditions and discontent are immediate, whereas those of rises in the price of manufactured goods may only occur some time later. In H1 as set out above, however, variations in the different variables are simultaneous. The hypothesis assumes, for example, that there will be an effect of the variation in food prices between t-1 and t on the variation in collective violence over the same period. It would, of course, be very easy to introduce other hypotheses which would take into account possible time-lags. We could assume, for example, that there would be an effect of a variation in the price of manufactured goods over the period from t-2 to t-1 on the variation in collective violence from t-1 to t. A hypothesis of this kind means supposing that a rise (or fall) in the price of industrial products takes a year to make its effects felt. Since there is a high degree of uncertainty where such time-lapses are concerned, the best method is to use as many hypotheses as possible in cases of this kind. This is what Snyder and Tilly did. In every case (i.e., whatever hypotheses about time-lapses were used) the influence of variations in price and production on variations in collective violence was practically nil.

It seems therefore that the *causes* of discontent do not have any influence on variations in the way in which that discontent is manifested. The causes of discontent may increase (or decrease) without manifestations of discontent showing a parallel increase (or decrease).

These negative findings are of major importance, for if there is no relationship between the level (A) of discontent and the intensity (B) with which it is in fact expressed, one wonders between what A and B elements a conditional law of the 'if A, then B' type could possibly be established. In fact, the hypothetical proposition 'if A (if there are causes of discontent) then B (the discontent is likely to be expressed) or, alternatively, 'the greater the discontent (A), the more it will be expressed (B)', tends to be seen as self-evident, since at the *individual level* it *is*. It is true that the more numerous the causes of an individual's discontent, the more likely he is to adopt discontented behaviour. At the individual level, the relationship between A and B is so obvious that not even the most empirically minded psychologist would be likely to bother to verify it. At the *collective* level, it is also obvious, but interesting because it is *false*. Why should it be so? The reason is not hard to find, for collective discontent is not simply the sum total of indvidual discontents. A situation S may cause discontent. However, determining whether this discontent will be expressed in an individual's participation ($m(S)$) in, for example, a demonstration, will depend on all sorts of conditions. Amongst the potential organizers, some will have to judge that *from their point of view*, the demonstration has a chance of succeeding (by attracting a sufficient number of people) and of paying off (by increasing their political credit). If these conditions are met, the individual who could participate still has to believe that the risk and costs involved are bearable and that the advantages to be gained are real and worth while. These risks, costs and advantages depend in their turn [$S = S(M')$] on variables. In a period of economic depression, for example, many people would no doubt prefer to struggle to keep their job rather than take part in certain kinds of collective action. If they feel that in such a situation the likelihood of mobilizing sufficient support is not great enough, the potential organizers might feel it better not to call upon their supporters. In such cases, the level of discontent will be high, but there will not be many massive or frequent demonstrations.

There is therefore no reason why we should expect to find any correlation between the degree of discontent and the extent to which it is expressed collectively. Discontent and the expression of it are likely to be related phenomena at the individual, but not at the collective, level. A slight increase in what Snyder and Tilly call 'hardship' might produce a great deal of collective demonstration. On the other hand, it is also easy to imagine situations in which the opposite would occur, with a major increase in hardship producing very little. Thus the 'obvious' law linking discontent and protest collapses completely once we realize that protest is an *action* which, depending on the situation of the actors, might seem to them more or less possible, valid, preferable or otherwise in comparison to other actions which are equally possible. The empirical analysis conducted by Snyder and Tilly shows in any case that in France between 1830 and 1960 violence was neither greater nor more likely when discontent was highest. Their empirical findings are also correspondingly much less surprising once we accept the idea that collective violence is an *aggregated* effect of individual behaviour.

In addition, there are many studies which show directly – and not indirectly, as that of Snyder and Tilly does – why A (discontent) may be followed by B (collective violence) or not-B. One of these is Oberschall's work on social movements.[7] The Black movement that grew up in the United States in the 1960s was often violent in the North and non-violent in the South. The reason for this lies not in the *personalities* of the leaders or their *preference* for violent or peaceful methods. The fact that disorder appears at the macrosociological level does not mean that the sociologist cannot make a valid contribution.

In both the North and the South, the root of the Black 'problem' clearly lay in the inequality between their conditions and those of the whites. But that inequality became a *problem* in the 1960s when, as a result of the application of the famous 'Thomas's theorem',[8] not only many Blacks, but a section of the cultural and political elites of both ethnic communities defined it as one, that is, as a situation that absolutely had to be rectified. As long as a social movement only has an audience amongst the subpopulation directly served by its objectives, it runs the risk of being seen as deviant, dangerous and reprehensible. Once that audience extends to subpopulations and sections of elites not directly affected by them, however, its cause can no longer be seen in the same light. Even if it is arguable, it becomes legitimate to argue about it. Thus a fundamental problem for leaders of socio-political movements is that of setting up, and of course maintaining, as effective as possible a system of alliances.

In the Southern States, the Black Protestant churches were the only institutions that were not largely under white control and did not have a significant white nucleus. There were many of them, and they were the basis of extended and diverse social relationship networks. Those churches, which Oberschall describes as being organized in the form of associations, hierarchical, fund-raising and elective,[9] were the sole places, in a South that had barely left behind the paternalist era, where Black leaders could be formed. Because of their function as poles of attraction and meeting-places, and of their influence in the Black community, the Protestant churches were potentially a very important ally for those who for one reason or another took on the task of promoting the Black cause. At the very least, such people had at all costs to avoid taking a different course from the Black clergy. This meant that the use of violence entailed a major risk for anyone tempted to resort to it, for it would alienate not only the Protestant clergy, but a great part of the Black population. The latter would include not only those recognizing the moral and religious authority of the churches, but also those whose religious convictions were not profound but who nevertheless took part in the various activities organized by the churches or, more simply, were aware that they were the only institutions not dominated by the whites. All the components of the situation in the South therefore urged a strategy of non-violence.

It was quite different in the North. The role of the churches in the social relationship networks was much less central, the Black proletariat much more fragmented than in the South, and the potential leaders had been formed by various backgrounds. A multitude of social problems emerged in the great Northern cities. They were *competing* problems, and the attention of political and cultural elites and of the general public was a scarce commodity, which could not be attracted to every problem simultaneously.[10] Here, organized violence and the recognition and 'recuperation' of spontaneous violence could seem effective strategies to political organizers. In any case, they successfully attracted the attention of intellectuals and politicians.

Although the basic data were by and large the same in both North and South, the two different contexts meant that in the South violence was a dangerous and ineffective strategy, whereas in the North it could be seen as advantageous. This simple example takes us back to a very obvious fact, which is that in a social system the concordance of two elements, A and B, depends on the structure of the system, and consequently there is no reason to suppose that it will be present in every case or even more frequently than the discordance 'A and not-B'. If trying to find causal laws were a fundamental aim of the social sciences, that conclusion would be distressing. But nothing indicates that this should be so. Why should it be more profitable to *establish that* the same causes always produce the same effects than to *explain why* the same causes can produce different effects in different situations?

Nevertheless, as Tilly has rightly pointed out, trying to discover the conditional laws governing violence is still an enduring aim in the social sciences.[11] As has been said, de Tocqueville thought revolutions were more likely to occur when a long period of economic or political stagnation is followed by a phase in which opportunities and possibilities of action are greater for everyone. This has certainly been observed in the past and will no doubt be observed in the future. What we have here is not a universal but a local law, that is, a relationship observable in certain conditions that cannot be described exhaustively. This implies that the relationship is formulated *existentially* ('if A, then sometimes B') and never *deterministically* ('if A, then always B') or *probabilistically* ('if A, then most frequently B'), as by de Tocqueville. There is nothing to justify maintaining that A will be followed more often by B than by not-B. The most we can say is that A *may* be followed by B.

Following de Tocqueville, other 'laws' of social and political mobilization were proposed. That of Davies, which maintains that revolutions are more frequent when a period of stagnation suddenly follows a period of steady growth, is a case in point.[12] In such a situation, it is held, individuals are likely to express unrealistic expectations and to form unrealistic aspirations, all of which will inevitably come to naught. It is, however, possible to maintain the opposite, and to say that a sudden cessation of growth can bring in its wake a hypersensitive kind of introversion that leads to a fall in collective action. Davies's 'law', like that of de Tocqueville and all conditional laws of the same type, are in fact expressing mere *possibilities*.

Gurr deserves separate mention.[13] In seeking to account for the fact that collective violence involves adversaries who have to mobilize resources in order to mount either collective action or resistance to it, he proposes a more complex law than his predecessors. In his view, the likelihood of collective action is a function of such variables as discontent, the resources enjoyed by antagonists in relation to each other, and so on. His law is no longer of the type 'if A, then B'. It is of interest to the extent that it is compatible with, for example, the lack of any link between A and B, since if A is to be followed by B, the conditions A', A'' and so on have to be met. Its area of validity is therefore greater than that of all those laws which seek to make collective violence a function of discontent alone. Nevertheless, it is still a local law. In addition, if we ignore the formula expressing it, we can see it rather as a *model*, since all it does after all is describe a formal framework and list a certain number of variables that have to be taken into account when analysing political mobilization.

From their study showing the lack of a relationship between hardship and collective violence, Snyder and Tilly do not seem to have drawn the conclusion that there can be no laws of collective violence. Their critical examination covers the nature of A rather than the form 'if A, then B'. In the second part of their article, they establish in fact that, although political violence in France between 1830 and 1960 was not affected by hardship, it *was* affected by the rhythms of political life (election years/non-election years), the severity of government repression, and a range of other political variables. They thus appear to be suggesting that the attempt to find conditional laws of the 'if A, then B' type is admissible in the case of collective violence provided that the conditions, A, are sought solely within the field of political variables. In fact, however, it has been noted in other contexts (particularly the British) that collective violence certainly can depend on *economic* ones. Thus in England, strikes seem at certain periods to have been closely linked to economic variables, but not in France.[14]

There has consequently been no general 'if A, then B' type of law formulated for the field of collective violence. All we can observe is relationships belonging to specific times and situations between certain A and B variables, the nature of A varying temporally and spatially. The differences between France and England in the particular case we are looking at are easy to explain. In modern times, the British state has been both more discreet in its interventions and more stable in its institutions and is seen as more legitimate. For their part, the British trade unions have been more powerful and more concerned with economic objectives. It is therefore understandable that in England collective violence has been more closely linked to economic variables than in France and, vice versa, why it has been more tied to political variables in France than in England. When there is a relationship between A and B, it is always subject to mediation by the *system* $B = Mm S(M', A)$. Depending on whether M' is different in this or that situation, A will or will not be accompanied by B.

To my mind, there are three reasons why the attempt to find laws of the type 'if A, then B' still occupies, implicitly or explicitly, a major place in studies relating to collective violence.

The first is of a general nature. The naturalistic way of thinking is still dominant in the social sciences. Conditional laws are seen as a part of the current production of the natural sciences, and producing them is *therefore* a sign of genuine science. It should be borne in mind that Popper himself is not immune to that argument in his *The Poverty of Historicism*.

The second reason lies in the fact that we are often only too ready to reduce the *aggregation* of individual actions to a mere *adding up*. Aggregation, however, although it may take that form, is not restricted to it. If every consumer wants less of a product, the overall demand for it will fall. If everyone is more discontented, the result is not the same kind of increase in collective discontent, for the 'sum' of individual discontents is one thing, and the collective expression of discontent is another. It should also be noted that writers such as Olson[15] and Hirschman[16] have identified some typical cases in which an increase in individual discontent is unlikely to produce collective protest. A situation of this kind will come about if, for example, everyone thinks he or she can get out of a fix more easily by using an individual defection strategy than by taking part in collective action, especially if it seems costly and not certain of producing the right result.

The third reason why conditional laws are so attractive in the area of collective violence has its roots in the holistic view of social movements. This view is based on the following postulates: in a social movement, the individual dissolves, and an 'individualist' analysis which sees the movement as an aggregated effect of individual actions is 'therefore' not relevant; 'consequently', all we can try to find is how to determine the *collective* circumstances A of *collective* action B. A historical epistemological study, which would be of enormous importance, would no doubt show that as far as the social sciences are concerned holistic paradigms have always been more fascinating than individualist ones.

THE LAWS OF DEVELOPMENT AND MODERNIZATION

This is another field, which I take here as a further example, where research has also very largely been directed towards the formulation of conditional *laws*. There are many such laws: the sociology of economic developments, that of political development, development economics, the sociology of modernization[17] and other disciplines have contributed towards this output. All or almost all laws of this kind now tend to be seen as of doubtful validity. In almost every case, a counter-example can be produced for each of them.

Parsons put forward the idea that industrialization leads to the replacement of the model of the extended family by that of the nuclear family. In his view, this 'law' was the result of the fact that in modern societies education tends to develop outside the framework of the family, social status to be more often acquired than transmitted, geographical mobility to increase, and so on. Such propositions are clearly acceptable, but cannot be regarded as generally valid. In Japan, if we are to believe what Ezra Vogel has established, an entrepreneur wishing to fill a post negotiated the recruitment of a candidate in discussion with the latter's family, who could therefore make full use of the resources of family solidarity in establishing the detailed terms of the contract and making sure that they were adhered to.[18] If the new employee was dismissed without good reason, the family could help dry up the supply of labour for the entrepreneur. In a situation of that kind, industrialization tends to *strengthen* rather than weaken the links of solidarity in the extended family, since they are a very valuable asset in negotiations.

Is this kind of discordance (A and not-B: industrialization plus stronger rather than weaker ties of family solidarity) *atypical* or simply less common than A and B concordance? It is hard to know in advance, and even to know after the event, for how can we determine the statistical population that would enable us to make comparative assessments? All that we can say is that there is no reason why discordance should be the exception rather than the rule and, indeed, that it can be the result of various configurations of factors. Let us simply take a second example, which most people would agree probably describes any number of real situations. When industrial wages are low and there is only moderate excess rural population, the pull-effect of industry and the push-effect of rural society will probably not be very marked. In circumstances of that kind, the wages of certain members of the family often supplement the family income from agricultural work and the family gives them in return facilities which enable them to survive on low wages. In such cases, far from breaking the solidarity of the extended family, industry helps to strengthen it.

Innumerable laws have been put forward in the field of economic development.[19] For example:

1. Development cannot occur if markets are purely local. When total potential demand is low, production will also necessarily be low. Indeed, there can only be any encouragement to increase productivity if total demand crosses a certain threshold. Thus, the owner of a workshop producing shoes will derive no benefit from mechanizing his production unless he expects to sell more than a few pairs a month.
2. Existing overhead capital (such as communications networks) is essential for development. In its absence, markets are purely local, and the processes described above occur.
3. When the ability to save is low, investment is impossible. This means that there can be no increase in productivity, with the result that individual resources remain static and the ability to save stays low. Consequently, development can only occur as a result of outside aid.[20]
4. When surplus resources in a society at a low stage of economic development are in the hands of an elite, that elite will tend to use the surplus for consumption rather than for investment, since investment presupposes the existence of sufficient demand, which is lacking when a large section of the population is living just above subsistence level.
5. In countries at a low stage of economic development, elites tend to consume rather than invest by virtue of the *conspicuous consumption effect*, which encourages them to adopt the consumption models of the 'rich' countries.

No doubt it would be laudable to mention a great many other laws. Those just described belong to what is generally labelled the 'developmentalist' school, but neo-Marxist theories of development have also produced numerous 'laws'. The same would also apply to all those currents of research centering on socio-economic development.

All such laws show mechanisms that it is *possible* to observe empirically and of which the logic can be easily seen at the theoretical level, just as it is possible to conceive of and observe, *in certain cases*, a *possible* cause-and-effect relationship between the rise in price of a product and a fall in demand for it. These mechanisms, however, are *ideal* ones, and only come into operation in the *real* world in certain very stringent conditions, exactly as an increase in price only produces a fall in demand in equally stringent conditions. If these are not met, we have a discordance, and not a concordance, between A and B.

Thus, we can counter the law that sees the prior accumulation of overhead capital as a precondition for development by quoting the example of Argentina at the beginning of the twentieth century, where spectacular economic development preceded rather than followed the development of a transport system.[21] Against the law positing the necessity of external aid for economic development, we can set the example of England in the eighteenth and Japan in the nineteenth century.[22] Similarly, by referring to the example of Colombia which, as Hagen has shown, developed very rapidly at the beginning of the nineteenth century despite the fact that trade between its regions was limited by its geography and the rudimentary state of its communications,[23] we can cast doubt on the universal validity of the law which sees fragmented markets as a bottleneck.

Should we take such cases to be exceptions that confirm the rule? Should some examples be seen as typical and others as atypical? The first of these two interpretations presupposes that we could make exhaustive frequency studies of an impossible nature. The second implies a definition of the pair of opposites 'typical/atypical' that could probably at best be only circular and hence, as Pareto has it, based on sentiments rather than experience. It is more pertinent to see that such so-called laws are in fact *ideal models* which can be more or less realized *in certain cases*, but whose area of validity cannot be exactly defined.

THE ANATOMY OF A THEORY OF SOCIAL CHANGE

It would be useful to stop at this point for a moment and draw this chapter to a close with a theory of social change – that proposed by Hagen – which provides an admirable illustration of both the influence exerted by the *nomological* or *nomothetic* concept of social change, by which we mean the attempt to find laws, and the impossibility of formulating such laws.

The starting-point of Hagen's 'theory of social change' is a critique of economic theories of economic development, which to his mind provide no explanation of important examples such as the development of Japan in the nineteenth century or Colombia at the beginning of the twentieth. Both countries developed without any outside aid. The flow of foreign capital into Colombia was insignificant until just after the Second World War, and its domestic markets were small and scattered. Until they began to develop spectacularly, Japan and Colombia were poor countries, but they did not obey the 'law of the vicious circle of poverty'. In short, none of the fashionable theories of the 1960s provided an explanation of their pattern of development, which clearly must not be under-estimated. And there are many other instances of resistance to theorizing.

Hagen casts a very critical eye on the ability of economic theories to explain economic development, concluding that the variables responsible for development are perhaps to be found in some other field than the economy. His critique is interesting in itself. He points out one of the annoyingly counter-productive effects of the division of labour operating in the social sciences: economists, sociologists and political scientists tend to take into account only variables arising in their own fields. The result is that if an economist or political scientist 'discovers' stratification, or a sociologist political institutions, budgetury constraints or the cost of information, it is something of an event. By suggesting that development might be a result of non-economic variables, Hagen helped to strike a salutary blow at the postulate of the independence of the economic subsystem, a postulate dictated more by the bad habits of a division of labour characterized by rigidity and anomie than by reasoned choice.

His *social* 'theory' of economic development is based on one or two case-studies and can easily be summarized. In all the cases examined, economic development was seen to be the result of the appearance of a group of entrepreneurs. Contrary to what the economic theories, so rightly criticized by Hagen, proposed, this was not a spontaneous phenomenon, occurring as soon as there was a demand. A demand for footwear is not enough to produce a dynamic boot and shoe industry. The existence of potential demand is perhaps a factor that will encourage the appearance of a corresponding supply, but it is not a sufficient condition for industrialization. In fact, both dynamic production and low demand and slack production and considerable total demand can be observed. Once the appearance of a group of entrepreneurs is no longer seen as the automatic result of the stimulation produced by demand, one of the basic problems of an analysis of development is that of attempting to discover the social conditions which explain its appearance.

Here, the cases Hagen examined convinced him that certain social variables made the emergence of such a group more or less likely. In Japan, entrepreneurs came to a disproportionate extent from the *samurai* class. Colombian statistics for 1956 giving the regional origin of the founders of 161 businesses employing more than 100 workers showed that a disproportionately high number of them came from Antioquía. The figures were 75 for this province as against a mere 25 from Cundinimarca, culturally and politically a much more important area, since it contained the capital, Bogotá. The interesting point is that the *samurai* and the Antioqueños had a common characteristic: both had come down in the social scale.

The *samurai*, who had served feudal lords, found themselves without employment or social status when the Tokaguwa emperors sought to strengthen the central power at the expense of such lords and keep them on a tight rein at the court in Kyoto. Like the Bogotanos, the Antioqueños were the descendants of Spanish colonists who had come to search for gold and silver in New Granada in the sixteenth century. They found both in Antioquiá, but not in the Bogotá area. The Antioqueños consequently became mineowners, whereas the Bogotanos began to work the land. From the middle of the seventeenth century, however, the gold and silver mines were more or less worked out, or at least brought in too little income for their owners to be able to keep on all the Indian workers they had employed for decades. They were thus reduced to a proletarian status. This meant that in the eyes of the Bogotanos or Caliños, Antioquía subsequently became a rather inferior hinterland. When Japan entered the Neiji era, the *samurai* became businessmen. When, at the beginning of the twentieth century, Colombia experienced economic growth similar to that of many other countries, the Antioqueños became the heads of companies.

From these shared characteristics of Japan and Colombia and those revealed by other case-studies, Hagen concluded that a collective decline in social status was one of the causes of the appearance of a group of dynamic entrepreneurs. In his view, both the *samurai* and the Antioqueños were encouraged, at a time when the first hesitant signs of economic development were beginning to appear, to become industrialists because they were obsessed with regaining their lost status. The trouble is that several generations passed betweeen the time the *samurai* first lost that status as a result of the strategy of the Tokugawa emperors and the point at which their descendants contributed to the economic rise of Japan. Similarly, there was a gap of several generations between the mid-seventeenth century, when the Antioquía mineowners took up the pick and shovel themselves, and the beginning of the twentieth.

Rightly convinced that his data – the fall in the social status of the Antioqueños and the *samurai* and the particular part both groups played in industrial development – were reliable, Hagen was unwilling to believe that the correlation between their loss of social status and their part in development was fortuitous. Rather laboriously and not very convincingly, he attempted to use the weight of certain psychological and psychoanalytical theories to show that the resentment caused by the withdrawal of status can be handed down from generation to generation. By being incorporated into the structure of the personality through the upbringing in the family, resentment could, he suggested, become a psychological determinant. The way personality was built up would thus be guided by a dominant value, achievement, and an unconscious aim, that of regaining lost status.

The theory clearly has all the weaknesses of theories that provide the personality of the actor with all the psychic setting, passions or determinants that induce him to adopt the precise behaviour they are seeking to explain: how can the existence of such determinants be shown, other than on the basis of behaviour?[24] But what hopes can one have that they will then *explain* it? Apart from being circular in nature, this theory is improbable on more than one account. How can it be possible for psychological factors of this kind to be transmitted over the generations in an even more rigorous way than genetic transmission since, after all, the latter presupposes a favourable *environment* and consequently cannot operate without it? It is true that studies have shown that loss of status can influence levels of aspiration. Children whose mother's social origin is higher than her current status often have, *ceteris paribus*, a higher level of aspiration.[25] A situation of that kind, however, is different from the one Hagen is describing, for although it is not improbable that a mother will remember her former social status, even if she has lost it by her marriage, it is much less certain that the memory of lost status can be maintained for generation after generation.

Ultimately, then, Hagen's theory is not too convincing. Nevertheless, it is interesting to note that it fails because of the nature of his investigation, which is still a model of its kind, but as a result of an epistemological bias towards the belief that a 'theory of social change' should eventually lead to the formulation of a 'law'. Effectively, Hagen set out to establish a *law* linking, in this case, the loss of social status and the entrepreneurial spirit. In doing so, he himself deeply obscured the extremely meticulous and highly credible theory of the development of Colombia implicit in his book. That theory takes the form of various *membra disjecta* that need reassembling, since he attempted to set out his contribution as an 'if A, then B' *law* rather than spell out the model $M = Mm s(M',A)$, even though he provides all its elements. We shall now try, albeit summarily, to reconstitute this model. We shall see that it will then be possible to dispense completely with the doubtful hypotheses of cultural transmission on which his 'theory' hinges.

The facts of Colombian geography meant that from the beginning of the seventeenth century there was in fact a social and regional segmentation of the country. The Antioqueños were reduced to proletarian status, with some of them working fairly uneconomic mines. At an appropriate point, some began to grow coffee. When this developed, others went in for transport. The whole enterprise, however, was risky. Until the beginning of the twentieth century, there was no road tunnel linking Medellin, the capital of the Antioquía province, with the Sabana, the area around Bogotá, and it was not until 1940 that it was linked to Cali, further to the south. The period 1800–1900 saw slow development in Colombia, similar to that experienced in neighbouring countries. It was, however, more marked in the Sabana than in Antioquía. Throughout the country, one or two banks, a textile industry, industry connected with consumer goods, breweries and transport companies grew up, but they tended to be concentrated in the Sabana. Subsequently, and particularly from the period just after the First World War, this regional imbalance was reversed. Until the middle of the nineteenth century, Antioquía had been the poorest and economically the least dynamic province. Three-quarters of a century later, it was an important centre of development.

Why were new firms founded to a disproportionate extent by Antioqueños, both in Antioquía and elsewhere? Contrary to what Hagen claimed, but in accordance with what his data enable us to say, there would be no point in resorting to the hypothesis of a collective memory trace of social status embedded in the structure of the personality. All that is needed is a consideration of the differences in the situation of the actors, which themselves arise from geographically and historically caused differences in the social structure of Antioquía and the Sabana. Four sets of data provide an explanation of them.

In the first place, the Sabana contained large estates, whereas in the 'Valley' (the province of Cali) stock-raising was the most important activity. For the historical and geographical reasons already given, landowning was a less significant activity in Antioquía.

Secondly, Antioquía was a cultural backwater. Its inhabitants were considered by those of other provinces as being a race apart and rather to be looked down on, a view resulting from the fact that the area had undergone a process of proletarianization over two centuries. Indeed, the general awareness of the Antioqueños as a different breed of men was so acute that myths grew up to explain the fact, and there were even some attempts to check them. It was thought that perhaps they were the descendants of Jewish or Basque colonists. The low esteem they were held in was even reflected in history books, which gave very little space to Antioquía's part in the country's past. The result was that when the education system developed, the province was unpopular and badly served. Even before independence, institutions of higher education and research establishments grew up more or less everywhere except in Medellin. Refugees from the civil wars settled there, thus helping to confirm that city's reputation as a ghetto town. In Antioquía, there were fewer contacts with the world outside Colombia than elsewhere.

Thirdly, although the region was poor, Antioquía also had its economic elite, which had a surplus at its command. Before the development of communications, the difficulty of transport and the needs of trade had produced long-distance haulage concerns. When roads, tunnels and railways began to appear, this activity declined, but it had served to enrich several families.

The final type of important data is that, within the framework of their mineworking activities, the Antioqueños had made use of modern forms of organization comparable to limited liability companies. Exploring for seams was a high-risk undertaking, and each project was financed on the basis of 24 shares, with a majority decision of the shareholders sufficing to suspend activities. If the enterprise failed, debts were honoured on a basis of equality by each of the 24. Shareholders were often kinsmen. As late as the beginning of the twentieth century, undertakings founded by Antioqueños were more often family concerns than those founded by others.

Now that we have established these four factors, we can determine their consequences $m(S)$. The elites of the Sabana and Antioquía had different types of resources and were exposed to different *opportunity structures*. The structure of the socio-professional environment encouraged the former to buy land, send their children to study and to encourage them to go into the liberal professions or take up administrative and political careers. For the latter, it was much harder to achieve such aims, and they were also seen as less desirable by the individuals concerned. In the eyes of Antioquía, education in the humanities was a speciality of Bogotá. The most esteemed establishments of higher education were all situated in other towns than Medellin. The structure of the situation was therefore such that there was no encouragement for the elites of Antioquía to seek careers in politics, 'culture' or the liberal professions, nor to invest their 'surplus' in land, since the landed upper classes, a marked feature of the Sabana, were no more than embryonic. Nor was there any equivalent of the 'pastoral aristocracy' of the Cali region, the 'Valley'. Thus, as between the Saban and Antioquía, the structure of opportunities and the system of values were inverted. In addition, the Antioqueños had a greater stock of organizational experience and family solidarity, and their disdain for the humanist culture flourishing in Bogotá inclined them towards pragmatic values. (At least this was the image of themselves, Hagen says, that they projected amongst the Bogotanos or Caliños.)

Thus the structure of the situation is enough to account for the statistical differences and in particular for the disproportionately greater importance of the Antioqueños in the industrial development of Colombia after the First World War. It may be that an age old feeling of reduced social status also played a part in this, but it is difficult to prove it and, *pace* Hagen, pointless to assume it.

In fact, if Hagen introduces that particular hypothesis, it is not so much because it is necessary as that it enables him to subsume several examples (Japan, Colombia, etc.) under a single law, that of loss of social status as the cause of the entrepreneurial spirit. That loss of social status and, more generally, a marginal position, *sometimes* create the conditions in which the entrepreneurial and innovatory spirit can develop, has been confirmed by many studies.[26] Nothing, however, permits us to give the relation between two terms the status of a *law*. In the case of Colombia, there is a link between them, but that link can only be understood if we realize that the data of the situation in Antioquía and the Sabana give rise to contrasting systems of encouragement. As for the part played by the *samurai* in Japan, it is due to quite different reasons.

From the epistemological point of view, Hagen's theory provides a very valuable example. In trying to infer a 'theory' (in this case a *law*) from his data, Hagen is led to provide an impoverished interpretation of them and to support the relationship between marginality and the entrepreneurial spirit with dubious hypotheses.

But once we separate his analysis from the nomological bias that blurs its essential features, we discover a theory that is a model of its kind. The emergence of a class of entrepreneurs in Antioquía is explained as an aggregation effect whose roots lie deep in a long historical process. Certainly it is the differential structure of opportunities facing the Caliños and Bogotanos on the one hand and the Antioqueños on the other that explains why during the second half of the nineteenth century the latter played a disproportionate part in the foundation of industrial and service undertakings. But that differential structure itself was the outcome of a long-term process. It was because the king of Spain, for readily comprehensible political reasons, attempted to impose the law of *morada* and *labor* that the colonists in the Saba developed large holdings of land worked by Indian agricultural workers and that there was an abundant agricultural aristocracy in the region. In the second half of the nineteenth century, the existence of that aristocracy was one of the macroscopic data that helped produce the differential opportunity structure Hagen describes so well. Similarly, it was the near exhaustion of the gold and silver mines in the seventeenth century that started the Antioqueños on their social decline, which probably accounts, for example, for the policy of setting up university institutions in the nineteenth century and the negative discrimination against Antioquía at that time. Similarly too, the 'materialistic' ethic of the Antioquía elites and the Bogotanos' taste for 'humanistic' culture were the result of this process. In short, the entrepreneurial spirit shown by the Antioqueños is well analysed by Hagen as an aggregation effect and the behaviour of the actors well explained as reactions to variable-structure situations. At the same time, however, he sees that differential structure as the outcome of a long cumulative process which is only completely *understandable* if we locate a certain number of macroscopic data set far back in time, such as the political principle summed up in the expression 'morada y labor'. In its logical structure, his theory is therefore a welter of analyses of the type $M = M\{m [S(M')]\}$.

Does the concept of *law* not hinder rather than help the social sciences? Is it appropriate to look for laws of change, even conditional ones, particularly when the systems we are trying to subsume under them are of a very high level of complexity, such as the national societies considered by Hagen? The answer, it seems, must certainly be in the negative, despite the nomological concept of *explanation* still dominant in many circles.

A critical analysis of Hagen's theory shows a further point: his investigation leads not to a *law*, as he claims, but a *model*. In addition, the model is not a model of *development*, but one which more modestly but rigorously explains the formation of a class of entrepreneurs in the particular context he is studying.

To return to a question raised in the last chapter, it certainly seems that the determination in the social sciences to establish conditional laws has its roots in an epistemology influenced by the natural sciences or at least by the social scientists' image of them. It is probably possible to establish certain regularities, but in order to do so the classical proviso of 'identical conditions' has to be applicable. It is clear, however, that that can only happen in particular cases. That is why the search for conditional regularities cannot be a major object of the analysis of social change. When there is an AB concordance, the problem is not usually that of demonstrating that it follows from an 'if A, then B' law, but rather that of showing that in the system under consideration element A encourages the actors to produce B, it being understood that in a different system it could encourage them to produce not-B.

Here, we are touching on a fundamental problem of epistemology. Contrary to what Hempel, for example, considered to be the case, there is no reason for believing that *explaining* a phenomenon always means subsuming it under universally valid propositions, namely, *laws*. The concept of explanation that I offered in the last chapter, on the other hand, allots the status of *consequences* rather than *principles* to the macroscopic regularities it might be possible to observe. This concept, summed up in the formula $M = MmSM'$, has the advantage of being more powerful and more generally valid than the other. And as Hagen's example shows, the 'Hempelian' concept of explanation can act as a distorting prism and inhibit knowledge.

4

Structures and Change: the Structuralist Bias

The notion of structure is polysemic in the extreme. We are justified in saying this in general and, perhaps more particularly, with regard to the social sciences.[1] However, although the term has many meanings and much of the uncertainty associated with it arises from the fact that one often does not know in what sense it is being used, some of those meanings are perfectly clear. We shall consider two that are of direct concern to us here, since they are consistently visible behind such notions as 'the *structural* laws of change', 'the *structural* conditions of change' and so on.

STRUCTURE AS 'TYPE'

First, the notion of structure is close to, if not synonymous with, that of *type*. A type is a set of characteristics. Thus, when we talk about an ethnic *type*, a *type* of novel or a *type* of car, we are saying that certain human groups, certain novels or certain cars have characteristics A, B, C . . . N, which define the type in question. In most cases, these characteristics are *linked* in the sense that, if one of them is present, all the others tend to be present too. If an individual has blue eyes, he or she also tends to have fair hair, or, more precisely, the probability of fair hair is greater than it would be in the case of a dark-eyed person. There will be many fair-haired people with blue eyes (type AB) and dark-haired people with dark eyes (type A'B'), but types A'B or AB' will be rarer. When, given a set of characteristics A, B, C . . . N, the frequency (or in some cases the probability) of the types that can be established on the basis of them varies greatly from one to another, it is often said that *structures* have been determined.

90

We can easily see why we talk about 'structures' in such situations: type ABC . . . N is very common, as is also type A'B'C' . . . N, whereas types such as AB'C' . . .N, or A'B'C . . . N occur much less frequently. This suggests that characteristics A, B, C . . . N tend to 'attract' each other and combine to form a structure. So too do characteristics A', B', C' . . . N'.

But although there is no difficulty in seeing why we talk of structures in a case of this kind, we must also see that it involves risks. A structure as just defined is simply a type. But whereas there is nothing mysterious about the word 'type', which merely indicates the end result of a process of classification, 'structure' evokes the notion of *essence* and gives the impression of mystery and depth. That is why structuralism, the aim of which is often simply to establish classification and typologies, has come to be seen by some as a method that makes it possible to reveal what is hidden, the essences that lie behind appearances.

Typologies are frequently used in the social sciences. Montesquieu's theory of political regimes, for example, is based on the identification of a typology: if a government is of form A, the relationships between the citizen and the state tend to be of the nature B, and the regime tends to be C from the point of view of stability. Another type of political regime might be A'B'C'.

Similarly, Tönnies's contrast between *Gemeinschaft* and *Gesellschaft* describes two types of society or two structures. In the *Gemeinschaft*, relationships between individuals tend to be affective (A), which is made possible by the fact that the community is a small one (B), in which formal rules are unimportant (C) . . . and, among other characteristics, the division of labour is perfunctory and distinctions of social status slight and by and large unquestioned (N). In the *Gesellschaft*, on the other hand, relationships tend to be impersonal (A'), the society in question is a large one (B') in which relationships between individuals are governed by formal rules (C') . . . and there is a complex division of labour and permanently disputed distinctions of status (N'). The *Gemeinschaft* is a structure (or type of society) with the characteristic features A, B, C . . . N; the *Gesellschaft* is a structure (A', B', C' . . . N') which presents an inverted image of it. The typology used by Tönnies shows that social groups and real societies tend to belong to one or the other of the two types and to be either *Gesellschaften* or *Gemeinschaften*.This means that types such as AB'C . . . N or A'B'C' . . . N are unlikely to occur.

The set of characteristics A, B, C . . . N tend to occur together, as do their opposites.

The hallowed distinction between *traditional* and *modern* societies can also be seen as a classic example of structural analysis. In traditional societies, kinship dominates and determines other types of relationships (A), tradition is venerated (B), change is seen as suspect and dangerous (C) . . . and personal relationships are highly affective (N). In modern societies, personal relationships are correspondingly reduced in importance (A'), behaviour is rational rather than traditional (or at least tradition is less important) (B'), change is seen as normal and desirable (C') . . . and interpersonal relationships are affectively neutral (N'). Once again, the two sets of characteristics have their own system of internal attraction, both forming *structures* with coherent elements. The neo-Marxist structuralism so much in vogue in Paris in the 1970s was also an attempt to establish a typology of societies with regard to their economic, political and cultural aspects.[2]

This first definition of the notion of structure is clearly of major interest to us, since a structure in this sense can be seen as a generalization of the notion of conditional laws. 'If A, then B', such laws maintain. 'If A, then B, C, D . . . N', is what structural laws say. More generally, a structure – in this first sense – can be defined as 'a set A, B, C . . . N of such a kind that if one of the elements of the set is present the others are present too'. Of course, structural statements, like conditional laws, can be defined more or less rigidly: 'If . . . , then (always, frequently, more frequently, most frequently, most probably)' and so on.

STRUCTURE AS 'ESSENTIAL CHARACTERISTICS'

The objects considered by the social sciences are complex in the sense that even intellectually it is impossible to list the characteristics that would exhaustively describe a society, an organization or even a group of moderate size. This means that we have to select and simplify. Some simplifications are inevitable in so far as they are directly imposed by the subject we are dealing with. Once I am interested in a *question relating to* a society rather than *that society as such* (for example, why is it economically stagnant?), a certain number of characteristics can be eliminated as irrelevant to the matter in hand. But it is not always easy to determine in advance whether a feature is relevant to a problem or not. Geographical factors may be either unimportant, or conversely they may be of crucial significance (as in the case of Colombia in chapter 3).

In reality, the relevance of a characteristic can only be decided a posteriori, once it has proved possible to construct a theory enabling us to explain the stagnation of the society we are examining, if that is the problem we are addressing ourselves to. Such a theory will be more or less complex, depending on the circumstances, and more or less convincing. In any case, it will take the form of a set of propositions in which stagnation will be seen as the result of a certain number of characteristics – A, B, C . . . N – of the society under consideration. In general, there will not be many of them (at least in relation to the theoretical and ideal set of characteristics that would provide an exhaustive description of the society) and they will also be interlinked in a certain way. Since they are few in number and form a more or less coherent whole, it will often be said, as a result of an understandable association of ideas, that they make up the *structure* of the society.

Such a label is, once again, both natural and useful. The notion of structure certainly brings to mind the notion of a 'set of basic characteristics'. It also contradicts the idea of a random collection. This means that when we talk about a structure in the sense under discussion at the moment, we certainly see, *by virtue of the fact that they come together as a whole*, its structural elements as interdependent or as helping to produce the effect that is being studied. The danger is, however, that the notion of structure is virtually synonymous with that of essence and might in this context suggest that the 'essential' features or the 'structural' data incorporated into the theory describe the 'underlying reality' of the society in question and that all else is simply trivial 'appearance'. The 'realism' of interpretations of this kind is, as we shall see, unhelpful and dangerous.

In the rest of this chapter, we shall look at, in turn, the problems raised by the notions of 'structural laws' and the 'structural causes' of change.

'STRUCTURAL' LAWS

These really raise the same problems and arise from the same kinds of analysis as conditional laws. The structure ABC . . . N will emerge if, for example, in a system presenting the characteristics C . . . N the actors are encouraged to bring about A and B, in such a way that $A,B = MmS(M',C . . . N)$. This means that the structure will be present only in conditions that it is hard to define *in general*. It is true that we can establish that if *certain particular* conditions are fulfilled, characteristics A, B, C . . . N will be present simultaneously. What we cannot do, however, is determine in a general way what conditions will or will not produce their simultaneous appearance. With regard to the question of whether the A, B, C . . . N combination occurs more frequently than say A, B', C' . . . N, it presupposes that the statistical population to serve as a basis for the enquiry has been defined, which is usually impossible. If we take only the example of the USSR and its satellites, we can see that despite a long-held structural law, a society can be at one and the same time industrial and military, in the sense in which Saint-Simon or Spencer used the terms. Does this AB' case occur more frequently than an AB one? The question is obviously meaningless, since it is impossible to give a precise and convincing definition of the statistical set to be used in calculating the relative frequencies.

We shall now look in detail at one or two examples of 'structural laws' that have given rise to persistent discussion in sociological literature. We shall take them from two fields: the sociology of ideologies and the socio-economics of development.

STRUCTURE AND IDEOLOGIES

What is known as the sociology of knowledge, the programme for which was outlined by Mannheim, provides a useful example on the basis of which it is easy to see how over-ambitious structural laws generally are. What we shall be looking at here is a particular example, but it should be noted that the basic principles of this branch of sociology mean that it will attempt to establish structural laws, since its aim is to demonstrate the links between the structures of society and those of knowledge. Its failure, which is universally admitted nowadays, is no doubt the result of that aim.

The bulge in the school population heralded in the 1950s led sociologists to reflect on its likely effects. Certain of them developed a theory of the 'proletarianization' of the intellectual classes that was much discussed at the time.[3] It can be summarized in the following propositions:

1. The development of industrial societies requires an ever-increasing number of people who have received higher education (A).
2. This 'functional' need of society is easy to meet, since at the same time complex factors ensure that the 'demand' for education grows. A higher standard of living plays a part in this, but universal competition is also important (as soon as certain people increase their demand for higher education, others have to do the same if they are not to be left behind). Finally, the belief that in the future jobs will call for higher levels of technical competence than they do at present has taken root. As a result of these varied factors, the number of intellectuals per qualification is inevitably bound to increase (B).[4]
3. From this follows (C): intellectuals, more frequently than in the past, will be obliged to occupy relatively modest professional or social positions. In other words, as a class they will be exposed to what one would call a tendential law of a decline in their status.
4. Simultaneously, their social importance will be growing (D), since modern societies are ever more dependent on both theoretical and technical know-how and the mastery and good management of growing masses of information.
5. Information is (will be) to post-industrial societies what energy was (is) to industrial ones. The history of the latter is dominated by the man/nature relationship, that of post-industrial societies by relationships between human beings. These developments (E), of which Daniel Bell has provided a good description, also imply an increase in the demand for intellectuals per qualification.[5]
6. In a situation in which such people are both more indispensable and less highly esteemed and their social recompense is declining and their contribution increasing, we can expect to see a new attitude of opposition to the social system (F) appearing amongst them.
7. A sense of solidarity will perhaps develop in their ranks. In any case, it is here that protest is likely to become evident in 'post-industrial' society, and to such an extent that, following the model of the nineteenth-century proletariat in Marxist doctrine, it will become the main cause of change (G).

This analysis leads to the formulation of a structural law to the effect that in post industrial societies elements A, B, C, D, E, F and

G are destined to appear simultaneously. The set of these (and other) elements is thus a *structure* which is characteristic of post-industrial society. In the same way as the contrast between traditional and modern societies, that between industrial and post-industrial societies can be expressed in terms of two inverted structures: ABC . . . G as against A'B'C' . . . G'.

The law is shaky because it does not bother to take into consideration the varied and complex nature of the situations which might emerge as a result of structural elements A, B etc. The consequence of this diversity, however, is that in certain situations A, B will in fact be accompanied by F (an attitude of opposition to the social system), whereas in others they will rather produce an attitude of allegiance and conformity. A simple example will illustrate this.

In the United States, the policy of the Great Society implemented by President Johnson brought about a considerable expansion of social programmes and the agencies set up to support them, which led to the creation of a large number of jobs. The specifications for many of them entailed higher education in the applied social sciences. Very often, students taking such courses have values of the kind ordinarily described as left-wing. They are very sensitive to social inequalities and injustices and often of modest origins themselves. The policy of the Great Society gave many of them a job and the chance to do something that was seen not only as legitimate but also as meeting a need. What they did was no doubt for the benefit of certain individuals and groups. The demand for it, however, came not from the beneficiaries themselves, but from the state speaking on their behalf. It is easy to see how, in a *situation* of that kind, a social worker paid from the budget of social programmes may find those programmes inadequate or directed towards aims of which he might not entirely approve, but hard to see why he should be radically opposed to the political system, since the institutions employing him are such that they see the case for eradicating inequalities and increasing social justice. He may challenge their methods, but would find it hard to reject their aims in any radical way or to see himself as serving an illegitimate authority in working towards those aims.

It is also possible to extend the scope of the example. Bell is probably quite right in seeing a likely growth of the 'quaternary' sector, that sector of socio-economic activity concerned with the relationships between social agents, which includes not only the social services but also trade unions and defence groups looking after the interests of this or that category or group. It is a sector which gives at least *some* of those who want it the *opportunity* of working for the rejects and misfits of the social system or for those suffering its 'injustices'. Such work is seen as legitimate and is possibly subsidized or even paid for by the 'system'.

In short, it is not too difficult to find examples and arguments that would support a 'structural' law saying the opposite of the one we have been examining. This would see the 'structural' features A, B and so on as producing a class of intellectuals not in opposition to the social system (F), but as an integral part of its mechanism (F'), despite their awareness of the injustices it gives rise to. Indeed, such a law has been suggested, and there has been a great deal of argument about which was the true one.[6] The answer, of course, is neither, since each is true in certain circumstances. Sometimes the structural elements A, B and so on give rise to situations in which the potential protesters tend to be integrated into the system and sometimes to situations in which they tend to be rejected by it. Totting up algebraically the effects of all these plus and minus signs is, of course, hardly a feasible undertaking.

We should also note that 'structural' elements are not the only ones that deserve to be taken into consideration. Nor, other things being equal, is it a matter of indifference whether the potential protesters are taken up by a revolutionary or a reformist union. The *same* structural effects will thus have consequences that *vary* according to the type of union system in operation. If it is revolutionary in its aims, taking up potential protesters may not rule out arguments urging the merits of breaking with the system.

Generally speaking, it is therefore quite risky to see ideological phenomena as the result of structural phenomena, although this is one of the major aims of the sociology of knowledge. The position of intellectuals can be affected in a variable and opposite way by some structural elements. This means that we shall sometimes have $F = Mm\,S(AB \ldots M)$ and sometimes $F' = Mm\,S(AB \ldots M')$ without having any way of determining a priori what the likely outcome will be. In cases of this kind, there is likely to be argument producing two conflicting and contradictory structural laws, as happened in this particular instance. They are, however, more an expression of the passions and feelings of their proponents than descriptions of reality. The truth of the matter is that even 'structural' factors are likely to give rise to variable situations which might in turn induce the intellectuals concerned to take up varying attitudes. As a consequence, *neither* of the two conflicting laws will be true.

Another way of expressing the same idea is to say that 'structural' elements are seldom the sole determinants. What they do is always mingled with what institutional or conjunctural elements do. The effect of institutional factors (for example, the development of institutions of what Bell calls the quaternary type) has been shown by what has been said above. That of conjunctural elements can be shown just as easily.

In the early years of this century, Sombart showed why there was no socialism in the United States. His view, as we have seen, was that the real chances of mobility and the belief in the virtue of individual solutions to individual problems (strengthened by the mobility made possible by the existence of the 'frontier') had made Americans unreceptive to ideologies legitimizing collective strategies of protest. During the years preceding the Second World War, however, socialist ideologies did indeed take root there.[7] The American Communist party was large and influential. Intellectuals – and not only those whose professions led them to observe, evaluate and possibly discuss how institutions worked and, more widely, the social, economic and political system, but also artists, writers, cinema directors, producers and actors – proclaimed their Marxist allegiance. The unions hesitated. Some people wanted to see a union movement that was apolitical and simply there to serve the interests of its potential membership, whilst others argued that if the movement was to widen its sphere of influence, it was very much in its interests to maintain and indeed make public its links with the political left.

There is really no great mystery about the way in which events occurring after the time at which he was writing disproved Sombart's assertions. The New Deal had made the notion of social policy respectable, and it was not seen as normal for the state to declare and meet its social responsibilities towards the individual. It was no longer a matter of protecting the citizen's life and assets, but of providing him with assets if his own were 'socially' insufficient. As for the American Communist party, it was based on Marxism, a doctrine little known to Americans, but managed to create the impression that it stuck to a non-dogmatic and not too sharply defined brand of it, and restricted itself in fact to one or two general lines of policy in no way incompatible with the principles of the New

Deal. Numerically smaller than the traditional large parties and not directly involved in the political arena, it had less to fear from compromise and managed to present itself as the watchful guardian of principles and the vigilant defender of the great causes that the two main parties had perhaps not exactly betrayed, but were at best only supporting half-heartedly. Very pragmatically, it supported every cause that could be seen to be a corollary of the principle of social justice.

During the 1930s and 1940s, therefore, a combination of factors meant that Marxism was the base and reference point for many of those who either needed to observe and evaluate the society around them for professional reasons or could find the 'social question' a source of artistic or literary inspiration.

In 1945, however, the American intelligentsia changed its perspective again. Sombart's observations became valid once more and remained so until the middle 1960s. Once again, there was no socialism in the United States, or at least Marxism was of considerably less appeal to American intellectuals than it had been before the war. The fact is that in the intervening years the American Communist party had moved much closer to Moscow and supported the German–Soviet pact. This had meant an immediate loss of influence. No longer social questions, but problems of international politics, were to be the great subjects of debate and the causes of dissension and conflict. The discredit it had brought upon itself meant that the party was also deserted by the unions. Those who wanted an apolitical movement were now in a stronger position. The warning signs had been clearly read, and all the risks involved in too close a link with a political organization like the ACP were so obvious to union leaders that the distance between the Marxist party and the union movement was now made quite clear. The *current circumstances* were really the exact opposite of what they had been in the 1930s. Social justice became less of an overriding concern, which meant that socialist doctrines lost their interest for intellectuals. Marxism in particular not only became less influential, but was also seen as suspect, and no influential institution any longer felt indebted to it. The ACP itself was routed. Its former sympathizers had abandoned it, and the unions would have nothing to do with it, since they had reaffirmed their apolitical stance, and it was the last party they would want any connections with. In the circumstances, any intellectual declaring his allegiance to Marxism could be more or less certain of total rejection and the loss of all *influence*. The one thing an intellectual must do, by the very nature of his role, is exert influence. He can, no doubt, choose the ways and means of exerting it and of applying his ambitions to various purposes. He can also, if he chooses, scorn honours, prestige and money. Unless he takes on a different role, however, he cannot choose not to exert an influence.

During the same (i.e., the immediate post-war) period, the situation of French intellectuals was quite different. Right-wing ideologies had been discredited for a long time to come.[8] The Communist party had played an important part in the Resistance and had consequently acquired credit and legitimacy. A significant section of the union movement was Marxist in inspiration and made no secret of its links with the French Communist party (PCF). The other large left-wing party, the SFIO, Section Française de l'Internationale Ouvrière (French Section of the Workers' Internationale), which had played an important part in the political life of the Third Republic, had had a bad passage through the pre-war slump years.[9] The supporters of Paul Faure and Leon Blum had clashed, having different views on basic questions. Some of the former had been receptive to the National Socialists' overt aim of crushing Bolshevism, although most of them were primarily pacifists and approved of the Munich agreements. In addition, the Socialists - who were unfamiliar with Leninist theories of clandestine political organization - had not managed to transform their peacetime institutions into an underground resistance organization. As a result of these factors, French intellectuals had every encouragement to adopt Marxist perspectives at a time when their American counterparts had none at all.

The dogmatic nature of the PCF - the fact that it was impossible to join if one did not subscribe to its teaching, at that time even more so than now - largely explains, if we are to believe accounts of the experience, why becoming a member of the party in those days was like entering a religious order. But the intensity of conviction and the 'inner' nature of that commitment do not in any way prove a lack of awareness of the facts of the situation. French intellectuals of the 1950s had just as good reasons, even if they were different ones, for accepting Marxism as the inevitable frame of reference and seeing their acceptance of its doctrines as the result of personal conviction, as their American counterparts had had in the 1930s.

I should like to make it quite clear that in propounding this analysis I am not arguing for a utilitarian theory of political conviction. Such a view would have as little justification as its opposite, that is, as seeing conviction as the result of an inexplicable 'commitment'. Subjectively, 'commitment' may be seen as an illumination or a conversion, but that, as our example shows, does not imply that there are no *reasons* for it. Thus, the modal choices of American intellectuals in the 1930s and 1950s, like those of French intellectuals in the 1950s, can be made intelligible on the basis of the circumstances in which both groups found themselves. These circumstances themselves were the result of macroscopic factors which determined the parameters of the individual's field of action. The parameters did not, of course, determine his behaviour, but merely provided the motivation and reasons for what he did.

With regard to our concern in this chapter, however, the main thing that these examples have to teach us is that in certain cases the parameters characterizing the situations in which people act may be determined much more by *institutional* or *conjunctural* than by *structural* elements. This mixture of elements and the fact that structural elements have locally variable effects on the situation of actors encourage caution and reservations with regard to the structural laws that, explicitly or implicitly, using the word 'laws' or some other, or not giving them any name, the social sciences often profess to be seeking. Structural causes are not always as *effective* as we suppose them to be, nor are their effects always as *positive* as we assume. Furthermore, they are not generally as *coherent* as they should be.

THE COHERENCE OF STRUCTURES IN THE FACE OF CHANGE

The notion of structure and 'structural law' necessarily entails seeing the elements A, B, C . . . making up a system as coherent. ABC . . . N and A'B'C' . . . N' are typical or likely structures, and any others atypical, deviant or transitory. That is the idea behind some classical typologies, such as *Gesellschaft* and *Gemeinschaft*, traditional and modern societies, folk and urban societies, and so on. The corollary is that any change affecting one of the component elements will always tend to affect all the others.

It is not hard to find large numbers of examples showing what a slender connection with reality this way of seeing things has. A change A → A' will have no effect on B, and *a fortiori* on the range B, C . . . N, unless that change affects the field of action of individuals in such a way as to encourage them to behave in a manner producing consequences B', C' . . . N' rather than B, C . . . N. An effect of this kind is obviously not the result of some transcendant necessity. It depends on the characteristics of a system of interdependence within which the actors involved move. *Depending on the nature of these characteristics*, A will or will not bring about a change at the leel of certain elements in the range B, C . . . N or perhaps of all of them. The following example will illustrate this point.

Just before the Second World War, the Indian government embarked on a large-scale irrigation programme. In a remarkable study, S. Epstein examines the effect of this exogenous change on two villages in Mysore, Wangala and Dalena, close to the city of Bangalore.[10] Because of its situation, Wangala directly benefited from the increased irrigation, whereas Dalena, where most of the land was too high for the water to reach it, received no advantage from it. The simple device of choosing these two villages provides a remarkable field of observation, the aim being to establish both the direct consequences of this exogenous change on those villages where land was irrigated and its indirect consequences for those where it could not be.

In studies of exogenous change and its effects on traditional societies, there are often two types of demonstrations or models. Sometimes, such studies are offered as confirmation of a reproduction model. In her *Cultural Patterns and Technological Change*, Margaret Mead presents a picture of a 'timeless and changeless' Indian village, where traditions are so deeply ingrained and inextricably interdependent that its structure cannot admit any change.[11] What she is doing is really no more than returning to the view expressly suggested by Marx, of an Asiatic village inexorably governed by an endogenous law of reproduction. The same view has been developed, albeit differently expressed, by many authors, amongst whom Hoselitz is the most outstanding example.[12] The other model is that of change as a snow-ball effect or a chain reaction. Here, if change is not purely and simply rejected or absorbed by the traditional society so that it affects certain elements of it, it finally affects all of them. Both the model of reproduction and that of generalized transformation as a result of a chain reaction look at first as if they are mutually contradictory, but both are really based on the shared postulate that the elements making up the 'structure' of traditional societies are *closely related*, i.e., that there is a very high degree of interdependence between them.

Epstein's study is extremely important because it shows that, for *Asian* villages, both models may be simplistic and false, and also that the effects of change are diversified (i.e., that they are not the same for the villages *directly* affected by irrigation and those *indirectly* affected). Thirdly, it demonstrates that not all the elements of the structure are affected with the same degree of intensity or in the same direction. Finally, it enables us to see that the effects of change can only be understood and established if we analyse the influence of exogenous change on the *situation* of the actors involved.

To sum up Epstein's findings very briefly, we can say that in Wangala (where the land was irrigated), the exogenous change A→A' had effects that were variable and in any case not coherent in terms of the social aspects considered. In some cases, that change modified a state of affairs (we can express this type of change as X→X'). In others, it perpetuated it (Y→Y).

As a result of outside influences, the village moved from a regime of subsistence economy to one based on trade (B→B'). Relationships between fathers and sons were also modified in a real sense in the direction prescribed by the theorists of modernization, with the latter becoming much more independent with regard to the former (C→C'). Those between men and women also changed, and the position of women improved. Their role within the division of labour increased in importance, which strengthened their autonomy (D→D'). On the other hand, however, change reinforced social stratifications and hierarchies within the castes (E→E: the old hierarchies were strengthened rather than overturned). Similarly, the hierarchies and subordination relationships involving peasants and Untouchables were also reinforced (F→F). The latter's traditional attitudes, solidarity and sense of belonging to the village community, were more obvious after than before the change (G→G). The standard of living rose (H→H'), but modernization brought about a decline rather than an increase in non-agricultural activities (I→I'). Despite the move towards a trading economy, contacts with the surrounding area remained very restricted (J→J), and there even seems to have been some evidence of an introversion effect on the village.

To sum up: as a result of exogenous change, the 'structure' ABCDEFGHIJ became the structure A'B'C'D'EFGH'IJ. There was neither generalized reproduction nor generalized transformation of all the elements of it. The latter were all interdependent, but some were changed and others confirmed and reinforced. In the 'arid' village, Dalena, exogenous aid (A→A') also had considerable consequences, even though it was of necessity not directly affected by irrigation. As in Wangala, although for different reasons and as a result of different factors, there was a change from a subsistence to a trading economy(B→B'). Relationships between generations were marked by an increased autonomy (C→C'). The sexual division of roles, however, was not affected to any great extent (D→D); women remained subordinate and enjoyed very limited autonomy. Social hierarchies within the peasant caste were modified, with some of the peasants gaining a higher relative status than the one they had enjoyed before irrigation and others being reduced to a lower one (E→E'). Clientage links between peasants and Untouchables weakened (G→G'). The sense of community that had characterized the latter declined and was replaced by lively competition. The standard of living increased (H→H'), with new activities growing up alongside the traditional agricultural ones. The move to a trading economy was accompanied by a noteworthy intensification of links with the surrounding area (J→J'). 'Structure' ABCDEFGHIJ is changed to structure A'B'C'DE'F'G'H'I'J'. This means that the village *not directly affected by irrigation* came closer to the chain-reaction model than the one which was, although with regard to one element, that of the sexual division of roles, change had a strengthening rather than a 'modernizing' effect. Figure 1 will help us to visualize the analysis.

If the basic aim of the socio-economic study of change was to demonstrate empirical regularities in the form of causal or structural laws, for example, the findings of Epstein's investigations would be

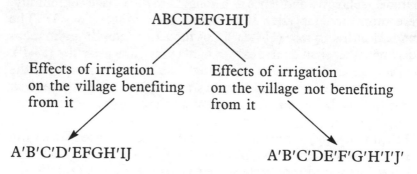

ABCDEFGHIJ

Effects of irrigation
on the village benefiting
from it

Effects of irrigation
on the village not benefiting
from it

A'B'C'D'EFGH'IJ

A'B'C'DE'F'G'H'I'J'

Figure 1

heart-breaking. The effects of irrigation were more evident in the village not directly benefiting from it. Far from being convergent, they were variable in portent, direction and intensity, and their complex nature discredits both the reproductive model of the 'timeless and changeless village' and the cumulative model of chain reactions. Thus we come back to the epistemological problem underlying this book. Should sociologists (or economists) looking at social change try to make *nomothetic* statements (i.e., attempt to show empirical regularities), or should they, once they have established that a structural system ABC . . . N at point t is characterized at $t+1$ by a different structure such as A'B'C . . . N, try to explain why that should be so? The latter course would mean showing how a change (such as A→A') modifies the situation of the actors involved in such a way as to encourage them to change their behaviour, and how structure A'B'C . . . N follows from the aggregation of such behaviour.

That is in fact clearly what Epstein does. Since I obviously cannot go through the whole of his analysis, I shall merely refer to its major elements.

Irrigation means that new crops, particularly sugar cane, can be developed. These offer greater financial gain than traditional ones such as *ragi* (a coarse millet), but also necessitate investment. The land has to be levelled and fertilizer used. On arid land, a wooden plough drawn by two decrepit oxen will suffice to turn, or at least scratch, the soil, and there is no need for fertilizer. Once it has been irrigated, however, a metal plough is essential, and large quantities of manure have to be applied. The investment necessistated by turning to sugar cane is financed by means of loans granted to the peasant by the factory buying the crop and by better-off neighbours. Financially, the peasant is more dependent, but enjoys a higher standard of living. B→B').

In addition, sugar cane and rice demand constant care, and keep the grower busy throughout the year, whereas crops grown on arid land (i.e., those that were the main ones before irrigation was improved) give a slack period from February to April, which was formerly occupied by various activities that took the peasants to the village or the neighbouring town. Under the new system, they were obliged to stay on their farms, and their network of relationships and social contacts became more restricted (J→J').

As an indirect result of both irrigation and the simultaneous introduction of new government measures, relationships between fathers and sons changed (C→C'). Since the cane was sold to a government-controlled factory, the government – by virtue of its *role* – had the twofold task of avoiding overproduction and treating the peasants in an egalitarian way. Per capita quotas were therefore established. This meant that the peasants, who earned more by selling sugar cane than by selling *ragi*, were encouraged to let their heirs have some of their land as soon as possible. In pre-irrigation days, it was normal for this to happen before the appropriate legal proceedings were begun. Once the new pattern of agriculture had been established, however, the sequence was reversed. The family farm dominated by the father was thus gradually replaced by one that could be described as federative, in which the sons, who had now legally come into their inheritance, were in a position to assert their autonomy.

The role of women (D→D') assumed some importance, for the surplus arising from increased wealth was invested in dairy production, which it was the job of women to organize and market. And locally everyone was quite aware that the normal way of judging the surplus produced by the farm was the richness of the clothes the women displayed on feast and market days.

As has already been said, however, this surplus was also used to help those who could not find the money to invest in fertilizer and equipment themselves. This meant that differences in income, prestige and status became more marked with the appearance of ties resulting from financial dependence. Economic growth, however, does not only produce increased indebtedness. It also leads to increased consumption, and the two factors tend to accentuate hierarchies. The rich not only get richer; they get more visibly and conspicuously richer. Moreover, if it is to be in the peasants' interest to acquire more land, their disposable surplus must reach a certain minimum level, since there is no point acquiring a new plot if they cannot afford the necessary means of production and, in particular, the draught animals needed to work it. It was therefore always the better-off peasants who added to their holdings. This meant that overall the distinctions between social classes tended to be perpetuated and indeed to become more marked within the peasant caste (E→E).

Agricultural development brought with it an increased demand for labour. Growing rice and sugar cane is a labour-intensive undertaking. That labour was provided both by those directly involved in the farm and by exchanging periods of work with other farms, and also by hiring day labourers. In addition, debts contracted by Untouchables were often repaid in the form of labour. In return for providing work of that kind, the latter could always count on the peasants' assistance when they had to pay out large sums for a funeral or a wedding or simply when they could not make ends meet. Client relationships between peasants and Untouchables are thus a kind of contract renewable from generation to generation in which complex exchanges of services are provided for. The peasants' increased demand for labour and the fact that the Untouchables could not afford to engage in growing the most financially rewarding crops tended to reinforce such relationships, since although the latter were to a modest degree better off as a result of the economic 'boom', they could not set up on their own account and would not benefit from moving to another area (F→F). As they were not in competition with each other, since their client relationship determined which employer was likely to provide work for them, their sense of community was very marked, and reinforced rather than weakened by the consequences of irrigation (G→G).

Despite the economic boom, Wangala was destined to remain an agricultural community (I→I). The crops produced there – rice and sugar cane – called for such constant attention that farmers had no time for anything else. They no longer had time to go to town, and their relationships with the surrounding area became more tenuous rather than stronger (J→J). Only the women still went to market. The new situation also meant that the peasants no longer had to transport their products themselves, since they could leave this task to hauliers who were very likely to come from 'dry' villages such as Dalena.

In Dalena too the standard of living rose, and the village moved from a subsistence to a trading economy (B→B'), although for different reasons. Here, those 'dry' crops that in pre-irrigation days had been and still were the only *agricultural* activity were being complemented by industrial and service undertakings. Since such crops leave a great deal of free time and consequently create chronic underemployment, Dalena had a large pool of labour anxious for opportunities for work. These came in the first place in the form of waged jobs in the sugar cane processing factory or in state-financed road and bridge building. The latter not only provided work for wage-earners, but also offered opportunities for those who felt that they were up to becoming public works contractors. Finally, those villages which, like Wangala, were directly affected by the irrigation programme lost the surplus labour available earlier. Their inhabitants no longer had time to transport their own produce, repair their own tools or grind their own grain, and it was easier for them to use the surplus arising from growing rice and sugar to hire the services of entrepreneurs from Dalena. The irrigation programme also brought about a vastly increased demand for draught animals. Dalena took advantage of this and became a centre of trade in them. The Wangala peasants went there to buy the oxen that the Dalena dealers brought in from a wide area.

The higher standard of living and the growth of non-agricultural management and service activities in Dalena indirectly affected family relationships. As was also the case in Wangala, the patriarchal structure became weaker, although for different reasons. The chief factor strengthening the autonomy of the young in Dalena was that more children went to school (C→C'). There was, however, little effect on the role of women, since agriculture in dry areas demands a larger female labour force than in wet ones. Whereas men increasingly became wage-earners or entrepreneurs, women were even more closely tied to the land than previously (D→D).

By creating a climate in which competition was an important element, the development of small service industries and public works contracting also contributed to the growth of an individualistic ethic. In Wangala, the symbols of social status were still the old traditional ones (the rich clothing worn by the women). In Dalena, however, there was a great demand for specifically urban symbols such as coloured lithographs, watches, bicycles and the like. The system of stratification was shaken, both by the appearance of new status symbols and the fact that the development of industrial or service undertakings produces a new business middle class (E→E').

Relationships between the Untouchables and the peasants tended to have a completely different basis. Since non-irrigated land does not require a large labour-force, the Untouchables left and went to work for the government, and as the peasants could not employ them full-time, they let them go. In addition, when they did employ Untouchable hands, the economic risks they were running encouraged them to do so on the basis of economic rather than cliental criteria. This meant a degree of dislocation of the traditional system of stratification (F→F'). The Untouchables were therefore obliged to compete with each other (G→G'). As a result, their sense of community became weaker. When they were required for a ritual service, they tended to go sick, something which would be virtually unthinkable in Wangala.

The standards of living rose in Dalena, of course, as a result of the developing secondary and tertiary activities, which brought about an increase in the links between the village and the surrounding area $(J \rightarrow J')$.

Epstein's study contains important findings and calls many of the assumptions in theories of change into question. Wangala and Dalena were clearly social systems with closely interconnected elements. Nevertheless, what the effects of irrigation show is not the kind of coherence that theories of change would lead us to expect, but incoherence and something that could be called a 'structural irregularity'. The incoherence is of course relative, in the sense that it is relative to expectations or rather to a hypothesis based on the 'classical' distinctions between *Gemeinschaft* and *Gesellschaft*, traditional and modern societies and the like, which maintains that only the structures ABC . . . N and A′B′C′ . . . N′ will be observed, all other combinations being purely transient. Such distinctions are perhaps no more than conventional notions. In any case, change may take place in *irregular* ways, but they are not incomprehensible. Because it gets down to the microscopic level and makes use of what I called in chapter 2 the Weberian paradigm, Epstein's analysis convinces us that what *would* have been inexplicable would be a transformation of the type ABC . . . N→ABC . . . N (i.e., identicalness or pure reproduction) or ABC . . . N→A′B′C′ . . . N′ (i.e., generalized transformation), despite the importance of these two cases in theories of social change.

If simple transformations of this kind do not occur in a social system as closely interconnected as that of Wangala-Dalena, we might well wonder how they could possibly occur in larger and looser ones. It is true that Dalena fits more readily than Wangala into the framework of 'theories of social change', and that the model of generalized transformation fits it pretty closely, but we must bear in mind that the modernization of Dalena and the abiding traditionalism of Wangala are two complementary aspects of a single process.

In a general way, Epstein's study enables us to examine comparatively or, more exactly, to perceive the 'ideal' (in the Weberian sense) nature of the typological distinctions that in various forms keep continually reappearing in the social sciences. An apparently minor exogenous change - the development of irrigation - was enough to reinforce the model of the *Gemeinschaft*, or at least certain aspects of it, in Wangala, while a few miles away and still within the same social subsystem, the *Gesellschaft* model was becoming apparent in Dalena. In Wangala the *mechanical* nature of solidarity was increasingly evident, whereas in Dalena what could be seen was something that the Durkheimian school would rather see as *organic*. *Homo hierarchicus* was the older model still dominant in Wangala, *homo aequalis* the newer one emerging in Dalena. Tradition prevailed in the first village, the symbols of modernity made their appearance in the second. In opposition to those realist interpretations of the two typologies that tend to associate the terms with particular social systems, seeing for example certain societies as being essentially *Gesellschaften* and others as essentially *Gemeinschaften*, Epstein's study draws our attention to the fact that not only can both categories apply at the same time, but both can describe closely interdependent elements. I shall simply use this observation to introduce a point I shall discuss in greater detail in chapter 7 and in the Epilogue. It is that theories of social change often get out of control because, despite Weber's warning (cf. the notion of the *ideal* type), they take a realist view of conceptual categories which as such are not literally applicable to any given situation in the real world.

STRUCTURAL AND NON-STRUCTURAL ELEMENTS

In the second meaning of the word that is appropriate here, when we talk of the 'structure of a social system', we are referring to those elements which taken together enable us to provide an explanation of the microscopic phenomenon we are dealing with. These may be, for example, the stagnation or the change (both seen from a certain angle) apparent in a social system over a given period of time.

There is no doubt that using the notion of structure in such a context is not only perfectly legitimate but also has a great deal to recommend it. When we are faced with a complex object like society, we naturally tend to simplify it. If, for example, we want to explain why a society is economically stagnant, we have to choose from an indefinite mass of factors observable in it those that seem to be relevant to the account we are trying to give. These basic or *essential* characteristics we often call *structures*. We can also see them as being 'essential' in so far as they provide a means of explaining stagnation or change. To return to an example already mentioned, the 'vicious circle' theory of poverty, which has been current since the 1960s, attempts to account for persistent poverty in terms of inability to accumulate wealth: poverty, inability to save, purely local markets, no opportunity to invest, no inducement to invest and so on are all, in terms of the theory, *essential* or *structural* features to the extent that, if taken together and seen as forming a system, they are *sufficient* to account for stagnation. Consequently, all the many other features of a poor society can be called *non-essential* or *non-structural*.

A rigid separation of this kind is sometimes seen as a characteristic of Marxist thought. It is true that in that particular tradition, there is commonly an attempt to identify the fundamental *structures* of social organization and to establish the laws governing the way they develop (which may indeed take the form of identical reproduction). Thus Guy Dhoquois, in a little book which is typically Marxist in character, attempts to draw up a typology of systems of production, or more exactly of systems of the conditions of production, and to establish what the laws governing such systems are.[13] It would, however, be wrong to see this way of thinking as being too exclusively associated with the Marxist tradition. A large part of both non-Marxist thinking on the socio-economic aspects of development and, more generally, of the sociology of change, is linked to the same 'programme'. This means that attempting to determine the nature of such structures and what the laws governing the way they develop might be is in no way linked to one particular doctrinal tradition.

Indeed, the argument between the Marxist tradition and others of a different type (such as the culturalist tradition) is not about whether such a programme is relevant or not, but about what *area of reality* we should try to find *structural* variables or data in. In Marxist thought, that area is more or less clearly defined as the way in which the conditions of production are organized. In non-Marxist theories, there is no such 'ontological' restriction, and not only the conditions of production but also, for example, values and, more generally, 'cultural' data are seen as having some right to be seen as 'structural' elements.

Thus in Hoselitz's theory, the close interdependence of economic, cultural and family activities within traditional societies makes such societies fairly unreceptive to both exogenous and endogenous change. A theory of this type is certainly different from Marxist theories in the *variables* and the data it takes into account. At the paradigmatic level, however, the difference disappears, for like its Marxist and neo-Marxist equivalents it assumes that it is possible to isolate a range of interdependent structural elements and link to it a law of development (in this case identical reproduction) ensuring that any society characterized by the *structure* in question would tend to be subject to processes which in Marxist terminology would be called *reproduction* processes.

If the 'structural' paradigm has imposed itself to such an extent that doctrinal boundaries are no obstacle to it, we may as well admit that it is because it is to some extent relevant and helpful. Accounting for a particular macroscopic change (or lack of change)

$$M_t \rightarrow M_{t+k}$$

really means seeing the change as the result of a system of relationships R(A, B . . . N) linking a set of 'structural' elements A, B . . . N. That having been said, we need to see that representation R depends on a set of conditions K, assumed to be (temporarily) present in the system under consideration but having no reason to be present in the same way in a different one.

Consequently, even if two societies are both characterized by the *same structure*, it does not follow that the *same changes* will occur between t and t + k. In other words, it does not follow from the fact that the model R(A, B . . . N) accounts for the development of a society

$$M_t \rightarrow M_{t+k}$$

that any society with the same structure will develop in the same way. Contrary to what many theories of change, Marxist or otherwise, all assume,

'if R(A, B . . . N), then $M_t \rightarrow M_{t+k}$'

does not follow from the proposition

'$M_t \rightarrow M_{t+k}$ because R(A, B . . . N)'.

This really comes down to saying that many theories of change are based on a *non sequitur*, that is on a false consequence of propositions which are, or can be deemed to be, true. The following instance will illustrate this fundamental distinction.

Once again, it is an example from the field of the socio-economics of development, this time from a study of West Bengal. The problem was to account for stagnation and in particular to find out why, despite government attempts to encourage peasants to adopt new techniques that would enable them to improve their agricultural production, they stuck to their old practices and thus helped to perpetuate a situation which was of no advantage to anyone and which was by no means inevitable.

Faced with such a situation, the observer's first reaction is often to condemn the *unreasonableness* of the actors involved, who are seen as deferring to tradition and hence as 'resisting' change which is nevertheless to their advantage. This 'weight of tradition' view of things has the merit of providing a simple explanation of the kind from which slogans are easily made, but at best it is tautologous and at worst paraphrastic.

The neo-Marxist interpretation proposed by Bhaduri is a great deal more acceptable, since it both assumes that the actors do indeed perceive their own interests and shows that the structure of the mutually dependent situation in which they are caught up produces an impasse.[14] They all work in their own interests and use all the assets they have at their disposal, but in doing so bring about a situation that is of no help to anyone. To use the vocabulary of games theory, the solution is a 'sub-optimal' equilibrium. Unlike explanations based on 'resistance to change' or the 'weight of tradition', an account of this type is neither tautologous nor paraphrastic. It deals with the rejection of new techniques as an emergent phenomenon following naturally from the aggregation of individual behaviour patterns which are fully comprehensible once the situation in which the actors find themselves is taken into consideration. Nevertheless, we must take care not to see the structure of the situation of interdependence as the determining factor, since it only contains the actually observed consequences because it is accompanied by a set of 'non-structural' circumstances. We shall return to this very important point later.

Bhaduri's interpretation is as follows. In the area of Bengal under consideration, the conditions of production are of a *semi-feudal* rather than a strictly feudal type, in so far as peasants cultivating land not belonging to them are not bound to the landowner by legal ties and are free to sell their labour. It can, however, be described as semi-feudal, since the tenants' assets do not permit them to achieve subsistence. This means that they are obliged to get into debt, which they can only do with the landowner. As their assets are so limited, they are not in a position to provide a bank with collateral and are consequently denied access to the financial market. Given the fact that they cannot increase their productivity and that their assets are chronically limited, they are permanently in debt. They are in fact tied to their landowner, because they cannot get away from him or her until their debts are cleared.

Let us now suppose that, as has in fact often been the case, the government tries to induce all those involved to adopt an innovation not requiring much investment and perhaps attracting subsidies, that it gives rise to increased productivity, and that it is in fact adopted (which did not happen in reality). In the first year (t1), landlords and tenants alike benefit from the innovation, production is higher than in the previous year, and both groups share the product of a bigger harvest in the usual proportions. In addition to the income from their own share of the harvest, the landowners have in their credit columns the interest paid by the tenants. The total amount of such interest is not affected by the innovation, since it is associated with loans received by the tenants in the previous year, that is before the innovation was introduced. This means that in the first year, the innovation will give rise to a *co-operative* game, with both sides benefiting from it.

As time goes on, however, the structure of the game changes. In the second year (t2), the crop will again be bigger than it was before the innovation was introduced (t0) and similar to what it was in t1. The tenants' income from their share of it will be of the same order as in t1 and greater than in t0. Their *assets*, however, may be greater in t2 than in t1. For that to be the case, they need only not to have consumed the whole of the surplus arising from the innovation in t1 and to have put part of it aside to reduce the loans that they regularly contract from the landowner every year. If this is in fact what happens, the two items making up the latter's receipts will develop in different ways. Their gains from the sale of their share of the harvest will go up from t0 to t1 but remain stable between t1 and t2, whereas those from interest on loans will fall as the sum still on loan to the tenant decreases.

If it is adopted, such innovations may therefore well affect the assets of the two types of actors in a complex and gradual way. Let us return to the rather convincing scenario we have just been looking at and try to determine the precise nature of the *threat* to which the class of landowners is exposed.

In t1, the game is co-operative and, in Rapoport's phrase, 'strongly stable', one in which any reasonable actor would agree to take part.[15] In t2, it *may* still be co-operative, since both classes gain at that stage in comparison with t1, but it is now merely 'stable', that is, with both classes gaining, but unequally. It *may* then become non-co-operative, and indeed it is possible that from a given cycle tk onwards, the total assets of the landlord might fall to the level they were at in t0, before the innovation was introduced, or even settle at a lower one. If this were to happen, the only beneficiaries at the conclusion of the process would be the class of tenants. It is also possible, of course, that the landlords' total assets could settle at a higher level than in t0 and that the innovation could benefit both classes. But in any case, unless we suppose that the tenants consume the whole of their surplus, they would benefit *to a greater extent*.

To sum up, the game brought about by the innovation in question is initially co-operative and has a 'strongly stable' equilibrium. Subsequently, it *is* at best co-operative and has a merely stable equilibrium (since one of the two classes enjoys relatively greater benefit from the innovation). It *can*, however, also become *non-co-operative* or *conflict-producing* if the landlord class is in a less favourable position in tk than it was in t0, with the rate at which that trend develops depending both on the effect of the innovation on productivity and on the way in which the tenants react to the increase in their assets.[16]

The importance of the mental experiment just described lies in the fact that it demonstrates that unless the tenants consume the whole of their surplus, the innovation produces *at best* a co-operative game with a merely stable equilibrium, which is more to the advantage of the tenant than to that of the landlord, and at worst (from the landowners' point of view) a non-co-operative game tending to be disadvantageous to the latter. In other words, landowners adopting the innovation cannot be certain that – in time – they will be able to avoid a dead loss. In the circumstances, they are not likely to be over-enthusiastic about the innovation. This means that in the conditions we have been looking at, they are the ones who can reject it or introduce it.

Thus, of the two groups of actors, one has the *ability* to introduce the innovation, but very little reason for doing so. Or, to be more exact, they have grounds for believing that it might entail unfavourable consequences for them. The members of the other group have certainly the reasons required, but are not in a position to make a decision.

Bhaduri's analysis has three characteristics. First, it accounts for the paradoxical phenomenon whose causes it is attempting to explain (i.e., the rejection of an innovation that looks beneficial) by picking out one or two essential elements from an indefinite list of all those that may characterize the social system under review. Once that has been done, it proceeds like all structural theories. In the second place, the theory can be seen as belonging to the subclass of neo-Marxist theories, since the structural elements it retains are taken from that area of reality to which Marxist doctrine grants a sort of ontological primacy, namely the organization of the conditions of production. Finally, it suggests a law of endogenous development: a society characterized by semi-feudal conditions tends to reproduce itself identically, since 'structurally' it tends to reject the innovations offered to it.

In fact, we must be very careful to see just what consequences we can legitimately draw from this analysis. To tell the truth, although it gives a convincing explanation of an event limited to a particular time and place (the rejection of a particular innovation in a specific region at a specific time), *it does not entail any consequence for the way either the system under review or structurally comparable ones will develop*, that is, systems characterized by a semi-feudal organization of the conditions of production. This is because the *structural* elements correspond only to the salient parts of the system of explanation, which also has elements that can be described as non-structural, but of which we must be aware.

The analysis demonstrates that landowners adopting the innovation suggested by the government would be running *risks*, namely the likelihood of a reduction in their differential status (considered here solely from the point of view of assets) and – what is much more difficult to evaluate – of a clear loss of assets in the medium term. Risks, however, are uncertainties, and the situation created by what the government is proposing is therefore *ambiguous*, in the precise sense that the actors involved in it have good reasons for choosing either of the two lines of action open to them. There are good grounds for the landowners to *reject* the innovation, since it entails risks. On the other hand, there are good reasons for *adopting* it, since it *also* offers them a chance of increasing their incomes in the short and medium terms.

Consequently, in order to be in a position to *deduce* what the actors in the structure of the situation are likely to do, we should need to provide the structural elements we have just been considering with a psychological hypothesis or law stating, for example, that in a risk situation, actors always behave in such a way as to minimize those risks, even if by doing so they forfeit a possible advantage. This is to universalize Wald's criterion of games theory. It is hard, however, to see what grounds there might be for formulating such a law. Games theorists have defined a criterion attributed to Wald, but also a contradictory one, attributed to Savage. When actors adopt it, they take risks to minimize their possible regret at not having made the most of their opportunities. For their part, the psychologists have never formulated a law stating that in an uncertain situation an actor will always adopt Wald's criterion. In short, we cannot see any acceptable general proposition enabling us to deduce how the actors in the structural situation are likely to behave. This is very probably because there is no such proposition.

In other words, we need to distinguish very carefully between the two elements contained in Bhaduri's explanation. One is a *demonstration*, the other an *observation*. The demonstration shows that the innovation puts the landowners in an uncertain situation, in which both possible lines of action entail the possibility of losses *and* gains. The observation has to do with the fact that, as things turned out, the landowners preferred to abstain. That, however, let it be said again, is an empirical statement that we have no grounds for seeing as necessary in character. Perhaps a more detailed study would have enabled us to *understand* why they abstained. Perhaps the wealthiest and most prestigious of them persuaded the others to do so, or perhaps the less well-off were afraid of being eliminated by the play of competition if they were not able to keep up with the richer ones in the work of modernization and used their power to stop the innovation being adopted. Bhaduri's study, however, does not enable us to make any firm choice from amongst the various hypotheses we can imagine in this connection. For whatever reasons the landowners decided not to go ahead, one thing is certain: those reasons are not explicable in terms of the elements that Bhaduri takes into account. This means that there is no relationship of *necessity* between the theory and the phenomenon it reports or, more exactly, the theory explains that if they had adopted the innovation, the landowners would have been running risks, but does not explain why they chose not to run them. It does no more than merely state the fact. The opposite might well have been true in a different context, even one characterized by the same structural features (the semi-feudal organization of the conditions of production) as those pertaining to the context discussed here.

When, if it is to be conclusive, a theory needs the addition of an empirical statement that is only applicable to the case in question, it is obvious that the conclusion cannot be extended to fit others. But that does not invalidate the theory or mean that it is without interest. It is quite plain that Bhaduri's theory is of greater help in understanding the phenomenon observed than any all-purpose 'general' theory about 'resistance to change' in 'traditional' societies.

Secondly, it is important to note that although Bhaduri's theory *explicitly* includes only elements characterizing the system of relationships involved in production, *implicitly* it includes many others. In other words, behind the structural elements, there lies a mass of non-structural ones.

Like any model, Bhaduri's includes parameters and variables. The variables consist of the following set of factors: the (average) income of landowners, the income of tenants, the value of the crop before and after the innovation is adopted, the value of the tenants' consumption and the degree of their indebtedness. The parameters include the real rate of interest, the share of the crop to which each contracting party is entitled under the terms of the lease and the marginal propensity of tenants to consume. All these elements and, of course, the interconnecting relationships between them, are the material expression of the 'semi-feudal' system that governs the relationships between the two classes of actors. The equations in the model state, for example, that the positive difference between the consumption and resources of a tenant represents the capital borrowed from the landowner and paid back with interest the following year. This is enough to indicate that the tenant is chronically in debt to the landowner. As a whole, the analysis assumes that the *ability* to accept or reject the innovation rests with the landowner alone. As for the value of the parameters, it is established by observation. Bhaduri notes, for example, that when a tenant sells only his labour and does not provide his own tools of production, the harvest is generally shared out on a 60:40 basis, with 60 per cent going to the landowner and 40 per cent to the tenant. He also observes that the nominal rate of interest is somewhere between 50 per cent and 60 per cent and the real one around 100 per cent, the difference between them being due to the fact that the tenants repay their debts after the crop has been harvested, when the price of rice is low, and borrow again some months later when the commodity is scarcer and its price is consequently moving towards its yearly peak.

All in all, the model implicitly includes all kinds of elements that are contingent upon the structural ones (the semi-feudal nature of the conditions of production). The financial market is not accessible to the tenants, but there is no reason why it should not be, or why they should not borrow part of what they need from government organizations if the government should so decide. There is nothing to prevent administrative measures being introduced to attempt to limit interest rates.[18] On the other hand, if the decision to accept or reject the innovation is to lie solely with the landowner, that innovation must have certain characteristics. It is clear that if it entails investment, only the landowners *can* decide. If it has to do with the way work is organized or teams of agricultural workers are made up, however, it will be harder for them to resist it.

In short, rejecting the innovation is not only the result of 'structural elements'. It also has something to do with elements that strictly speaking have no part in the theory or the model that expresses it. And, other things being equal, if another type of innovation were proposed, it might be adopted, as the landowners would not be able to oppose it. In such circumstances, even a low degree of interest-bearing government financial assistance to tenant farmers would modify the relationships within the model and the conclusions that could be drawn from it. In other words, the model assumes a set of constant conditions. There is, however, no indication that they have to remain constant. This means that intellectually we need only change any one of these conditions to produce an obvious transformation of the data of the analysis. Ultimately, a semi-feudal organization of the conditions of production will only lead to a refusal of innovation, stagnant productivity and reproduction of the conditions of production because it is accompanied by a complex set of implicit conditions that the analysis assumes to be constant and which are observable *hic et nunc*. That is another way of saying that the analysis is only valid *hic et nunc*, or in other words that the same structural elements will not necessarily produce uniform effects *as a general rule*.

It is therefore dangerous to try to set up a strict boundary between the structural and non-structural features of a system and above all to interpret the distinction in realist terms. We have to realize that the structure of a system does not enable us to see how it will develop, since that *structure* is always associated with 'non-structural' elements which in general cannot be seen as certain to remain constant.

In this chapter, I have tried to suggest that certain ambiguities in theories of change are the result of interpreting the notion of *structure* in *realist* terms. Certain typologies are *useful*, and we tend to use this as a pretext for assuming that they reflect real distinctions. By the same process, we tend to see structural and non-structural characteristics as existing *in reality*, and therefore conclude that the latter can be ignored, which has all sorts of disappointing results.

A realist interpretation of this kind, however, has two unbeatable attractions. The first is that structural distinctions (such as that between community and society, between traditional and modern societies or the notion of the semi-feudal structure of the conditions of production) often correspond to emotional, sentimental or ideological *truths*. The second is that when the notion of structure is interpreted, as usually happens, in realist terms, the result is an artificial inflation of the social sciences' power of prediction.

5

The Search for the Prime Mover:
the Ontological Bias

In their desire to seem and to be scientific, sociologists, economists and political scientists tend to keep rather quiet about their continuing interest in all those great arguments that in the nineteenth century were lumped under the general heading of the philosophy of history.

A recent American work on social change claims to be based on the proposition that conflict between social groups is the main cause of change.[1] Others are more specific, seeing the primordial factor as being conflict between *classes*, which can either induce change or perpetuate in various forms the deep division between the dominant and the dominated class. The opposite point of view has had its supporters, of course, with Durkheim maintaining that social conflicts are secondary phenomena, occurring when the social fabric deteriorates and the regulatory mechanisms ensuring order within a society are no longer effective. There are also more recent writers who share such a view.[2]

Although they usually avoid using the word, some of the latter favour a 'materialistic' way of looking at change, maintaining that it is the result of the interplay of interests that are strictly controlled, and perhaps even determined, by the social position of the actors involved. In the most orthodox versions of neo-Marxist thought, ideas are seen as being strictly governed by interests. In its more flexible varieties, groups brought into conflict by their differing interests vigorously make differing 'cultural' demands, and those which are inevitably in a position of increasing 'functional' importance, are very likely to obtain satisfaction. Future cultural innovation is thus seen as very closely linked to the present 'social structure' which is determined by groups opposed to those in whose hands the future lies.[3]

In contrast to such 'materialistic' ways of seeing change, there is an ever-present 'idealistic' interpretation. The traditional distinction is nicely preserved, even though, in order to make it quite clear that the social sciences have nothing to do with high-flown philosophical debates, the latter adjective is virtually never used. If we cannot see that the debate is still going on, we cannot understand, for example, why *The Protestant Ethic* has become a 'popular' book while the rest of Weber's work is not only unknown to the educated public in general but also has a very restricted influence on the current output of the social sciences. We now know that his main argument, which was certainly not put forward crudely or simplistically, needs to be filled out and seen in relative terms (a point that we shall return to later). Rather than doing that, however, we generally present it dogmatically: the Calvinist ethos inspires in those who subscribe to it the desire to control commercial undertakings and is therefore responsible for the appearance of a social type, the capitalist entrepreneur, and consequently for the growth of capitalism itself. The only way of explaining the success of the popularized version of Weber's thesis is to see it as the demonstration of a *metaphysical* proposition to the effect that a social change as important as the development of capitalism *can* be seen as the result of the emergence of the new *values* or *ideas* rather than of changes in 'structures'. More generally, it can be interpreted as suggesting the primacy of ideas and values in an area where the Marxist tradition, for example, sees the 'conditions of production' and structures as being all important.

Major questions like the part played by conflicts, ideas and values, and the primary or secondary nature of such factors, are all ever-present in the output of the social sciences. Parsons is one of the very few writers to have explicitly acknowledged this fact, and his personal authority was great enough to make it possible for him to publish an article explicitly on 'The Role of Ideas in Social Action' without seeming to be a purely speculative thinker or to run the risk of exclusion from the fold of true social scientists.[4] It was written a long time ago, but in my view the questions raised in it are by no means out of date. Indeed, I am quite willing to go further, or even too far, and suggest that a large part of the social sciences is devoted solely to such matters.

As Nisbet has made abundantly clear, there is another question that is always present in theories of social change, namely that of whether change is *essentially endogenous* or *exogenous*.[5] He is right,

I think, to suggest that we most often choose the first alternative, not only in sociology, which is his prime concern here, but also in a considerable area of economics and political science.

Most theorists of social change set out to show that the $t+1 \ldots t+k$ state of the social system they are interested in follows from its state at t; the future is contained in the present, which in its turn has its origins in the past. Sometimes it is the 'contractions' of the system at t that are supposed to account for changes at $t+1$. In what can be called 'functionalist' thought, it is rather the 'dysfunctions' of the system at t that determine the pace of change between that point and $t+1$.

My own view coincides with that of Nisbet, for we both see the preference of sociologists for an endogenous concept of change as a matter of fact. The reasons for that preference are complex, and for the moment I propose to defer any discussion of them. One reason, however, should be mentioned at this point. If change can be seen as 'essentially' endogenous, the autonomy of the social sciences, and in particular their independence with regard to the traditional and ancient discipline of history, can easily be asserted. On the other hand, if 'exogenous' factors loom too large, it is harder to separate the historian's field of enquiry from that of the political scientist or the sociologist. We can see a symptom of this in the fact that when, in the middle 1970s, the social sciences lost some of their standing, that of history went up to such an extent that some sociologists, political scientists and economists announced that they were ready to convert to that discipline.[6] Of course, the fact that the social sciences are drawn towards a view of change as endogenous is not due to 'corporatist' reasons alone, but also – and perhaps particularly – to epistemological ones, as endogenous change is seen as more predictable (which is undeniable) and more intelligible (which is not quite so self-evident).

I do not think it would be hard to show that in all theories of social change a stand is taken on the three issues mentioned above, namely the part played by conflicts and ideas and the essentially endogenous or exogenous nature of change. This is very evident in the case of the classical theorists. For Durkheim, conflicts, as has been said, were derivative, values of secondary importance (he saw the 'individualism' apparent in the Renaissance and the Reformation as a result of the process of individuation connected with the greater division of labour), and change chiefly endogenous.[7] A theory such

as that of the vicious circle of poverty sees conflicts as being of
secondary importance, is materialistic and reflects a strictly
endogenous concept of change, or more precisely, a lack of change
and stagnation are held to be the inevitable effect of strictly
endogenous causes. The next logical step is to assume that in a poor
society change can only occur as a result of *exogenous* intervention.
These three questions (to which we could add one or two others,
such as the argument about whether change is unilinear or non-linear)
are as far as our choices go. It would not be at all hard to show that
any 'theory' of social change simply encapsulates and labels in a
particular way one of the possible combinations.

In the *Critique of Pure Reason*, Kant showed that certain questions
are of such a kind that we can answer them in contradictory ways
and defend each answer by means of apparently irrefutable
arguments. The ultimate questions that underlie theories of social
change and (implicitly) set the limits of a major part of the
'programme' that such theories indicate seem to me to be of the same
kind. A properly presented *set of arguments* can provide an apparently
irrefutable case for any general proposition relating to questions
concerning such matters as the primary or derived part played by
conflicts or ideas. My own view is that the debate will obviously
go on forever and that there can be no final answers.

The way to resolve such antinomies, to keep the word Kant used
for them, seems to me to be through a critical response which takes
into account the fact that there are no answers to many questions
about social change, although they are always asked in the same way.
There is no point in trying to demonstrate that its ultimate or chief
causes lie in a particular sector of the real world, whether we are
talking of values, ideas or the relationships involved in production.
Nor does it serve any purpose to suppose that change is necessarily
fuelled by one set of mechanisms rather than another, whether we
are reflecting – to take one or two classical examples of such
mechanisms – on group or class conflicts, 'dysfunctions' or
'contradictions'.

In contrast with speculative theories of this type, *scientific* analyses
of social change meeting what Popper saw as the demands of rational
criticism have three characteristic features. In the first place, they
have *definite* objects. To put this in another way, they try to answer
clearly formulated questions generally expressed in the following
way. 'We note that at point t, social system S has the characteristic

features A, B, C . . . N, and that at t + k these become A', B', C' . . . N'. Why is this so? For example: 'Society S is economically stagnant (A), despite efforts made by the state (B') to induce such-and-such a category of actors to modify their behaviour. Why is this so?' Secondly - and here we come back to a point that we have had occasion to stress in the two preceding chapters - a scientific analysis is one which can show that changes in certain features between t and t + k has the effect of modifying (or not) the situation of this or that category of actors in such a way as to induce them to bring about the aggregated results A', B' . . . N' that we in fact observe at t + k. Thirdly - and this follows from the last two points - depending on the process under consideration, we shall be led to take this or that type of variable as either dependent or independent.

I must beg the indulgence of those readers who are not social scientists for inflicting on them propositions that they will probably quite rightly consider to be extremely trite. However, they should realize that if everyone, and particularly social science specialists, had always seen them in that way, the history of those disciplines would have been profoundly different. No one would have wondered whether ideas are determined by structures, whether the part they play in change is a primary or derivative one, or whether conflicts are primary or secondary phenomena. In short, there would have been no Marxists, culturalists or structuralists. No one would have defended a 'materialist' or 'idealist' concept of change. Parsons would not have attempted to contrast functional and conflict theories.[8] All such questions would have been classified once and for all as forming part of the antinomies of sociological reason.

The history of the social sciences being what it is, there is perhaps some point in stressing the fact that the mechanisms of change can vary from one process to another and that the conceptual tools that are helpful when we try to analyse it *are determined by* the process under consideration. Reciprocally, no general (or would-be general) theory of change can a priori be held as better than any other when we are trying to account for this or that specific process.

In the rest of this chapter, we shall consider three problems: the part played by conflicts in change, that played by ideas and values, and the relevance of the endogenous model of change.

THE PART PLAYED BY CONFLICTS

It is one thing to see that there are often conflicts between social groups, but quite another to see them as the essential mechanism of change. The first proposition is acceptable, whereas the second is not, for the simple reason that there are a great many examples of processes leading to important changes in which conflicts play a less important or secondary part. We have already seen some of these.

All theories attempting to 'demonstrate' that intergroup conflict is the *main* mechanism of change are in fact based on rhetorical or sophistic techniques incontestably stemming from Marx (and it is interesting to note that it is in his writings that the best refutation of the theory of the class struggle as the universal cause of change is to be found).

In *The Poverty of Philosophy*, Marx expounded the famous thesis, that history is the history of the class struggle, which was to be developed the following year in the *Communist Manifesto* :[9]

> Feudalism also had its proletariat - serfage, which contained all the germs of the bourgeoisie. Feudal production also had two antagonistic elements which are likewise designated by the name of the *good side* and the *bad side* of feudalism, irrespective of the fact that it is always the bad side that in the end triumphs over the good side. It is the bad side that produces the movement which makes history, by providing a struggle . . .
>
> After the triumph of the bourgeoisie there was no longer any question of the good or the bad side of feudalism. The bourgeoisie took possession of the productive forces it had developed under feudalism.
>
> Thus feudal production, to be judged properly, must be considered as a mode of production founded on antagonism.

If we look at the text closely, we cannot help being struck by its very Hegelian character. There are two mutually antagonistic elements in feudalism, we are told: the 'bad side' (the lower class) struggles against the 'good side', and as a result of what Hegel would have called the obscure work negativity, the 'bad side' finally wins, since serfdom contains all the seeds of the bourgeoisie. This is a perfect example of the endogenous model: when the conditions for its emancipation are achieved, the group that was the inferior class in the feudal system becomes a dominant class, the bourgeoisie, opposed by the new inferior class, the proletariat.

Their text is less interesting for its contents, since the same ideas appear in the *Manifesto*, than for its context. In it Marx is open to the criticisms that a few pages earlier he had made of Proudhon.[11] Marx was a devotee of economics and very alive to the principle of what we would now call methodological individualism. Consequently, he attacks Proudhon for reifying society and not seeing that it exists only by virtue of the individuals who make it up:

> M. Proudhon personifies society; he turns it into a *person-society* – a society which is not by any means a society of persons, since it has its laws apart, which have nothing in common with the persons of which society is composed . . . M. Proudhon reproaches the economists with not having understood the personality of this collective being . . .

Marx therefore goes on to defend economists. Later, on the same page, he quotes with approval the American economist Thomas Cooper, who declares the need to avoid seeing society as a reasoning entity and to see it rather as a collection of persons: 'The moral *entity* – the grammatical being called a nation, has been clothed in attributes that have no real existence except in the imagination of those who metamorphose a word into a thing . . . '

These methodological observations are completely forgotten in the pages in which the theory of the class struggle is developed, where classes are substantialized and Marx forgets that they are made up of persons. The antagonism described in the first passage quoted above is not that between serfs and their lords, but one between two 'elements' or 'sides'.

There would be no point in stressing the weaknesses in a text written during Marx's early life if it did not provide an almost exemplary illustration of the shifts of meaning to be found in the theoretical writings of all those who see conflicts as the factor producing change. In the first of the extracts quoted, Marx falls back on a piece of sophistry, saying in effect that classes are *by definition* mutually antagonistic and that *therefore* there can be no classes without a class struggle at the same time. The latter, it is implied, would of course be futile and meaningless if it was not bound to produce the emancipation of the 'bad side'.

Even more interesting is the divergence between the passage in *The Poverty of Philosophy* in which Marx develops the theory of the class struggle and one a few pages further on where, in connection with the argument about the causes of the division of labour he is conducting, he returns to the question of the disappearance of the feudal system and the development of modern industry.[13] Proudhon's contention was that workshops and manufacturing had developed endogenously, as we should say, quite simply because they made increased productivity possible. Marx is opposed to that idea, and reminds Proudhon that 'history cannot be made with formulas'. This means that he is teaching the latter history and developing a theory of the disappearance of the feudal system that has very little connection with the earlier passage about the class struggle.[14] Here, Marx analyses the decline of feudalism – exactly as Keynes was to do later – as an exogenous (and no longer as an endogenous) process triggered off by the discovery of America.[15]

> One of the most indispensable conditions for the formation of manufacturing industry was the accumulation of capital, facilitated by the discovery of America and the import of its precious metals.
>
> It is sufficiently proved that the increase in the means of exchange resulted in the depreciation of wages and land rents, on the one hand, and the growth of industrial profits on the other. In other words: to the extent that the properties class and the class of workers, the feudal lords and the people, sank, to that extent the capitalist class, the bourgeoisie, rose.
>
> There were yet other circumstances which contributed simultaneously to the development of manufacturing industry: the increase of commodities put into circulation from the moment trade penetrated to the East Indies by way of the Cape of Good Hope; the colonial system; the development of maritime trade.
>
> Another point which has not yet been sufficiently appreciated in the history of manufacturing industry is the disbanding of the numerous retinues of feudal lords, whose subordinate ranks became vagrants before entering the workshop. The creation of the workshop was preceded by an almost universal vagrancy in the fifteenth and sixteenth centuries.[16]

I have quoted the passage *in extenso* because it seems to me to be of absolutely fundamental importance. There are two reasons for this. The first is that it shows that *there was no class struggle* between the feudal lords and the bourgeoisie. As a result of the influx of precious metals from the New World, there was chronic inflation. The consequence of this was that the seigneurial class became poorer, since it was difficult for them to adjust their income to the rate of inflation if they did not want to take the risk of sparking off a peasants' revolt. They were therefore obliged to reduce their standard of living and dismiss their followers. On the other hand, the influx of metals freed capital and stimulated the creation of manufacturing. Thus, at one and the same time, 'circumstances' favoured the bourgeoisie and worked against the feudal lords. The rise of the former and the decline of the latter, however, were not the result of a *struggle* in which the lords came off worst.

The second is that the process was by no means a result of any endogenous necessity. The opposite was in fact the case, for the rise and fall were brought about by a *conjunction of circumstances* and a welter of linked effects resulting from the influx of precious metals. The inflation also had a further classical effect that Marx was of course well aware of. This was that low wages did not rise as fast as inflation, especially as a large labour force, swollen by the dismissals to which the lords had been forced to resort, was available on the market. That effect, however, as Marx himself well knew, is not enough to prove the existence of an endogenous class struggle in the phase of primitive accumulation.[17]

This means that we cannot reconcile the passage on p. 185, in which Marx shows himself to be an excellent economic historian (many of his conclusions were later confirmed by Keynes in particular and are still accepted as valid) with the dogmatic passage on p. 174 unless that one assumes that 'struggle' is used metaphorically. In the passage on p. 185, the class struggle takes the form of the process of succession well known in the ecological field, a process which occurs when a modification of the environment encourages the developmment of one species and discourages that of another.[18] In such cases, one can no doubt talk about the 'struggle' between the two species, but only metaphorically, since in them there is no struggle or even competition between them, merely 'opposite sign' effects produced by an exogenous factor.

In short, only rhetoric and sophistry can reconcile the three passages from *The Misery of Philosophy* that we have been examining. In the first, Marx, the conscientious pupil of the Anglo-Saxon economists, reminds us that it is essential not to personify groups, which are simply made up of individuals. In the second, like the good historian he was, he applies this principle and demonstrates that the rise of the bourgeoisie and the decline of the feudal ruling class were emergent effects from the aggregation of the behaviour of individuals in conditions which were changing under the influence of a particular conjuncture of circumstances. In the third and last, he goes against all the principles stressed in the first two and maintains that history is the result of the antagonism and 'struggle' developing between the two classes.

There is nothing exceptional about a recourse to sophistry in his work, and indeed it is apparent at another key point in Marxist doctrine, namely the definition of the notions of surplus value, exploitation and surplus labour. These notions enabled Marx to conceive of the relationships between the bourgeoisie and the proletariat, the two classes of capitalist society, as being antagonistic. He could thus at once affirm the existence of both classes (which was anyway hardly in doubt in nineteenth-century capitalism) and the struggle between them. The struggle might be apparent to varying degrees in different circumstances, but even when it was not directly observable or reflected in confrontation, it was *there*, since it was an integral part of the antagonism arising from capitalist conditions of production as defined on the basis of the notions of exploitation and surplus value.

The theory of surplus value, which has given rise to all sorts of learned arguments that need not concern us here, is in fact based, like the demonstration of an antagonism between the feudal rulers and the bourgeoisie, on arguments of a rhetorical type that it would be worth while to bring out into the open.

First, we need to make one or two obvious points. The very notion of the division of labour – a phenomenon which Marx, following Adam Smith, wrote a great deal about – implies differentiating and co-ordinating a range of elementary tasks. Consequently, the production costs of a manufactured product depend not only on the costs of *labour*, which Marx defines as the act of transforming matter, but also on the cost of *organizing that labour*, which is clearly not non-existent, since it includes such things as foremen's wages. It is, of course, more than compensated for by the increased productivity following from the division of labour. In addition, a firm has to be informed about its customers' orders and to receive payment. The sales side therefore also entails costs.

Marx was, of course, aware of these obvious points and said so explicitly on several occasions. However, he removed such distinctions and reduced the costs of firms to a single element. To do this, he resorted to a classical rhetorical distinction that Pareto often stressed. When we are uneasy about the dangers to freedom inherent in policies that we support, we contrast *real* freedom and [mere] freedom, and when we want to justify questionable actions, we contrast true virtue and [mere] virtue.

It is a device of this kind that Marx is implicitly using when he defines labour. [*True*] work is that work that contributes directly to the transformation of matter, and hence the value of a product is the value of the work of the *workmen* involved, since they are the only ones who act on matter. The costs of the organizational and sales side can therefore be ignored. The work of a clerk managing a stock of information or an executive co-ordinating the management of such information come under the heading of [mere] work. In the last analysis, surplus value is no more than the difference between the value of [mere] work and that of *real* work, although Marx does not of course define it as such.

The distinction between [mere] work and real work is obviously a piece of sophistry. But, as Pareto says, sophistries are effective when they confirm *feelings*. That is what has happened here. It may well be that the metaphysical and religious representation that portrays mankind's struggle against nature and matter is no stranger to the feeling that lies at the root of the credibility of the rhetorical distinction between work and *real* work.

It is by using the same kind of rhetorical distinction as a basis that Marx 'demonstrates' in his analyses of the history of law that *ideas* are of a derived nature, whereas that of the conditions of production is primary. *Real* law, he suggests, appears once the latter demand that the worker be able to sell his or her labour. Consequently law (i.e., *real* law) is a mental construct meeting a necessity inherent in the capitalist system of production.

If I have dwelt at some length on the case of Marx, it is because his propositions and techniques of 'demonstration' are not only still very much alive in the social sciences, but are also a source of inspiration for all those who are determined that conflicts between groups and particularly between social classes shall be seen as the main motive force behind change or, where appropriate, the absence of change. The point of examining Marx's work itself is not only that he invented all the propositions and techniques to which the neo-Marxists have chiefly added variations. It is also that to Marx himself the Marxist construction was profoundly equivocal, for his own familiarity with economics and his enormous historical culture meant that his own analyses in those areas continually went beyond the doctrinal framework he tried to draw from them. Hence the contradictions (in the strictly logical sense of the word) that are apparent, as I have tried to show, in a work such as *The Poverty of Philosophy*, in which the doctrine of the class struggle is already present in a more or less definitive form, even though it squares badly with the historical developments shown in other parts of the work.

The modern neo-Marxists have kept Marx's idea that classes are necessarily antagonistic and that the very notion of social class implies the idea of a permanent class struggle, even when that struggle *is invisible*. This means that any social differentiation or any form of inequality can be seen as indicating and confirming it. In Marx's own writings, there is an attempt to demonstrate this 'antagonism' in the theories of value and exploitation. In those of the modern neo-Marxists, class antagonism is often put forward as a prime truth apparently requiring no verification. This is perhaps because the theory of value and exploitation it is based on becomes less and less credible as the division of labour becomes more and more complex. Once that stage is reached, it does indeed seem very difficult to assume that the costs of *organization* and *information handling* are nil. That is why there are attempts to adapt classic Marxian theory to the modern economic world. Some writers restrict themselves to the theory of surplus value in its orthodox form and turn, for example, clerks into petty bourgeois, the lowest members of the bourgeoisie.[19] Since their wages are taken from surplus value, such petty bourgeois are part of the bourgeoisie, but they are *petty* bourgeois in the sense that their wages are low. Such arguments clearly imply that, far from being self-sufficient, class theory is completed by a theory of stratification.

Others go further and see it as permissible to include marketing and organizational costs in the *value* of a product.[20] If that is the case, clerical and manual workers can both be seen as part of the working class, with the means of establishing a distinction being the use of the criterion of authority (the differentiation between 'management' and 'subordinate' functions). When that happens, class theory is completely dissolved in stratification theory.

Such adaptations of Marxian theory are of interest, since they show that the theory of value and the distinction between work and *real* work that underlie them are seen as being hard to view as compatible with modern economic systems. But if the distinction between work and *real* work is abolished, the theory of value and also the possibility of defining surplus value and the idea of exploitation itself all collapse. There is thus no longer any demonstration of class antagonism, and classes are no longer *necessarily* engaged in a struggle. Nor is it any longer possible to talk about an invisible class struggle originating in a structural antagonism between them.

It is for that reason that certain kinds of neo-Marxism have tried to remove the class struggle from the economic to the cultural field.[21] So far at least, however, this area has produced no equivalent of the theory of value that forms the basis of class antagonism. It is no doubt true that in industrial societies not all individuals enjoy the same access to culture, and that there are all kinds of differences and inequalities between them. Weber, in a series of classic texts, has shown that individuals belong to different *classes*, have a different *status* and enjoy differing degrees of *power*. These obvious facts apply to both modern and to many 'traditional' societies. But, Weber says, the fact that classes exist does not imply that there is any permanent of 'structural' conflict between them or that we can presume that such conflict exists even when it does not show itself. Once again, if such a presumption is to have any proper basis, some theory implying the antagonism in principle, such as the theory of value, is indispensable. Without it, we can only assume the existence of a class struggle when we can demonstrate that we have actually encountered it.

It seems to me that the way the social sciences have recently developed tend to show that Weber was right and that Marx was wrong, and that there is now no credible theory of the 'fundamental' antagonism of classes. In conformity with de Tocqueville's prediction, however, the 'general and dominating passion' for equality has produced a situation in which any equality, of whatever kind, can be seen as the result of unseen conflicts between antagonistic groups of unequal strength.

This is because if we restrict ourselves to visible conflicts, we can see that they sometimes occur during processes of change but clearly do not in any way represent the fundamental mechanism of either change or of the perpetuation of social structures (assuming that the latter can in fact be seen as unchanging). As the Machiavellian tradition, represented by such figures as Pareto and Mosca, had clearly seen, conflicts are chronic and endemic only in a political subsystem. Now political conflicts do not reflect exclusively class or social conflicts; they may also, for example, reflect rivalry between competing sections of the elites.

The only support for the principle that social conflicts are the essential motive force of change comes from a logic of the emotions.

THE PART PLAYED BY IDEAS AND VALUES
(WHICH IS SOMETIMES GREATER THAN WE IMAGINE)

A second antinomy in sociological reason includes the thesis that ideas and values are the product of structures. It also includes the antithesis that they are independent variables which explain the differences between social systems and the processes of change and reproduction. The thesis and its antithesis are seldom expressed so crudely, but they are implicitly present in much of the current output in the field. Very often, the success of a book in sociology or the political sciences is attributable to the fact that it is directly or indirectly seen as supporting either thesis or antithesis. The size of the readership that McClelland's *The Achieving Society* attracted in the United States certainly has some connection with the general idea behind the specific analyses it presents, which is that values produce the 'dynamism' and progress as well as the stagnation societies are imbued with.[22] The popularity of Weber's book on *The Protestant Ethic* can also, as I have suggested, probably be accounted for in the same way. The same would be true of the success enjoyed in its time by Michel Foucault's *The Order of Things*, which presents Western history as dominated by a succession of apparently inexplicable 'epistemic' swings.[23] As for the thesis, it is still present in different varieties of neo-Marxist and 'functionalist' thought.

There can be no overall answer to this second antinomy, any more than there could be to the first. That is why the debate goes on but we get no nearer to a conclusion. Analysis of social change can only be *scientific* – and by that I mean once again that it can only meet Popper's conditions for rational discussion – when it concerns itself with partial processes clearly defined in spatial and temporal terms. When that is achieved, it can be seen that *certain* of these processes can be convincingly analysed if we postulate that ideas and values (or, to use a deliberately vague and general term, the data of mental life) are *autonomous*, whereas others imply that such data are to be seen as *heteronomous* or, to use the language of statistics, as dependent variables. In the terminology of econometrics, the former would be described as *exogenous* and the latter as *endogenous variables*.

The study by Epstein referred to in the last chapter belongs to the second type, since it treats ideas and values as dependent variables. To recapitulate the main features of his analysis: irrigation creates new opportunities of different kinds for different actors. They are not the same for both peasants and Untouchables, and are different for the landowners in the two villages concerned. Epstein then supposes that the actors grasp the new opportunities as far as they are able and that their main aim is to improve their own conditions. We could therefore say that he interprets the situation in a *materialist* way, since structures account for behaviour, and also in a *utilitarian* one, since the actors are guided by their own interests. He also observed changes at the level of values, with the Dalena peasants still setting great store by symbols of modernity and those of Wangala prizing only the traditional signs of prestige and status. But such changes in values are interpreted as the readily comprehensible consequences of opening up Dalena to its surrounding region and the breakdown of social structures brought about by irrigation. Similarly, the strengthening of traditional symbols in Wangala is ascribed to a strengthening of hierarchies within the peasant caste and of the links of clientage between them and the Untouchables following the introduction of irrigation, which at the same time tended to cut the village off from its surrounding area. *In this specific case*, therefore, it is possible to see both the changes in values in Dalena and the persistence of traditional values in Wangala as derived and secondary phenomena.

There are of course also cases in which values have to be treated as independent variables. In this connection, it is interesting to compare Epstein's study with one by Dore of Japanese agriculture in the nineteenth century.[24] In it, the author gives a fascinating account of how an apparently innocent traditional practice played a crucial part in setting in motion a process of modernization in an agriculture that had remained extremely stagnant until very late in the nineteenth century. In particular, Dore's analysis shows that *in this specific case, a* decisive role has to be ascribed to *ideological* or *axiological* variables which have to be treated as independent variables, even though the influence of ideology in this case as well as in others has to be understood from the standpoint of the situation of the actors in question.

The practice Dore describes created a twofold obligation for landowners. They had to reduce their income in bad years and not increase it in good ones. The explosive effect of this obligation arose from the fact that it gave rise to a system of *contradictory encouragement*. Landowners had in fact good reasons for seeking to increase their productivity, since doing so could mean that they need not lower their income in bad years, but they also had good reasons for not introducing innovations, for their tenants were used to having no increase in rents in a good year and found it hard to accept that there should be one on the grounds that the higher yield was not due to favourable weather but to increased productivity.

There were other factors, that perpetuated and increased the ambiguity of the landowners' position. At the end of the nineteenth century, the Japanese government launched a propaganda campaign containing proposals for subsidies to develop irrigation. All those wishing to avail themselves of these, however, had to have the records of their land holdings brought up to date. When the records were first introduced, in the Meija era, landowners had often used bribes to 'persuade' the officials to underestimate the value of their lands. Revising the records therefore meant that there would be tax repercussions for them, and this put them in a dilemma. As income was based on the area shown in the records, those landowners whose holdings were set at a higher value could not try to increase it without the risk of incurring protest from their tenants, but neither could they refuse to increase it without having to face recrimination from their peers.

The ambiguous situation brought about by both the existing custom and the government's proposals rule out the possibility of applying in this case the classical utilitarian model so appropriate to the Indian situation we have just examined. Landowners could not come to a decision by weighing up the pros and cons of the various possible lines of action, and it is not immediately clear where their best interests lay. That is why Dore noted that *ideology* seems to have played a decisive part in the attitudes finally adopted by both sides.

Indeed, in the first place at least, the modernization of agriculture seems to have been the work of men who had been exposed to the influence of the physiocratic views the Dutch had managed to introduce into certain circles of Japanese society. Their influence, it should be added, went hand in hand with that of certain conjunctural or situational factors which served to strengthen it. The mobility of tenants living near the towns was higher, since a wider range of occupations was open to them than to those living in the depths of the countryside. Landowners in the former areas therefore had a greater incitement to decide to innovate, since they could use the departure of their tenants to put up rents and thus obtain a maximum return from the effects of that innovation on production. This explains why in the first stages of the process the innovators belonged for the most part to the category of landowners living near an urban centre and fed on physiocratic ideas. Subsequently, there was a halo effect. The innovators were imitated and – a particularly important factor – they put their more traditionalist peers in a difficult position. In so far as their own production costs were lower, they indirectly encouraged their peers to change their traditional practices.

What chiefly needs to be stressed, however, is that in the situation we are examining the ideological factor cannot be overlooked and was indeed a consequence of the situation in which the actors involved found themselves. That situation did not of course determine the contents of the beliefs they subscribed to, but it did induce them to summon up ideological reasons that would enable them to find the right answer when it was by no means clear what it might be. That is why those who had been nurtured on the philosophy of the European Enlightenment were more tempted by innovation, in a given comparable situation, than those who had been brought up to revere local traditions and practices.

It should be noted in passing that at this point we need to make an observation similar to that in chapter 3 concerning the theory of development in Colombia set out by Hagen. In both cases, it is important to realize that the analysis only appears to cover a medium-term process. In the first place, it should be noted that if we examine the process studied by Dore in its subsequent stages, then from the time when the first centres of innovation begin to form (for reasons he studies) they bring with them a whole train of cumulative stimuli. Clearly, if X produces rice at a lower price, there is an external effect that Y cannot afford to ignore. It can be seen that such stimuli effects develop over the long term and give rise to the transformation effects so brilliantly described by Dore but which, for reasons of space, cannot be dealt with at length here. One such effect is the erosion of clientage links (since the process may encourage landowners to get rid of their tenants), the appearance of the phenomenon of classes, the spread of political mobilization to the countryside, and the consequent opening up of such areas to the political fermentation originating in the towns. Looking at the process retrospectively, we can see that if we analyse the appearance of the innovation at point t as an aggregation effect resulting from the structure of the situation characterizing a given category of actors at that point, then the structure itself follows from factors from the very distant past. Although I have had to isolate one or two factors from Dore's analysis here, it can be seen that he views Japanese development as having been a gradual process taking place over a long period, with each separate point in the development only comprehensible if macroscopic data from a very wide time sector are taken into account. Again, we must note that the Weberian paradigm of methodological individualism is not restricted to short or medium-term processes and can also be applied to long-term ones.

The part played by ideas, values and, in general terms, mental data, thus depends on the structure of the situations we are induced to examine when investigating a particular topic. Some of these situations raise problems involving decisions and can only be easily dealt with by someone who has ideological convictions. Others – of the kind we have just been examining – can, however, be the subject of 'rational' or quasi-rational reflection, since the actors involved can easily see what course of action they can take and decide which seems best.

Comparing these two types of example once more shows (to make the point again in passing) just how pointless it is to discuss in a priori and general terms the validity of the rational model of action. It *is* valid in certain cases, but not in others. This is because the hypothesis that the actor tries to adapt to the situations he is confronted with is universally valid, whereas the form that adaptation takes varies according to the structure of that situation. Pareto had already made the same point when he said that one can build a bridge by using what he called 'logical' actions (that is, by making rational choices based on scientific propositions), but one cannot choose one's member of parliament in the same way.

That common but often misunderstood idea of the relationship between the structure of a situation and 'the part played by ideas' is of such great importance that it deserves deeper investigation. More exactly, what I would like to do is to use an example borrowed from Hirschman[25] to emphasize the fact that when we are considering complex decisions – and more particularly *collective* decisions – they may be based on more or less coherent systems of beliefs that could, if we so wished, be called *paradigms*, since by virtue of both their nature and their function they come very close to what Kuhn means by the term.[26]

The nature of the paradigm selected in a given situation is to some extent, but largely negatively, determined by reality and the problem to be overcome. There are some paradigms which do not seem to be capable of providing a solution. The one selected is also affected by 'social factors' such as influence or the demands of certain categories of the actors involved. However, although its content can be *explained* by the structure of the system in which it occurs and by the situation of the actors, it cannot be *deduced* from them. We must therefore grant it a certain autonomy. In other words, it cannot be trated as a *dependent* or endogenous variable.

If we make all due allowances, we can see that the situation is in fact rather like that described by Kuhn with regard to the history of science, where a paradigm is a system of propositions determining the general direction of the research undertaken by the members of the scientific community and is the object of a more or less uniformly shared collective belief. As long as it is not openly contradicted by reality or threatened by the approach of any conflicting paradigm, there is little resistance to it. If it is increasingly unsuccessful, or if adventitious hypotheses capable of accounting for the contradictions between reality and the theories based on it seem to be *ad hoc* in nature and created 'to meet the needs of the cause', then some people will be tempted to search for a new one that, at the appropriate time, will be likely to oust the paradigm in current use.

As the example from Hirschman's work has shown, the same type of process can be observed when the problem to be resolved is one of achieving practical goals rather than interpreting observational data. In both cases, it can be seen that the solution is defined on the basis of more or less coherent and clearly formulated systems of collective beliefs, to which we must grant a certain degree of autonomy. Thus it is possible, if one so wishes, to use a more exact term and talk of 'ideological paradigms'.

Hirschman's study deals with the way in which the 'problem' of north-east Brazil was handled between the end of the nineteenth century and the Second World War. The interior of the region, the *sertão*, has a particular rainfall pattern. There are seven months of *certain* drought (June–December), coming after an *uncertain* period in which the rainfall varies and, indeed, it may not rain at all. This means that the *sertão* is not a desert, and indeed agriculture and cattle-raising are quite highly developed. There is always, however, the threat of the catastrophe of drought. In bad years, the peasants move to the banks of the São Francisco or Parnaiba rivers or to the towns of the south or the coast, looking for temporary work and assistance until the rains come again and they can go back to the *sertão*. Economic conditions in the area are of course a political problem for the government.

At first, over a long period covering several decades, the 'solution' to the 'problem' of the area was seen as being a *technical* one, consisting of regulating the watercourses, building dams and reservoirs and digging wells. Between 1877 and 1879, a period of drought followed an exceptionally long spell of sufficient rainfall, and there had in fact been no catastrophe since 1845. An imperial commission of enquiry was set up. It recommended the development of communications, in particular several railway lines, and the construction of 20 small and large dams. The work was carried out, but the undertakings were badly run and did not solve the problem of drought.

During a further period of drought in 1888–9, there was talk of political corruption. The siting of the dams and the routes taken were alleged to have been mainly decided upon for political reasons and in particular to have served the interests of local leaders. The opposition, of course, had every reason to support these allegations. The results of their investigation – which had been partly disinterested and partly for their own advantage – were that the policy of building dams was seen as having failed not because of its own weaknesses but because of the way it had been implemented, and in particular because the way it had been carried out had given too much influence to people with political aims. As a consequence, it was decided, in 1909, that a government agency attached to the ministry of public works, the *Inspetoria*, would be set up. All the key posts were given to scientists and engineers.

The authority given to these specialists was the result of a whole range of convergent reasons. In the first place, there was the desire to use the slowly acquired understanding of why things had gone wrong in the past to avoid any failure due to political corruption. Secondly, there was a vague general agreement that the paradigm favouring a technical solution to the region's problems was correct. Thirdly, largely as a result of the influence of French positivism in Brazil, the major engineering colleges of the country were held in high – and envied – social esteem. The idea of building reservoirs seemed, as a solution, to be all the more *natural* and *obvious* as the nature of the terrain in question was eminently suited to it, since the irregular watercourses often came down through narrow gorges. As a complementary – and equally obvious – measure, it was judged necessary to dig wells and develop transport systems so that the peasants could move to wetter regions and materials and products could be carried as necessary.

It was probably felt in some quarters that emigration was a more appropriate solution to the problems of the area than struggling against drought, but it was not politically viable. It first came up against the obstacle of regional feelings in the north-east, as the area had been politically important in the past. In addition, the *Inspetoria* more than met the wishes of those who were against emigration, since it too planned to develop communications to allow peasants to move closer to the dams. There was a further objection to emigration, which was that agriculture and stock-raising had long been traditional activities in the *sertão*. Crops suited to the climate (xerophilous plants) had been developed, and although the irregular rainfall created difficult problems, other factors such as the absence of insects were favourable to agricultural activities and stock-raising.

Here, as in Kuhn's classical analyses, we have a range of factors working together to produce a paradigm to the effect that 'the problem of the North-East is of a strictly *technical* nature'. Around it there emerges a consensus which is both positive and negative and which continues despite failures, which are ascribed to the fact that political corruption had emasculated the policy implemented in 1877. The process is very like those described by Kuhn. If we use his terminology, we can say that the policy of constructing dams launched in 1877 was an *anomaly* and that it was *resorbed* by means of the *adventitious* hypothesis of the effects of corruption.

But the strictly *technicist* nature of the paradigm used to solve the region's 'problem' was bound at some time not only to come up against the inevitable difficulties in the way of implementing a programme of such a kind and political and economic contingencies, but also to be affected by an endogenous erosion process. Both the strictly technical nature of the paradigm and the habits of thought of the scientists and engineers involved combined to overshadow the social consequences of the technical measures taken. As those consequences ultimately became increasingly visible, the credibility of the paradigm became correspondingly less self-evident. Unlike what had happened in 1877, it was no longer simply a case of blaming the – relative – failure of the policy that had been implemented on all kinds of unforeseen circumstances and interferences (which had to some extent, however, upset the way it had been introduced and the attempts to carry it out efficiently). It began to be felt that the purely technical perspective in which the problem of the region had been seen for decades was perhaps not the right one. Once the question of a paradigm shift, as Kuhn calls it, began to surface, it came into contact with political forces determined to exploit the growing resistance to purely technical solutions. Certain intellectuals helped this trend by beginning to attempt a first definition of the competing paradigm that was starting to seem necessary, although initially at least the process was vague and unfocussed. The new paradigm was not of course developed by the scientists and engineers, who had neglected to take the social consequences of their policy into account, but – naturally – by specialists in the social sciences.

The problems produced by the policy of building dams were first brought to light by a department of the *Inspetoria* in charge of co-ordinating the activities of the stations built along the major reservoirs, which had been constructed without very much thought for the problems of irrigation. This was partly because building such reservoirs in the gorges seemed such a 'natural' thing to do and was of great political benefit, since it showed that something was clearly 'being done'. It did mean, however, that there were good reasons for hurrying the work along rather than stopping to take proper steps to set up an irrigation system. The reasons were in fact of an *economic* as well as a *political* nature, for building the dam meant not only that certain types of need for water could be met, but also that there was considerable protection from drought. The universal feeling, of course, was that irrigation channels were vital, but should be judiciously planned for a later stage of the programme.

In the meantime, however, the *social* consequences of the policy had had a chance to develop, and from 1940 onwards it was these effects that occupied the centre stage. Furtado, an economist who was later to play a vital part in the subsequently adopted policy of redistributing land, gives a brief account of them. The major one was that the crops that benefited least from these major undertakings were those most directly useful to the greater part of the population and the poor in particular. Since the state had not assumed responsibility for irrigation, it had chiefly been developed, in a modest way, by big landowners who often had holdings near the reservoirs. For the greater part, however, they had used it to increase the amount of land used to produce sugar cane, which meant greater profits from selling sugar or *aguardente*. The cultivation of food plants, on the other hand, scarcely increased. Although the reservoirs meant that it was considerably easier to keep stock alive in times of drought, this too was of benefit largely to the landowners.

All in all, what happened was the exact opposite of what had been aimed at. The policy of building dams had given more of a stimulus to industrial crops such as cotton and sugar-cane and stock-rearing than to subsistence crops, which were still not produced in sufficient quantities during periods of drought. In addition, the large-scale public works projects had kept in the *sertão* impoverished peasants who might otherwise have left the region. This meant a plentiful supply of labour at a low cost to the major landowners, since there was no inducement for the peasants to try to adopt more efficient methods of raising stock or growing crops. Consequently, agriculture production settled at a very low level, and this brought in its wake a self-perpetuating stagnation in wages.

Building dams was therefore no solution to the problems of north-eastern Brazil. Indeed, they had helped to make the inequality between large landowners on the one hand and small landowners, agricultural workers and tenant farmers on the other a great deal more marked.

With regard to the matter in hand, Hirschman's analysis demonstrates first that the policy implemented in the first period cannot be reduced to an expression of collective interests. It probably worked to the advantage of the better-off and to the disadvantage of the most deprived, but class interests offer no explanation of the fact that it was in fact implemented. Indeed, we need to see its inegalitarian effects as the *unwilled* consequences of a quasi-unanimous *will* to reduce the effects of drought on the part of the political class. For their part, the influence of the 'technicist' paradigm and the ways and means by which it was put into effect must be considered as being an emergent effect, in the sense that as a result of a set of macroscopic factors various categories of actors were induced to *believe* that the solution to the region's problems was technical in nature.

At a more general level, the analysis shows that once a 'problem' reaches a certain degree of complexity, a solution to it is arrived at via a more or less implicit elaboration of 'theories' or 'paradigms'. Although such constructs take real data into account, they are also influenced by social variables and the facts of specific situations (such as the prestige enjoyed by engineers), in rather the same way as a scientific theory can be influenced by both those groups of phenomena. Once they have been established, such practical 'theories' are also subject to a fate rather like that of their scientific counterparts, in that the length of their life span depends on their ability to absorb falsification by comparison with reality, the existence of 'alternative' theories, the credibility of the latter, their attraction for certain categories of actors (for example, the economists in the second period we have examined) and the means such actors have at their disposal for disseminating their views.

Since I have already made observations of this kind in connection with the theory of Hagen that we looked at in chapter 3 and that of Dore in the present chapter, there is no need to dwell on this point, and I propose simply to draw the reader's attention to the temporal dimensions in which Hirschman is operating here. As is the case in the two other examples, it is a *long-term* one. For example, Furtado's influence after the Second World War only makes sense if the earlier stages of the process are kept in mind and, if like Hirschman himself, we go back to the middle of the nineteenth century.

Finally, the analysis shows the mutual interdependence that, as Pareto stressed, links ideas, values and the data of stratification and the consequent impossibility of isolating the effects of any of these categories of variables.

THE PART PLAYED BY IDEAS AND VALUES
(WHICH IS SOMETIMES SMALLER THAN WE IMAGINE)

Certain traditions, such as that of Marxism, tend to underestimate the autonomous nature of 'ideas' and 'values'. In other cases, however, we can see in the social sciences an opposite tendency to see values and, more generally, mental data as having the status of a *first mover*.

J. Baechler quite rightly objects to the way Weber's *The Protestant Ethic* is frequently seen as providing a picture of the Calvinist who is certain that he is one of the Elect and looks for signs on earth of his predestination in the life to come and consequently feels induced to strive and succeed.[27] If he is engaged in business, he is led to invest rather than to consume, thus inadvertently helping to develop capitalism.

There are two reasons why an interpretation of this kind fails to carry conviction. In the first place, it takes absolutely no account of the social environment in which Calvinist entrepreneurs frequently found themselves. There is no *aggregation* of microscopic behaviour. All that happens is that a microscopic hypothesis is simply *transposed* to the macroscopic level. Secondly, it is hard to see the relationship between the 'signifier' and the 'signified' in the popular version of Weber's thesis. Why should economic and commercial success be a sign of salvation in the world to come? A more satisfying aspect of the problem is that interpretation which goes no further than showing the autonomy that Protestantism in general and Calvinism in particular give to the social subject. Durkheim also suggests that the growth of Protestantism helped to spread individualistic values, which no doubt encouraged the entrepreneurial spirit.[28] Both interpretations, however, have the defect of introducing a direct link between the appearance of new values and the aggregated effects that they are supposed to produce.

Popular ways of interpreting *The Protestant Ethic* should be seen as a particular illustration of a much more general phenomenon. Many theories introduce the hypothesis that values directly influence social change and see a correlation between the two as sufficient demonstration of such influence. Thus, for McClelland, society is entrepreneurial and dynamic when the need for achievement is highly valued by the individual. Certain of Parsons's writings contain the same idea,[29] and the dynamic nature of American society is seen as arising from the fact that the values of achievement and success are profoundly embedded in it. He also attempts to account for certain differences between American and certain European societies (and particularly German society) on the basis of differing values. As for neo-Marxist sociologists, they stick to their received doctrines and have an *endogenous* concept of values, which in their view are produced by structures. Once this proposition has been accepted, however, they have no difficulty in conceding that values play a fundamental and direct part in social change or, quite the opposite, in perpetuating 'social structures' which give rise to class 'subcultures' explaining how social classes are reproduced.[30] A few years ago, theorists of social development proposed similar schematic representations, suggesting for example that the appearance and consolidation of democratic regimes is very closely linked to that of certain individual values.[31] Similarly, some theorists of economic development have implicitly taken up the popular way of seeing Weber's thesis and suggest that such development depends to a large extent on that nature of the values inculcated during the 'socialization' process of individuals.[32] Generally speaking, the idea of socialization has assumed such an importance in the field of the social sciences that it is sometimes treated as an autonomous area of research.[33] To some extent, this is no doubt the result of the division of labour that has taken place, but it has only become possible because it is based on an implicit theory that a direct relationship between the *values* interiorized by the individual and certain macroscopic phenomena ('political' and 'economic' development, 'social reproduction' and so on) can be established. This theory, although it most frequently remains implicit, has acquired currency because it need not clash with many differing schools of thought.

As Durkheim rightly stresses, the division of labour can produce anomie. That, it would seem, is what has happened here. If we make socialization into an autonomous process, we run the risk of exaggerating its importance and, above all, of obscuring the macroscopic phenomena we are seeking to account for. With regard to Hagen's theory, we have tried to show that development in Colombia in the early twentieth century becomes much more intelligible when seen as the aggregate effect of behaviour no doubt guided by values but also by situational data; when, in other words, we are quite aware that values were by no means as primal as Hagen would have them be.

The considerable interest of H. R. Trevor-Roper's writings is precisely attributable to the fact that they subject Weber's theory of *The Protestant Ethic* (or, more exactly, the popular interpretations of it) to a similar kind of correction. It is worth spending a little time on this matter, as Weber's book is a major reference for all those who insist on the primacy of values as an agency of social change.

In the first instance, what Trevor Roper demonstrates is based on pinpointing a certain number of facts that had escaped Weber's attention. It is true that most of the sixteenth-century entrepreneurs were Calvinists, but none were produced by Scotland, Holland, Geneva or the Palatinate, the four outstanding Calvinist societies. Nor can it rightly be said that every Calvinist businessman led an ascetic life, in the sense of Weber's *innerweltliche Askese*. Many lived comfortably, some amassed considerable personal fortunes, and not all were Calvinists to the same degree.

No doubt the entrepreneurs of the sixteenth century often were Calvinists, even those who gravitated around the courts of the Lutheran princes of Denmark and Sweden, and it is true that the Hamburg bank was created by Dutch Calvinists. There was, however, one other characteristic that they shared: almost all of them were *emigrés*. None of those active in Geneva was of Swiss origin, and they often came from provinces of Spanish Flanders. Even the prosperity of Holland was due to Flemish entrepreneurs. Similarly, the business world of Hamburg and Germany as a whole was dominated by Dutchmen of Flemish descent. The Catholic entrepreneurs in Cologne or Holland generally came from Antwerp or Liège.

Thus the sixteenth-century entrepreneurs were often Calvinists and often came from Calvinist Flanders, but their chief common characteristic was the fact that they were immigrants, mostly from the great industrial and commercial centres of the fifteenth century – Augsburg, Antwerp, Liège, Como, Lucca and Lisbon (in the last of these, they were Jews rather than Calvinists). As Trevor Roper points out, it is also difficult to follow Weber in his insistent suggestion that there was some sort of fundamental difference between fifteenth and sixteenth-century entrepreneurs or in his contrast between the 'adventurers' of the fifteenth century and the 'entrepreneurs' of the sixteenth or seventeenth.[34] It is true that there were more Fugger-style entrepreneurs in the sixteenth century than in the fifteenth, and this difference in 'frequency', together with his hypothesis of the influence of Calvinism on the development of capitalism, are no doubt the two factors that combined to encourage Weber to see the Fuggers as 'adventurers'. The rather fragile distinction can however be demolished as soon as we interpret the influence of Calvinism in the world of business as the result of a reaction involving adaptation and also observe that the plentiful supply of capital in the sixteenth century facilitated the appearance of 'entrepreneurs'.

The reason for the correlation between the growth of Calvinism and the development of capitalist undertakings are therefore a great deal more complex than Weber suggests. In the sixteenth century, the industrial and mercantile bourgeoisie was naturally aware of the thought of Erasmus, with its view of the equal worth of the lay and clerical state, its stress on the interior nature of faith and its view of the right of the man of action to attend to his secular affairs without failing in piety. The middle classes who were imbued with such beliefs - like those of Milan, for example - later moved imperceptibly towards Calvinism, which took up the main themes of Erasmus's thought. They tended, however, to identify with international Calvinism and to form links with it, particularly once the pressure of the Counter-Reformation began to mount. Their emigration to towns less threatened by it - amongst the chief of which were those of the Netherlands - meant that the old economic elite of Europe was fleeing a power that saw such thought as heretical, increased taxation in favour of the Church, thus causing a flight of capital, and generally tried to increase the hold of the bureaucratic state on entrepreneurial activities. The children of those men of affairs who preferred not to emigrate were directed towards the profession of arms. Capitalism perished in Milan and Antwerp and flourished in Amsterdam.

When the corrections suggested by Trevor Roper are built in, Weber's famous thesis becomes a great deal more credible. At the *microscopic* level, the mechanisms become simple and conform to the Weberian precepts summed up in the notion of comprehension. We can *understand* why men of affairs welcomed the thought of Erasmus, since it legitimized their activities and took the wind out of the sails of their detractors, *why* they sought to make good use of the support that international Calvinism could give them, and *why* some of them tried to settle in more welcoming lands when they were threatened by a power which attacked such thought, increased the burden of taxation on their undertakings and generally tried to step up its supervision. We can *see* why those who remained urged their children to take up professions that the Counter-Reformation saw as prestigious, and that in doing so they helped further the decline of the entrepreneurial spirit in that type of society. Whilst providing a perfectly acceptable explanation of why men of affairs were sympathetic towards Calvinism, Trevor Roper at one and the same time manages to get rid of the doubtful causal relationship which sees engaging in commercial undertakings as the consequence of a belief in predestination.

At the microscopic level, he analyses the relationship between Calvinism and the growth of capitalism as an aggregation effect resulting from the adaptative reactions of men of affairs to changing conditions largely arising from the appearance of the Counter-Reformation. This means that the end result is a system of explanation that fully meets the rigorous traditional criteria proposed as a basis for testing the validity of a scientific theory. Indeed, Trevor Roper's theory accounts not only for the part played by Calvinists in the growth of capitalism, but also for a considerable number of facts that Weber's theory in itself fails to explain. Why were the Geneva entrepreneurs not of Swiss origin? Why were their German equivalents often of Flemish origin? Why were there also Catholic and Jewish entrepreneurs from the provinces affected by the Counter-Reformation? Why did Antwerp decline and Amsterdam prosper? Why were men of affairs in *Lutheran* countries often *Calvinists*? (This last question probably lay at the root of Weber's decision to stress specific aspects of Calvinism as distinct from other forms of Protestantism and of his view of the decisive role of the doctrine of predestination.) From a negative point of view, it enables us to avoid certain historically unconvincing and hence undesirable corollaries of Weber's theory, such as the view that the Fuggers, who were Catholics, were mere 'adventurers', whereas the sixteenth-century Calvinist men of affairs were 'entrepreneurs' in the modern sense of the word. Overall, Trevor Roper's theory is more valid than Weber's both from the point of view of the latter's criterion of comprehension and Popper's criteria.

In Trevor Roper's work, *ideas*, *values* and *beliefs* are correspondingly seen as elements in an explanatory system that includes a range of other factors. Thus, the fact that men of affairs were drawn towards the thought of Erasmus and subsequently (particularly when they found themselves thrust into opposition) towards Calvinism, together with their flight from the Counter-Reformation, is interpreted as responses to changing situations and hence as dependent on the characteristic features of such situations.

It must be stressed, however, that since Weber's death the arguments about his *The Protestant Ethic* have in no way detracted from the essential matter of his theory. It is indeed manifestly true that the economic elites of the sixteenth century were attracted to Calvinism much more than to Lutheranism. The reasons for this are much more complex than Weber maintained, and particular attention must be paid to Trevor Roper's insistence on the close intellectual relationships between Calvinism and the thought of Erasmus. It is also true, however, that Calvinist discourse, in its stress on asceticism in this world, was more likely to appeal to such elites than Lutheranism, in which the Christian could glorify God just as much by enjoying the things of this world at their true value ('Pforzet und rülpset Ihr nicht? Hat es Euch nicht geschmeckt?' proclaimed Luther) as by successfully attending to his affairs. On the other hand, as Troeltsch emphasizes in his *Soziallehren der christlichen Kirchen und Gruppen*, which completes Weber on this point, the belief that grace was revocable meant that the Lutheran could not enjoy the assurance and serenity that the Calvinist could derive from his own irreversible election.

EXOGENOUS OR ENDOGENOUS CHANGE?

I shall now examine very briefly a final antinomy (to return once more to Kant's term) very rightly stressed by Nisbet. Very frequently, the social sciences consider that a theory of change worthy of the name must be *endogenous*, with the change a system undergoes between t and t+k hence being seen as a function of the state of the system at t. For example, 'dysfunctions' (to use the functionalist terminology) or 'contradictions' (to use the Marxist vocabulary) are observable at t and explain changes occurring in that system between t and t+k. The *antithesis* in that change is generally the result of exogenous causes. The chief argument for the proposition is as follows: in a closed system (that is, one which is isolated or situated in a constant environment) a state of equilibrium will normally be reached after a certain time. Theories based on this antithesis normally see change in 'traditional' societies as being generally brought about by exogenous interventions. We cannot be sure that Nisbet, who was hostile to endogenous theories of change, offered enough resistance to the temptations of the opposite thesis. Anthropology provides a further classical illustration of the two terms of the antinomy. The functionalists, who see change as being endogenous, are at the opposite end of the spectrum from the diffusionists, who see it as exogenous.[35]

The desire to decide between thesis and antithesis no doubt comes partly from certain deeply held metaphysical convictions and partly from the social need political scientists, economists or sociologists feel particularly keenly at certain times rather than others to dissociate themselves from history, a question to which we shall return later, in chapter 7. What needs stressing here is that the endogenous or exogenous nature of change is completely determined by the problem which is to be resolved or, to put it differently, the phenomenon we propose to account for. As a useful way of illustrating this idea, we can use the example of the analysis of racialism in American trade unions after the Second World War put forward by Merton.[36]

Merton asks why, despite the egalitarian values that the union movement generally paid lip-service to, did discriminatory practices against Blacks grow during the period in question? The answer lies in bringing out into the open a self-sustaining endogenous process, which can be described as follows. Black workers, who came from an under-industrialized region, the Southern states, and had often been agricultural workers, had no experience of trade unions or any cultural affinity with the movement. Trade unionists, when faced with a choice between two applicants and in a position to control recruitment, preferred - *in the interest of the movement* - to offer membership to a White worker from the North rather than to a Black from the South. Since this happened repeatedly, the result was that *in general* Blacks experienced much greater difficulty in finding work than Whites. At that time, the unions were much less recognized, accepted and institutionalized than they later became, and employers were often tempted to break strikes by bringing in Negro labour. Since Blacks found it hard to get work, they tended to jump at the chance. The result was a spiral effect, with the doubts the Whites felt about Black solidarity with the unions being 'confirmed by facts'. Imperceptibly, the former moved from simple *distrust* based on a desire to protect union interests to an attitude of *discrimination*.

If that is as far as we go in the sequence of events and if all that concerns us is explaining the appearance and strengthening of anti-Black racial feelings in White workers, we are dealing with an *endogenous* process. It develops within a *closed system* composed of four categories of actors, these being White workers, union officials, Black workers and employers. Each of these reacts 'comprehensibly' to its own situation at t; once they are *aggregated*, these reactions produce a new situation at t + 1 (Black workers find it even harder to get jobs than at t, the employers can make use of them more easily, and so on) which produces equally comprehensible reactions at t + 2, etc., etc. The spiral effect – the imperceptible movement from distrust to discrimination – is the result of an endogenous combination of actions and reactions. It would be easy to express this endogenous model in mathematical terms. What we would have would be something like those used by economists to account for certain spiral effects in the economic field (like the so-called 'spider's web' theorem, for example).

But let us suppose that we observe the process *over a longer period*. After a time, the fact that discriminatory practices in the unions have become institutionalized will attract the attention of actors who have so far been passive or inactive. These practices may go against values seen as fundamental to American society and therefore may, when the right time comes, mean that politicians, intellectuals, journalists and so on will intervene. An exogenous effect (i.e., one produced by actors outside the system as already defined) will intervene to correct the spiral effect by modifying the norms governing the relations between actors in the preceding phase.

I think that the example I have just given is of general significance. A social system is not an immediately observable or identifiable datum like a stone or a road. It is only defined once the phenomenon we are claiming to explain has been determined. The racialism of American trade unionists in the period after the Second World War was an aggregation effect, developing exogenously in a closed system defined by four categories of actors, each of which obeyed easily 'comprehensible' principles. If, however, we want to explain *simultaneously* both the growth and the diminution of discriminatory practices, we have to see the original system as an *open* one, that is as one likely to be exposed to possible exogenous reactions on the part of actors situated within its *environment*.

The endogenous or exogenous nature of a process is therefore very closely linked to what kind of process it is and what temporal limits we are considering it in. This means that it is pointless to opt *generally* for an endogenous view of social change (as Marxists and functionalists usually do) or for an exogenous one (as Nisbet does, for example).

Arguments about the part played by conflicts or values or about the endogenous or exogenous nature of change, which have loomed so large in the social sciences, are ultimately attempts to solve insoluble problems. Their chief interest is the degree to which they indicate that *ontological* beliefs are in operation. Such beliefs may serve a purpose and help to provide an interesting direction for research, but they may also distort analysis. Weber's *The Protestant Ethic*, with all its strengths and weaknesses, and Marx's rhetorical legerdemain are in the last analysis a witness to the complexity of the interaction between science and metaphysics.

6

A Well-Tempered Determinism

There is a deep-rooted prejudice that insists that the postulate of determinism is the indispensable foundation of scientific knowledge.[1] Given the state of a system at t, that state can only be the result of a range of data, which may be internal or external to that system, existing at $t-1$. No doubt a *real* observer may not know all the facts and therefore feel that there is no determination, but that of course can only be an impression. An *omniscient* observer would be able to see the world at point t on the basis of its situation at $t-1$. Unfortunately, Laplace has never explained how a *non-omniscient* observer could know, without becoming omniscient himself, what his famous demon knew.

In the social sciences, Laplace's demon is still whirling about, even though he is no doubt a harmful rather than a useful fiction. In the first place, this is because certain processes reveal *open* situations and others *closed* ones (for the sake of brevity, we shall speak of *open* and *closed* processes). Only the latter, however, make it possible to establish the state of a process at $t+1$ from its preceding state.

We can illustrate that distinction with the help of explanatory examples. Imagine a system of interaction involving two people in which each has repeatedly to choose between two options and is free to choose either A or B. This means that in choosing they may help bring about four situations: AA (in which both choose A), AB (one chooses A and the other B), BA (the choices are reversed) or BB (both choose B). Let us also suppose that the four situations have characteristics that mean that anyone would automatically prefer AA to all the others. In that case, every time the choice is proposed, each will choose A, and the situation AA will be brought about. Neither of the two people involved can choose that *situation*, since it is the result of choices made by two mutually autonomous individuals, but each of them can rule out certain situations. By choosing A, the first person involved rules out BA and BB. The second, if he or she makes the same choice, also rules out AB and BB. By ruling out BA and BB, however, the first simultaneously makes AA or AB possible, and it is up to the other one to choose between the two possibilities. Similarly he or she too, by excluding B, leaves two possibilities, AA and BA, neither of which he or she is in a position to impose. Both of them are therefore in a position to open up a totality of possibilities from amongst which the other participant must choose. In certain cases, the result may be unacceptable to one or both parties, but that is not so here, for in making a choice between the options the other makes possible for him or her, each helps to bring about AA, which it is assumed that both prefer to any other situation. Each time the choice is offered, both will thus choose A and hence do their bit to bring about AA.

Let us call the *structure* of the process all the hypotheses involved in it, namely that both participants repeatedly have to make a choice between A and B and that both strongly prefer AA to any other possible situation. A process of this type would be foreseeable for an external observer who had mastered its structure: AA, then AA, and so on. This fictional process is subject to the same rigid determinism as Newton's apple, because it places the actors in a *closed situation*. From an *ontological* point of view, the fact that they are capable of reasoning and anticipating no doubt distinguishes them from Newton's apples, but the example shows that even with such actors a determined and foreseeable process can be constructed. Conversely, a determined and foreseeable process does not imply passive subjects. In more general terms, the deterministic character of a process depends not on the nature of the constituent elements but on the nature of their relationships.

Let us now look at a process analogous to that just described in every way except one. Again, both participants have to make repeated choices between A and B. This time, however, they are not in total agreement about which situation they would prefer. One strongly prefers AB to any other situation, whereas the other feels the same, but with one modification, preferring BA. It is not hard to imagine social situations leading to symmetrical preferences of this type. Two children may both declare that there has to be a leader and that it has to be him or her. In formal terms, this everyday example is expressed in the following preferences: the first prefers AB to AA, BB and BA, the second BA to AA, AB and BB.

Here, the first participant can rule out either the range of BA–BB situations (by simply choosing A) or of AA–AB situations (by simply choosing B). None of the possible choices, however, is very satisfactory either for him or her or the other participant. He or she can only hope to bring about the situation he or she wants to see (AB) by choosing A. If he or she chooses B, there is no chance of it happening. But is there any advantage for him or her in choosing A? For that to be the case, there would have to be some chance of AB coming about, that is, of the other participant having good reasons for opting for B. That is scarcely so, because if the latter does in fact choose B, he or she rules out the possibility of obtaining what he or she prefers, the BA combination. Both, therefore, have good reasons for choosing A. Since, however, they both have the same reasons, they also have good cause to expect that neither AB nor BA will be achieved. Thus there is no point in either of them choosing A. That particular choice would be meaningful for each of them if BA and AB were, respectively, combinations that they feared. In our hypotheses, however, there is nothing that leads us to believe that BA would be a worse combination for the first participant than AA for example, or AB than AA for the second. Our only supposition has been that the first will prefer AB and the second BA to any other situation.

It is impossible to predict what will happen. The system of hypotheses leads to total indeterminacy. The structure of the process (that is, the total of the hypotheses) is such that neither participant has any real reason for choosing A rather than B, and produces an *open situation*. One can, of course, introduce adventitious hypotheses. We could, for instance, suppose that only the first participant has a dominating personality, and can impose his or her preference for AB on the second. We can, however, also postulate that there is no psychological distinction between them, which would mean that it would be impossible to forecast how the process would work out. In short, the example shows that it is just as easy to imagine *totally determined* elementary social processes (i.e., those giving rise to *closed* situations) as to imagine those that are *totally non-determined* (i.e., which give rise to *open* situations).

Contrary to what one type of current orthodoxy would have us believe, non-determined processes are just as interesting from the point of view of knowledge as rigorously determined ones. This may seem quite paradoxical, but it is obvious if we refer to our two illustrative examples. In the first, an observer can forecast with complete certainty what will happen whenever the two people involved are faced with a choice between A and B, and he or she can also see why it is so easy to forecast how the process will work out. Since the preferences are what one would naturally expect – by hypothesis, the participants would have to be mad not to prefer AA – there is no reason to expect any other outcome. In the second case, he or she cannot predict the choices they will make, but he or she can readily see why that should be so, since as their situation is an open one, neither has any reason to choose A rather than B or vice versa. Our observer cannot know beforehand what the state of the process will be at t, but he or she can know and explain why that kind of prediction is not possible. In other words, the inability to predict is a consequence of the structure of the second kind of process, just as the ability to predict flows naturally from the structure of the hypotheses defining the first kind.

In short, no general relationship can be established between the ability of an observer to understand a process and the rigorously determined, partially determined or totally indeterminate nature of that process. Nor is there any relationship between the *interest* of a process and the degree to which it is determined. It is just as interesting to understand why those involved in the second kind of situation have no reason to choose A rather than B as to see why those involved in the first kind have every reason to do so. There seem to be no grounds for supposing one to be more interesting or intelligible than the other.

In the social sciences, therefore, Laplace's demon comes up against the first obstacle, that of the existence of *non-closed* situations. The second hurdle he meets is the fact that there are such things as incompletely foreseeable innovations (which does not of course, mean that they are unintelligible. The third is what I shall call, making use of a classical reference, Cournot effects. Non-closed structures, incompletely foreseeable innovations and Cournot effects rule out a Laplace-type representation of social processes. It follows from this that the postulated determinism often seen as the indispensable foundation of our knowledge of the real can, in the case of social processes at least, have the effect of thwarting or inhibiting analysis and knowledge.

OPEN AND CLOSED PROCESSES

French sociologists specializing in questions of organization are familiar with M. Crozier's study of firms, presented under the code name of *Monopole*.[2] It presents a process with closed situations, in which those involved are constantly faced with options. As in the first theoretical example above, however, the way they respond is largely predictable. We need to look in some detail at why this should be the case.

As the name implies, the Monopoly is a group of firms with the monopoly of manufacturing a product. Each of the factories is run by a director who has an assistant director as his right-hand man. The director is responsible for the proper running of the firm, the assistant director for production. The latter has authority over a qualified technical director. The management team also includes a financial controller whose task it is to check that the financial decisions taken by the director are in order. As for the workers, they are allocated to production shops under the supervision of a foreman. Repairs and maintenance for the machinery are carried out by maintenance teams. Maintenance and production units are the responsibility of the technical director.

The undertaking as a whole and in its component parts is riddled with conflicts, not very efficient or dynamic, and routine bound. Curiously enough, the causes of conflict are the same in all the firms in the Monopoly. In every one, the technical director has far greater real power than his official job description suggests, and the assistant director seems incapable of exerting in any real way the authority that, according to the organization chart, he is supposed to have over his technical colleague. Throughout the Monopoly too the maintenance workers seem to make the production workers obey *their* rules and behave like a privileged caste hand in glove with the technical director. Why should this be the case? Why should such a *dysfunctional* system, satisfactory neither collectively nor from the point of view of several actors and categories of actors, reproduce itself identically over time?

The reply to that question is as follows. The organization has a structure of such a kind that:

1. Each actor or category of actors can theoretically choose from amongst several ways of interpreting his role. Let us call all these possible interpretations (I_i). For example, $(I_i = (I_1, I_2)$.

2. Each actor or category of actors is greatly encouraged by the 'structure' (a concept to be defined later) to choose one particular element of (I_i). For example, I_1.
3. By choosing the interpretation of their role suggested by the structure, certain actors put themselves in an unfavourable position, for the situation that they help to create by their choice is not the best from their point of view. The inducement to make that choice emanating from the structure, however, is so effective that they are helpless and so feel both impotent and frustrated. In other words, the interaction system leads to *deficient equilibrium*.[3]
4. In cases of deficient equilibrium, innovatory behaviour on the part of the actors can sometimes be observed. If the rules of a game are such that they make me lose constantly, I may be tempted to change them. If I can, of course. In the case of the Monopoly, however, the actors are in a situation which never gives any of them both the *ability* and the *motivation* to do anything about the rules.

In short, no actor can really choose between the possible interpretations of his role that are theoretically offered. In theory, he could choose between I_1 and I_2, but the inducement to choose the former is so powerful that the choice is theoretical. Such a *reduction* in the area of choice is naturally not a general feature of interaction structures, but it can occur in certain cases. When it does, we need to explain *why* it does. A structure can also tend (as is the case here) to inhibit innovation, in these particular circumstances the creation of a new area of choice. A *reduced* area of choice and the lack of any action by the actors on that area produce a closed process subject to a 'reproductive' law.

Let us consider, for example, the interaction system formed by the production workers, maintenance workers and foremen. The wages of the production workers depend partly on their output, and consequently it is to their advantage to ensure that any breakdown in the machinery is rectified as quickly as possible. (It should be pointed out that as the raw materials are heterogeneous, such breakdowns are frequent and hard to foresee or avoid.) It is also to the foremen's advantage for repairs to take place as quickly as possible, since they are responsible for the proper working of the shop and their authority can only be undermined if operations proceed by fits and starts. The maintenance teams, on the other hand, have quite different interests from those of the other actors. If they make it a rule to meet the demand for their services as quickly as possible, they create unpleasant working conditions for themselves, with periods of idleness alternating with bursts of feverish activity. There is no need for them to accept such conditions, since their output, unlike that of the production departments, cannot easily be quantified, and their wages have therefore very little to do with the way in which they carry out their job. In addition, since they are in a monopoly situation, they cannot by the nature of things be subjected to the same moral sanctions they might encounter if they were less efficient than a competing team.

The consequences of these technological and institutional data are at once clear. The maintenance workers have in theory a choice between two ways of carrying out their job (I_1, I_2). They can (I_1) behave altruistically and decide to take responsibility for all the erratic performance and hold-ups due to the difficulty of telling when the machinery is likely to break down. Alternatively (I_2), they can pass the buck back to the production workers by straightening out their own operations, even if it means letting queues form when breakdowns occur simultaneously in several workshops. Of course, the area of choice (I_1, I_2) is theoretical, or rather *potential*. The maintenance workers have every inducement to choose I_2, since it is to their advantage and has no drawbacks as far as they are concerned. Consequently, it is not hard to understand that I_2 is the behaviour that they are observed adopting on the ground.

The only disadvantage for the maintenance workers if they choose I_2 would be the criticism of their workmates on the production side. The latter have in theory the possibility of relating to the maintenance workers in one of two ways. They can simply put up with the situation and, if a breakdown occurs, wait for them to act (J_1). An attitude of this kind would of course entail disadvantages for them, since the production workers' pay-slips vary according to their output. In addition, it is not pleasant to work irregularly, with alternating rush and slack periods. Or (J_2) they could try to make the maintenance workers feel sympathetic and guilty and try to push them into speeding up their operations. J_2 is of course a better line of action to take, provided it is likely to work. If not, it will not be as advantageous as J_1, for if the production workers harassed the maintenance teams to no avail, it would merely make the general atmosphere in the shop and the firm as a whole get worse. What is more, they might be held responsible for the inevitable split between the two types of workers and accused of breaching working-class solidarity and affecting the smooth running of union machinery. In short, J_2 is a better strategy for the production workers provided that one condition is met: it must intimidate the maintenance teams and make them change their own strategy, or, to put it another way, it must persuade the maintenance team to choose I^1 when their own interests urge them to choose I_2.

If they choose J_2, this will lead to situation I_2, J_2, which is in fact worse for the production workers than the situation that would arise if they opted for the strategy of acceptance (J_1). In other words, the production workers run considerable risks if they choose J_2. They might simply run up against a brick wall and break working-class solidarity, all to no avail. Faced with a J_2-type of initiative on the part of the production workers, the maintenance teams can easily let it be known that there is no moving them from I_1. Nor is it likely that the production workers will try to make a move towards J_2, since the facts of the situation – i.e., the advantages enjoyed by the maintenance workers as a result of their monopoly position and their guaranteed wages – are enough to dissuade the former to try intimidation. The maintenance workers cannot be swayed by the risk of the moral disapproval of their production-line colleagues (which is the only weapon those colleagues have), because if they do not start on repairs in a particular shop as soon as their help is requested, it is because they are busy elsewhere.

So everything combines to produce a situation in which the maintenance workers 'choose' the 'selfish' (I_2) interpretation of their role and the production workers realize clearly that they have no power to intimidate or threaten them. In a word, the production workers have no choice. Their area of choice is *reduced* to J_1, since to all intents and purposes all the organizational and technological facts of the situation compel them to select that option.

We can now see why that part of the process is closed: of the four combinations of strategy or situations that are theoretically possible, three are potential and only the fourth occurs in reality.

When the foremen are included in the interaction system, we have a potential area of choice containing eight theoretical situations. Like the production workers, the foremen have some advantage in harassing the maintenance workers (K_1), for if the latter turn up to repair the machinery in their own good time, they put the foremen, who are responsible for the smooth running of the shop, into a difficult position, as the production workers may well accuse them of inefficiency and their authority may consequently be undermined. Even if the production workers do not criticize them, they may still feel that they cannot meet the responsibilities of their 'role'. But they are caught in the same trap as the production workers. For a foreman, K_1 is only a good strategy if it works. If it does not, there are serious risks in using it. Since he is required to exercise leadership, he needs to try to keep his moral authority. In the eyes of the production workers, it would be greater if he could organize the maintenance teams into working for his shop and diminished if he tried to influence them and only succeeded in (at worst) giving them a chance to show their independence or (at best) in demonstrating how powerless he was. In short, K_1 is a good strategy if it is likely to work and a risky one if it is not. It is, however, very likely *not* to work, since a foreman has no power to intimidate the maintenance workers. This means that he is likely to choose K_2 (acceptance), even though in so doing he helps to create an unpleasant situation for himself. If he chose K_1 (taking positive steps), however, it would be even worse.

Thus, the *potential* area I_1, J_1, K_1 to I_2, J_2, K_2 is reduced to the *real* area I_2, J_2, K_2: the maintenance workers impose their way of working on the other two categories, who can only accept it. The situation is pleasant for the former and unpleasant for the latter. One can of course imagine the production workers and foremen asking for the rules to be changed to avoid being put into a situation that makes them help create conditions that they are justified in seeing as unpleasant for themselves. The 'rules', however, are the result not only of *institutional* but also of *technological factors* that it is difficult to manipulate in the short term (heterogeneous raw materials and unreliable machinery). This collection of data, which forms a *system*, creates a favourable situation for the maintenance workers which they are naturally not anxious to lose.

All the analyses of the Monopoly are in the same vein and show that institutional data and practices help to set up strategic areas involving this or that group of actors. In almost every case, however, those areas are reduced. Thus, the assistant director and the technical director are caught up in a system of ambiguous relationships resulting from the fact that the former is theoretically above the latter but has much less practical experience in his job, being a *polytechnicien* simply waiting for another posting, whereas the technical director has considerable on-the-job experience and everything at his fingertips. If there is a conflict with the assistant director, he is likely to have the final word. As in the case referred to above, the potential area of strategy is reduced to a single course, with the assistant director resigning himself to the fact that the technical director will retain the situational advantage conferred on him by the recruiting practices and operational rules of the undertaking. The potential area of strategy is thus reduced to its minimum. As in the previous case, the 'end' of the 'game' leaves the participants equally dissatisfied. The technical director, who has *real* authority, is scarcely inclined to try to modify the rules. Nor is the assistant director, who merely has *formal* authority, since his time in the firm is merely one stage in his career.

Monopole provides a nice example of a structure leading to a *closed* process which is fairly rigorously determined. Behaviour is predictable and repetitive, since the characteristics of the system have the effect (1) of reducing all the areas of strategy that they determine to their minimal level and (2) of dissuading those involved from acting to obtain changes in the rules.

It must also be emphasized, however, that the *closed* nature of the process is dependent to a large degree on *all* the conditions. If one changes, then it may no longer be closed. Should the breakdowns become less frequent as a result of technical innovations, the area of strategies corresponding to the interaction system among the three categories of actors – production workers, maintenance teams and foremen – is opened up again, and this means that the game can no longer be *determined*. Should the system of appointment and recruitment to positions of responsibility be changed, other areas of strategy will be opened up. If there are modifications to the organization chart, the structure of the various interaction subsystems may also be modified. Thus the *closed* and predictable nature of the process is not the result of tiresome cultural habits which stop the actors involved facing squarely up to their problems, but rather of a relatively complex- and hence fragile - combination of technological and institutional data.

We can draw the following conclusions from the example we have been considering:

1. In the social field, there are processes which are rigorously

determined. The behaviour of those involved in the Monopoly is consequently totally predictable.

2. A process of this type occurs when those involved are placed in conditions of such a kind that the areas of strategy defined by their interaction are reduced to their minimum level.
3. The closed nature of a process is always highly dependent on a complex system of conditions. Corollary: if one of the conditions changes, the system may be no longer a closed one. The behaviour of the actors may no longer appear determined and predictable.

It should be noted in passing that the same kind of remarks could be made about the conclusions Crozier draws from his analysis as those made in chapter 3 with regard to Hagen. The 'blockage' in *Monopole* is obviously very closely linked to the characteristics of the interaction system described in its code name. This means that it cannot be seen as illustrating the propensity the French are said to have (which is cultural in origin) for avoiding face-to-face discussion and thus unintentionally creating blockage situations that could only be resolved in the crisis mode. In other words, 'blockage' in the Monopoly cannot be seen as the particular illustration of a general process that could be inductively rediscovered.

'Forced choice' situations characteristic of closed processes do not of course enjoy any ontological or scientific primacy, since it is clear that although there are situations in which choice is forced, there are also situations in which it is real, and because there is no reason why the former should be more interesting than the latter. Showing that a set of conditions leads to a more than minimal reduction of the field of choice is of no less scientific interest than showing that other sets of conditions do lead to a minimal one. Observing that a game is closed and explaining why is neither more nor less 'scientific' than observing that another is open and accounting for the fact. At least, that is so unless one believes that without determinism there is no science. If that is in fact what they believe, researchers will behave like the drunk looking for his key under a lamp-post because there is more light there and tackle closed processes, not because they are more interesting, but because they are more predictable.

Several of the studies mentioned in earlier chapters illustrate cases of open processes, as witness Bhaduri's work on Bengal or Dore's work on the changes in Japanese agriculture.[4] To recapitulate the latter briefly: at the end of the nineteenth century, when the government was anxious to encourage Japanese landowners to increase their productivity, they only succeeded partially at first. This was because practices relating to a readjustment of income provided good grounds for both investing and not investing. The reason for investing was that by increasing productivity the landowner could hope to resorb the shortfall in income caused by a downwards adjustment in income in bad years. The argument against investing was that there was little inducement to do so, since the agreement was that income should not go up when the harvest was good. The logic of the situation created an area of two options, namely to invest or not to invest. A landowner could not ignore the problem, since the government was offering subsidies and he had to make a choice. The same logic, however, gave him good grounds for choosing either of the two possibilities.

This example demonstrates – if any demonstration is needed – that there are open processes in which the logic of the situation defines a range of options but does not offer any a priori convincing reason for choosing one rather than another. This proposition is generally accepted when individuals in a position of 'responsibility' are involved, but less readily accepted when it is a case of the 'minor decisions' that are the subject-matter of the social sciences, be they economics or political science. Here, the tendency is to agree that in general the choice made is determined by the logic of the situation or, if that is not what happens, that it is of no interest. That, however, is a view that is produced by metaphysics rather than anything else. Processes characterized by reduced areas of choice are the exception rather than the rule, and it is hard to see what criterion could make them the only ones worth examining. There is a second propostion that the open or closed nature of an area of choice is an essential factor in any analysis. If we do not see that the Japanese landowners were faced with an open area, we cannot understand why some did invest and others did not, since objectively they were all in the same situation, or what influence ideology and beliefs exert. The latter can, in fact, provide an actor with reasons for choosing this or that line of action pecisely *because* the logic of the situation creates an open area. If they did *not* do so, then their influence would no doubt be limited. In short, all the facts observed by Dore can only be explained if we see that (C) creates an open space. Recognizing the indeterminacy of the process is a *sine qua non* for any analysis of it.

INNOVATION AND SOCIAL CHANGE

The existence of open processes is one major reason for believing that there are no good grounds for accepting a deterministic representation of social change. Another is that action does not necessarily take the form of a choice between two predetermined options, but can also be innovatory. The objection to this is sometimes that innovation does not necessarily rend the fabric of determinism, since it is always the result of a need ('You would not be looking for me if you had found me'). Since in this way of looking at things the innovation adopted at t + 1 is a response to a need formulated at t, being aware of the need means foreseeing the innovation. We must, however distinguish between situations in which innovation results from a clearly formulated demand and a situation or situations in which it should rather be understood as a *specific* response to a wide-ranging question. In the latter case, innovation may be largely unpredictable and create 'breaks'.

It is of course true that an innovation is only adopted by a system when that system has the capacity to accept it. To put it more exactly, the innovation must appear to certain actors to entail desirable consequences. Certain actors must also be in a position to take on the costs of adopting it. Whether an innovation is adopted or not by a system is thus a function of certain characteristics of that system. As Linton points out, it is hard to make societies where shoes are unknown adopt the use of spades.[5] Similarly, White has clearly shown that ploughs with metal shares were originally only brought into use in regions with a certain minimal population density.[6] Since a plough of this type is more powerful than a swing plough, it can turn heavier and more fertile soils and hence increase productivity considerably. It also requires more energy, however, since it can only be pulled by a team of several strong oxen. The development of agriculture and the standard of living in the period examined by White – medieval Europe – were such that the average peasant did not have access to enough suitable beasts to provide the energy without which metal-shared ploughs simply cannot be used. This explains why they were brought into use in relatively densely populated regions where the peasants could pool their resources to get a team of oxen together. In the examples we have just looked at, adopting innovations is certainly a function of the characteristics of the system. It does not follow, however, that those characteristics offer a sufficient explanation of technical change. If a metal ploughshare is to be adopted, someone has to be able to think of it and make it. The fact that an innovation can only be adopted if it fits in with the *demands* of a system is not therefore a sufficient reason for seeing the spread of the innovation as merely a consequence of the characteristics of that system. Demand must have a corresponding supply, and the latter does not necessarily influence the former.

It is true that the appearance of innovation *sometimes* depends to a greater degree on the characteristics of a system than is the case in the examples given above and that a demand for innovations can be seen as being directly responsible for the supply of them. When that happens, the appearance and spread of innovations can be seen as constituting an endogenous process, and innovations, although some aspects of them cannot be predicted, as a consequence of the particular features of the system. In eighteenth-century England, the first looms appeared at the same time as the first weaving-shops.[7] Whether the latter were profitable, however, depended on how easily the weavers could get supplies of yarn. The yarn, however, was traditionally spun on the farm, and spinning was of course only one of the farmer's many activities. For a time, weavers could not get all the yarn they needed by linking their weaving-shops to spinning-shops. Since the level of production in the latter was low, the cost of yarn would have been excessive. The consequent bottleneck therefore led to an explicitly formulated demand from the weavers, namely for technical innovation. Anyone inventing a device for spinning more cotton in less time was certain to do well. In cases of this kind, the system encourages certain actors to formulate an *explicit* demand. In this specific instance it was of course not possible, when that demand was making itself known, to see in detail the technical inventions that would make it possible to improve productivity in the spinning processes (if it had been, the word 'inventions' would have been inappropriate), but it could reasonably be expected that innovations that would meet the weavers' needs would appear fairly quickly.

The fact that such examples exist is a godsend for those who want to see innovation as not incompatible with a determinist view of change. It is true that *in certain cases* it looks very much like supply meeting an explicit demand and that consequently it can be considered as a consequence of that demand. Since the demand itself follows from the 'structure' of the system, the innovation – although it *is* an innovation – can also be seen as a consequence of the structure of the system. It matters little to the historian, the sociologist or the economist what the particular technical solutions to the 'problem' of increasing productivity were. The only important fact for them is that the increased productivity was in response to an explicit demand and that it involved an exclusively *technical* answer.

It must, however, be repeated that, interesting as this example is, it is no more than a particular case. The earlier example of the metal ploughshare is quite different. There, supply cannot be seen as a consequence of demand. It came about independently and was retained because of its adaptative value. And all White's examples follow the same pattern. Innovation, whether it be a matter of the metal ploughshare, the bit or the four-stroke engine, appears in rather the same way as a *mutation* in a population.[8] If it has an adaptative value (such as making it possible to increase productivity) and is acceptable (that is, if the demands imposed by introducing it are not impossible), it has been *selected*. There are, however, innovations whose adaptative value is harder to define. Coleman rightly stresses that the notion of the moral person is a legal innovation that meets, but cannot be reduced to, certain demands.[9] It has an adaptative value in so far as it facilitates exchanges, but one which is not as easily definable as that of the bit, for instance. The same is true of a new organizational feature such as the Anglo-Saxon closed shop, which has now become established. It perhaps has an adaptative virtue, to the extent that it allows the union movement to extend its influence, but the fact that it has been selected should be seen as the result not only of its advantages for unions but also of conjunctural factors. The spread of another well-known innovation, the Leninist type of political party, is also very difficult to see in terms of the mutation/selection concept.

We should perhaps not get too involved in this particular discussion, but restrict ourselves to one or two points. In the first place, as the foregoing examples suggest, we must distinguish between several types of innovation, even if in practice the distinctions we can make remain ideal ones. That is, it may be difficult to decide the particular type a particular innovation belongs to. Nevertheless, the existence of such types and the aptness of the distinctions they introduce seem to me to be fundamental. Certain innovations are an unsurprising response (although from a technical point of view they may be astonishing) to a perfectly explicit demand. They are compatible with a determinist view of social processes and, since they manifest themselves in reply to a demand, they can be seen as arising as a result of the characteristics of the system. Other innovations can more easily be likened to mutations, since they are not the product of the situation, but are selected by it (or more exactly by certain actors who form a part of it) because of their undeniable adaptative value. In that case, the adoption of an innovation at t follows (partly, at least) from the characteristics of the system at $t - 1$. In regions with low population density, the metal ploughshare will not be adopted, even if its existence is known. But *here* supply is independent of demand. There are other cases in which innovation cannot be seen as the result of demand or as meeting it. We shall also have to make the typology more complex and distinguish between *demand* and *adaptative value*. I might, for example, see that a given innovation is of interest, without having even implicitly formulated a demand for it. Between the two ideal types, a range of intermediate types is possible. Of course, the fact that an innovation has been 'selected' for its adaptative virtues does not imply that it is preferable to other 'solutions'. The closed shop is adaptatively valuable for trade unions, since it enables them to keep a restive membership, but other and perhaps better 'adapted' solutions are obviously a possibility.

Curiously, the social sciences often tend to put all innovations under the first heading and to see them chiefly as a response to an explicit or implicit endogenous demand. If it is explicit, the term *demand* is used. If it is implicit, it is more usual, depending on the problem under consideration and the intellectual tradition in question, to talk of *functional requirement, dysfunction, contradiction, bottleneck* or *structural requirement*.

There is an example of this way of thinking in an important article by Gudmund Hernes, in which innovation is presented as generally being a response to a functional or structural requirement.[10]

The example of the development of spinning-machines in England mentioned above provides an illustration of a *functional* requirement. *Structural* requirements are illustrated by Hernes by means of the example of the history of numbers. The impossibility of solving an equation of the type $x = 2 - 4$ in a system involving only positive numbers (which would provide an immediate solution for $x = 4 - 2$) is said to *explain* the invention of negative numbers. Similarly, the impossibility of solving an equation of the type $x = 2{:}4$ in a system involving only whole numbers (which would provide an immediate solution for $x = 4{:}2$) is also seen as the *reason for* the invention of 'rational' numbers, and so on. Thus, the history of numbers could be seen as an endogenous process set in movement at each stage by the *structural requirements* arising from the preceding phase. In fact, the causal imputations that Hernes claims to establish are the result of a posteriori rationalization, and he rewrites the history of numbers from the viewpoint of the form given them by modern mathematics.

It is true that in definitions of set theory, negative numbers are no more mysterious than positive ones. Clearing up the mystery, however, presupposes a purely formalist concept of numbers, which is a modern innovation. It means, in other words, that we have to be able to forget that mathematical structures can be applied to the real world if we want to see negative numbers as being as 'natural' as positive ones, or 'rational' numbers as being as 'natural' as whole ones. But making mathematics into something quite autonomous in relation to the real world is the opposite of a simple process. That is why 'structural requirements' (such as those arising from the impossibility of solving the equation $x = 2{:}4$ in the set of whole numbers) have sometimes only been met after the lapse of centuries. To see this afresh, we need only recall the astonishment that Hegel still felt at the idea that an equation is not modified if one of its terms is taken across to the other side, provided its sign is changed.[11] The operation seemed to him to illustrate the obscure laws of 'dialectics'.

In an otherwise very suggestive article, the biologist Garret Hardin likewise suggests that the invention of the right to strike should be seen as a response – to some degree natural – to the 'positive feedback' of power: since the power of capitalists was affirming itself, it was bound to create (as a result of a structural requirement or of a functional necessity?) an *opposition*.[12] This was an *inevitable* innovation meeting an explicit demand of the system. To see that this is purely an a posteriori rationalization, we need only note that although it seems so 'natural' to us it never occurred to Ricardo, who was nonetheless an informed observer and analyst of the capitalist system.

The iron law of wages supposes that it does not occur to workers to combine and thus influence their rates of pay. Why did Ricardo not realize that his iron law (the expression is that of Lassalle) ran the risk of being disproved by the appearance of union opposition? Probably because, as was the case with many of his contemporaries, the idea of combining evoked in his mind the idea of the ancient guilds, which were universally seen as an outdated form of social organization.[13] In any case, the 'iron law' shows – by the very way in which it is formulated – that the lack of any opposition or, to use the language of cybernetics employed by Hardin, of any negative feedback to correct the positive feedback of power, seemed quite 'natural' to Ricardo. Nowadays we have the opposite situation, with Hardin seeing its appearance as 'natural'. This perhaps shows that we should think twice before deciding that an innovation is simply a response to an explicit or implicit demand or the consequence of a structural or functional 'requirement'.

This wrong interpretation is encouraged by three temptations. The first is the temptation to *generalize*. There are innovations that *actually are* brought about in response to a demand, so why should not all of them be?

The second is that of determinism, in which any state of affairs observed in a system is determined by earlier states of affairs. However, although this outline is acceptable when the matter in hand is an explanation of the appearance of spinning-machines in eighteenth-century England, it is not when we are trying to account for the appearance of the metal ploughshare in medieval Europe. It is true that innovations are accepted because of certain characteristics of the system, but in itself it is a kind of inexplicable *deus ex machina*. There is nothing in the system itself to provide an account of it, and supply is not the result of a demand. This determinist view is *a fortiori* unacceptable in the case of an innovation like that of parties of the Leninist type.

The third temptation is that offered by an endogenist view such as that proposed by Nisbet, who suggests that since all systems are closed, all change therefore has in the last resort causes deeply rooted in the system itself. 'Ultimately' any innovation is a response to a functional requirement. This proposition is not entirely absent from the thought of Parsons, who sees innovation as a response to an imbalance occurring in a system.[14] That view is only acceptable in certain cases, however.

In his *Business Cycles*, one of the major books in the field of economic sociology, Schumpeter is perhaps the writer who has most successfully brought out the insufficiency of any *structural* theory of innovation. In the case of industrialization in England, the *inventions* put to use by industrialists under the Tudors and Stuarts were in most cases importations from abroad. German methods were used for pumping out mines, for example, and techniques introduced from Germany or Holland transformed iron and steel manufacture. As the energy used came basically from wood, the increased production of iron and steel in particular brought with it not only an increase in the price of that commodity but also measures for the protection of forests. In this case, innovation was not a response to a demand formulated by the environment or the consequences of, for example, an earlier extension of markets encouraging producers to step up their productivity. It was rather a consequence of the fact that entrepreneurs decided to produce at home goods that had hitherto been imported and to use methods of production that had been developed abroad. In doing so, they caused disturbances in the existing equilibrium – such as a shortage of wood – which gave rise to adaptation reactions on the part of other actors and also offered them the *opportunity* of developing other innovations. Resistance by the environment to the consequences of certain innovations (for example, measures to protect forests) can also make it easier for other innovations to occur. Thus replacing wood by coal, which had for long only been used in certain particular activities such as the glass industry, was the result of a long and complex process, of which one factor was the exhaustion of supplies of wood.

What Schumpeter proposed in his analyses is that innovation should be seen as the result of a strategy that is based on but does not mechanically follow from the data of the environment, since the latter provide *opportunities* which may or may not be taken. In addition, it must be emphasized that the characteristic features of the environment need to be seen as the convergence of independent series, in Cournot's sense of the term. Thus in Stuart times the ironmaster was in a *situation* that provided cheap energy (in the form of wood) and the chance of using processes developed abroad.

This strategic and interactionist view of innovation, which can be contrasted with the 'structural' image of it, also entails an important corollary, which is that any analysis aiming to provide a spatial and temporal location for any large-scale process and to see it as the consequence of dominant *factors* is generally no more than an illusion. As Schumpeter ironically notes, one can, if one wishes, use an expression like 'the English industrial revolution', provided that one does not let oneself be trapped by words and picture the 'revolution' as a phenomenon that can be called a 'break', explicable by one or two simple causes, and that one takes care to remember that the 'event' or 'break' took place over a period extending from the thirteenth to the nineteenth century. As we have seen, these observations also apply to the cases, examined above, of development in Japan or Colombia. The analyses of both Dore and Hagen, although dealing with defined processes, are situated within a very long time-scale. The same is true of Hirschman's studies of Brazil mentioned in the last chapter. These observations are enough to rule out any theory claiming to reduce the processes of social change to dominant factors, whether they be dependence, cultural change, the resorption of bottlenecks, extending markets, the class struggle, the features of political organization, or the like.

CHANCE AND THE PART IT PLAYS

In the social sciences, chance is generally thought to be a very unwelcome guest, ubiquitous but studiously concealed, ignored and even denied the right to exist by virtually everyone. There are differing opinions about the ontological status it should be given. Some see it as having objective existence, but most think of it as merely the result of our ignorance, holding that we only see a phenomenon as not being fully determined because we do not have access to all the variables that shape it. Opinions about what chance is exactly, may vary, but if there is one point on which there is more or less total agreement in the social sciences and perhaps in even wider circles, it is that by its very nature it is of no interest from the point of view of knowledge. How could the fact that an event is due to chance interest the sociologist or economist or, more generally, anyone concerned with understanding why that event occurs? When we say that it is due to chance, are we not really saying that it has *no* cause, or at least none that we know? In fact, not only does it certainly *exist*, but it is important to *recognize* that it exists if we wish to account for an enormous number of phenomena.

In an excellent book on Leninism, Colas has convincingly shown that throughout his life Lenin was dominated by an orchestral image of social order and the organization of societies.[15] An admirer of Taylorism and fascinated by the docile way in which musicians obey the conductor's baton, he was also captivated by the capitalist firm, with its order and discipline and the clockwork precision with which each of the workers in it carried out his allotted task. So it is not surprising that his chief contribution to Marxism was his theory of the party as the guide, conscience and organizer of the masses. Just as musicians cannot play without the conductor, or workers create a complex product without management, so the revolutionary fervour of the masses was doomed to remain a mere potentiality without a party to co-ordinate its energies and organize its activities. Where Marx had hesitated, Lenin decided swiftly: the party was to go ahead of the masses, direct their activities and provide them with a doctrine. By means of a careful and brilliant analysis of his writings, Colas shows that from *What Is To Be Done?* onwards not only the political thesis of the party as the guide and conscience of the masses, but also representations of the social order on which the thesis is based are a persistent feature of his work. The metaphor of the orchestra, the admiration for Taylorism, military discipline and the division and meticulous co-ordination of the modern factory appear again and again as a leitmotiv. In addition, he insistently expresses his distrust of what was later to be called worker-management and his distaste for collective spontaneity, which seemed to him to be inevitably a 'hysterical' form of expression.

Quite deliberately, Colas refuses to try to get into the mind of his 'author'. He also refuses to put Lenin's writings into their political context. All he sets out to do is to show the recurring themes of Lenin's discourse and illustrate their organization, coherence and stability. With a man of action and a maker of history, it was a bold but justified choice. Throughout two decades, the writings were rigid and repetitive. No doubt pragmatism and opportunism caused him to change his position with regard to practical questions, but where essential matters – the role of the party, the principles of organization and the effectiveness of political action – were concerned, the texts remain surprisingly unyielding and profoundly insensitive to current circumstances. Very skilfully, Colas convinces his reader of the validity of the hypothesis that Lenin's political action and doctrine were the product of a system of representations of the world and of the social order that barely changed from those in *What Is To Be Done?*

But not from earlier ones. A few years before the pamphlet was published, Lenin had defended ideas diametrically opposed to those in it, which are perhaps the expression of a system of beliefs. They are also – as we shall see – the product of a Cournot effect, that is, of the convergence of two independent causal series. Cournot, of course, illustrated the idea by means of very simple examples, such as that of a falling slate stunning a passer-by. The fall of the slate was certainly predetermined. It was not properly fastened on the roof and was at the mercy of the slightest gust of wind. The fact that the passer-by was walking just below the roof was also the result of an easily traceable causality. He was going about his business that day as on any other day and was thus bound to pass below the roof in question. So we are dealing here with two causal series. The fact that they converge, however, is, according to Cournot, not causally determined, since there was nothing to make the slate fall just as the man was passing by.

If a writer uses simple explanatory examples to illustrate a concept, this sometimes means that the field of application of the concept is not very well understood. This seems to have been the fate lying in wait for Cournot's theory, for, even when it is accepted, the temptation is sometimes to think that it can only be applied to trivial cases of the kind he uses as illustrations. The example of Lenin, however, shows that it is to the advantage of students of social change to keep Cournot's theory of chance constantly in mind if they want to avoid going against their own wishes and principles and being obliged to detect the hand of Providence at work.

In 1895, Lenin maintained that the role of the intelligentsia was merely 'to join up with the workers' movement, to bring light into it, to assist the workers in the struggle they themselves had begun to wage'.[16] Why should that be so? It is not hard to imagine why, and all we need do is examine the political and economic situation in Russia at the time. Major industrial expansion was under way in 1890, as has been shown by Gerschenkron in particular.[17] Investment from abroad was high and unemployment low and, as is often the case at times of rapid growth, there were many strikes. They began amongst workers in small craft industries in the large towns and in Moscow in particular, but subsequently spread to large concerns. The workers were naturally happy to be able to call on intellectuals for help and to benefit from their assistance in matters of organization and propaganda. At the same time, however, they were mindful of the populist agitation that had occurred a few years earlier and did not forget that extremist intellectuals had sought to shape the course of history by resorting to political terrorism. That was one of the reasons why they had certain reservations about them.

Thus the economic situation, the intensity of the working-class struggle and the reservations that the workers had about intellectuals combined to force upon Lenin, that committed intellectual, the 'theory' that he in fact defended at the time, namely that the workers are the chief agents of social change and the initiators of their own struggle, and that the intellectuals can help working-class movements by acting as auxiliaries and assistants. Since he was both a professional politician and an intellectual, it was natural for Lenin to express an opinion about the problem of the relationship between workers and intellectuals. If he wished to retain any influence, he could not diverge from the 'theory' that the circumstances dictated. Seeing this as mere opportunism is pointlessly simplistic. If was of course to his advantage to espouse the 'theory' of the working-class movement currently accepted by, or at least widespread in, working-class circles. If he had taken up the opposite position, as he was to do a few years later, he would have lost all his influence. It is quite likely, however, that he actually believed the theory. The upheavals arising from the lightning industrial growth taking place in Russia were making their effects strongly felt, as were also the massive strikes. In a situation of that kind, it was not only difficult to express publicly the populist theory of the intellectual as the conscience and guide of the passive masses, but no doubt also quite simply hard to believe it.

A few years later, there was a major slump. Despite the earlier boom and the scale of the working-class movement, the workers did not have a sufficient level of either organization or wages to amass any appreciable collective or individual assets. As a result, agitation declined and then disappeared. On the whole, the workers were more concerned with keeping their jobs and their resources than with engaging in political action. The new economic situation meant that the workers were more likely to defend their own individual interests than to engage in protests and collective action, and the working class no longer seemed to be the vehicle of history.

Over the same period, and without any clear link between the two phenomena, the enlightened elite was also engaging in 'class' behaviour. Economic growth had meant an increase in the numbers of those receiving an education. The St Petersburg students, who had been harassed by the tsarist authorities, began to agitate and were soon joined by others. A cycle of alternating violence and repression set in, and gradually the students became a pole of attraction and a focus not only for malcontents of every ilk but also for many who were politically opposed to the regime. This was so to such an extent that in 1901 it seemed to be the enlightened intelligentsia rather than the working class that was the vehicle of history. It was that intelligentsia that provided the resistance to authority. And indeed, had not students played a considerable part in the politics of Europe throughout the nineteenth century and formed the kernel of movements producing profound political and social change?

It was in such circumstances that Lenin was writing *What Is To Be Done?* In that pamphlet, he distinguishes between workers who are politically unaware and workers who are not, tells intellectuals what their essential role in organizing the working-class movement will be and draws the distinction between the enlightened elite and the masses who are unaware of the centralizing and authoritarian principles of organization. From this point onwards, we are acquainted with what happened, which was that these principles were inevitably accepted and shaped the real world. *What Is To Be Done?* sets out the principles that in fact guided the organization of social democracy in Russia. When in the years leading up to the First World War the economic situation changed once more and strikes broke out again, it was not as influential a factor as it had been in 1901 or 1902. Henceforth, the social democratic movement was a party organized on Leninist lines and no longer a nascent political organization. In 1912 Lenin thus simply recognized in his words the spontaneously revolutionary character of the working class and in his practice kept up a certain degree of democracy in the life of the party, without modifying its organizational principles. The war decimated the working class and thus meant that it was possible to introduce the rigorous form of Bolshevik organization that was to be perpetuated for many long years to come.

In my view, it is impossible to understand that history if we do not detect the presence of a series of Cournot effects in it. Obviously, neither the worker movements occurring around 1895, nor the fact that they lost their thrust after the depression at the turn of the century, nor the reappearance of student movements in the early 1900s, are inexplicable phenomena. However, although the chains of cause and effect are easy to discover, they are not completely linked to each other. No doubt industrialization accounts for the appearance of worker movements and the birth of political parties claiming to have their origins in them, but there was no logical necessity for the iskrists to lay the foundations of their organization at a time when the working-class movements were at their nadir. The partial linkings are intelligible, as is the way they converge, but the *synchronization* between them cannot be seen as the result of a rigorous determinism. The fact that two series converge at a given stage of development can have crucial and irreversible consequences. There was no logical necessity for the worker and student movements to be out of phase with each other or for one to be growing while the other was fading out. Separately, the two phenomena could be explained, but neither was the cause of the other and it was not foreordained that they should succeed each other in any particular order.

The foregoing story has a typical structure that is very often detectable when social processes are being analysed. The linkings A C B (with A being the cause of B) do not make up a total order A c B c C c . . . , or even a partial order (A c B c C and B c D). What they *do* make up is a set of partial linkings (A c B, B c D and so on). The fact that the latter coexist in time causes *sui generis* effects, the nature of which depends on the synchronization between the series. The latter can be observed *post factum*, but is seldom predictable.

Chance is therefore not *nothing*. It is a particular *form* that sets of cause/effects linkings *as perceived by a real observer* can take on. Some of them have a total form of order (the match causes a fire that causes the fire brigade to arrive). Others have a partial form of order (the match causes a fire and also causes the person holding it to cry out in pain). Others contain contingent links (the series 'A causes B, which causes C' occurs at the same time as 'P causes Q, which causes R') but it is impossible to decide whether the synchronization is really between B and P, B and Q or C and Q. It is therefore impossible to tell whether event BP, BQ or CQ will necessarily be brought about. And the three events can have very different consequences.

So there is such a thing as chance, and here we can follow Cournot's thought, which is both simple and profound, in all fidelity. To do that, we must see chance not as a substance, a variable or a set of variables, but as a *structure* which is characteristic of certain sets of causal chains as perceived by an observer. In any case, it can to my mind be seen as something quite different from the entirely empty, negative and scientifically uninteresting concept that Thom talks about.[18]

The theses Lenin put forward in *What Is To Be Done?* were perhaps more in line with his personality than those he had defended a few years earlier. Perhaps – at first without knowing it and later quite consciously – he always had an orchestral view of social order. That, however, seems to be a part, and perhaps a small part, of the story. If we are to *understand* why Leninism and its authoritarian face became essential, we need to take into account the (contingent) circumstances in which the doctrine was formulated.

If it is true that a *chance* event is generally of very little scientific interest, then taking into account the place of chance may be indispensable if we are to understand an event. Certain things I do are basically explicable in terms of the structure of my personality, others can only be understood if it can be seen that I found myself in particular circumstances. There was no compelling necessity for me to be in them, but an external observer who was unaware of them would not be able to understand why I acted as I did. Similarly, what Lenin did and what positions he took up cannot be understood without a perception of the circumstances he found himself in.

7

Giving Disorder its Due

It is time to tie up the loose ends. To a high degree, the programme underlying theories of social change seems, as Nisbet diagnosed, to be a failure. The perpetual search for the first mover has been unfruitful, and the absolute and conditional laws of change are more or less void. There are numerous exceptions to structural regularities. Should we go the whole way with Nisbet and suggest that this programme, which is common to most of the social sciences, is doomed, and that theories in the field of political science or economics are bound either to fail in the face of reality or to become merely another aspect of history? In my view, that would be going too far, and the real problem is that of defining the logical status of the programme. With rgard to Nisbet's position, what we need to know is whether, if we assume that it is based on the failure of theories of social change, it is also the result of his adherence to the realist view of the explanation of social phenomena that Ranke in his own period had sought to impose. In this connection, there is no lack of very curious ramblings in the history of ideas, for it was in opposition to Ranke's realism that classical German sociology as exemplified by Max Weber and Georg Simmel defined itself.

POSTULATES AND OBSERVATIONS

Theories of social change are often characterized by an initial logical shift, in that they treat as generally applicable *postulates* ideas that should rather be seen as observations of *local* relevance. There are, for example, as we have already seen, processes that are determined in that their state at $t+1$ can be established on the basis of our

180

knowledge of their state at t. But this property is not a general one. Indeed, it depends on the structure of the process, and if it is to appear a whole set of conditions putting the actors involved in a *closed* situation must be present and persist. It is obvious that this is not always what happens. There are also *open* situations, in which the actors are faced with a range of options and have no compelling reason for choosing one rather than another. There are also situations of such a kind that those involved are encouraged to produce an innovation. Once again, however, cases in which innovation is the result of a specific demand and its content is therefore largely determined are particular rather than general in nature. In others, innovation is only partly dependent on the demands of the system. There are also yet others in which it is completely *independent* of it. Notions such as *structural* or *functional requirement* are therefore pointless. They do, however, entail dangers, such as the risk of not seeing that there are generally several possible responses to a structural demand, or that certain innovations do not occur as a response to any requirement. Finally, certain innovations are largely due to Cournot effects. If we bear in mind the example of *What Is To Be Done?* we can see that the Leninist party, one of the major social innovations of the twentieth century, cannot be explained without reference to the political and social *circumstances* in which it occurred.

With regard to the social sciences therefore, determinism is not an indispensable *postulate*, but an *observation* which needs or does not need to be made in this or that situation. It is not a condition of knowledge, but a property peculiar to certain processes, and whether it is absent or present depends on the structure of the process in question. Contrary to what is often stated, the only essential postulate is that we may, or indeed may not, detect determinism at work. If we do not recognize the latter possibility, we run the risk of denying ourselves the means of understanding certain facts. For example, we shall not understand the influence of Enlightenment philosophy on the behaviour of Japanese landowners if we do not see that they were in a situation that obliged them to choose between option A and option B when there were good reasons for choosing both.[1] Nor shall we see the *low degree* of correlation between their education (traditional/modern) if we do not see that those who had received an education deeply influenced by the teachings of the physiocrats had good reasons for not following their precepts.

The epistemological model of 'patchy' or 'well-tempered' determinism that I set out to defend in the preceding chapter is far from being universally accepted in the social sciences, where it is more usual to encounter two positions. The first is to see indeterminacy as essentially subjective in nature, that is, as caused by the prohibitive cost of information and the observer's total inability to identify or observe all the variables responsible for a phenomenon. The second is to think that only processes characterized by deterministic features are of interest to sociologists, economists or political scientists. Nisbet is perfectly right about one thing: sociologists and other specialists in the nomothetic disciplines (to use Piaget's term) are either chiefly interested in endogenous processes or see every process as endogenous. In both cases, they also accept that an endogenous process is by definition one in which the state at $t+1$ is determined by the state at t.

The first of these positions (in which indeterminacy is seen as always subjective) is untenable, since it goes against the straightforward observation that open situations can exist and that innovation is not always narrowly determined by a demand. Although the second, in which scientific interest and determinism are linked, is apparently more prudent, it has no real basis. There is no visible reason for thinking that it is less interesting to show that a situation is open than to show that another is closed, or for holding that it is of less value to show that an innovation is partly explicable because a Cournot effect is involved than to show that another innovation has its source in a specific demand.

The same *reversal* must be effected with regard to all those questions to which theories of social change claim to give a general answer. The primacy accorded to values by, in particular, theories that see change as essentially the product of socialization mechanisms is an undesirable postulate. The importance of values depends on the process under consideration. Like determinism, it is a function of that process. According to circumstances, values may or may not be a variable that it is important to take into account. Depending on the situation, they may be seen as primary or secondary, or it may be impossible to decide which they are.

In Epstein's study of the effects of irrigation in southern India, changes in values are secondary.[2] In Marxist language, the process would be said to be a matter of a 'materialist' interpretation, and changes in values in that case would be the result of changes in the forces and relationships of production. As the land owned by the peasants of Dalena was not affected by irrigation, they could not take advantage of it to make it more profitable. However, the movements created by the irrigation of nearby land gave them, or at least the wealthiest of them, the opportunity of investing their surplus in public works, transportation or service undertakings, and these new activities meant that henceforth they had permanent relationships with people in the towns. The result was that they adopted their status symbols. The Untouchables in the Dalena area were chronically underemployed. Once irrigation came, they had opportunities to obtain employment in town or in the service undertakings. Their sense of community was weakened, especially as they were recruited on the basis of merit rather than *ascription* and found themselves working in teams with individuals from many different backgrounds. As a result of the dislocation of social structures indirectly brought about by irrigation, the Dalena villagers began to pay more attention to pan-Indian deities and neglect their local gods. Any analysis can be conducted in strict accordance with 'materialist' principles. And yet in the case of Dore's study of Japan the 'idealist' model is more appropriate, for if the Dutch had not introduced their physiocratic ideology, the history of development in Japan would probably have been quite different. In yet other cases, it is impossible to say whether ideas and values are of primary or secondary importance. In the Weber–Trevor Roper theory, the Calvinist view of the world encouraged the entrepreneurial spirit, but its attraction and hence its influence were also the *consequences* of the difficulties and obstacles that entrepreneurs laboured under as a result of the policies of the Counter-Reformation. Thus we can see that the part played by values and ideas, whether it be of the first or the second importance, is not established once and for all and that there are cases like the foregoing example in which it cannot be determined, since it is simply a function of the process in question and is often indeterminate.

The same observations apply to the importance of social conflicts, which must also be considered as a function of the structure of the process under investigation. There are no doubt situations which place the groups of actors concerned in a position of mutual opposition. If, for instance, we consider the sharing of profits and wages *at a given moment*, it is a no-win situation, since the higher profits are, the lower wages are, and vice versa. *Over a period* of time, however, union pressure to push up wages might stimulate productivity and help to raise the level of both profits and wages. Depending on the time-scale used, the conflict between wages and profits can therefore be either a 'game' in which interests are diametrically opposed, or one in which conflicting and co-operative elements are inextricably mixed, even if the co-operation is involuntary.

With regard to the importance of conflicts, however, there are two points in particular that must be stressed. The first is that the notion of class does not entail the notion of class conflict, a proposition that Marx involuntarily defended when he observed that the replacement of the feudal landowners by the bourgeoisie was the result not of a struggle from which the latter emerged victorious, but of a process of which examples can be found in the plant world. The flow of precious metals from the New World enriched the bourgeoisie and impoverished the feudal lords, just as a change in climate can favour one species and be harmful to another. It is true that at the end of the process one of the two species was 'dominated' by the other but, at least if we are to believe *Marx*, there had been no conflict between the two. Similarly, there was no *real* conflict between the feudal and the bourgeois classes. In any case, in this context, 'conflict' has quite a different meaning from that in the nineteenth century between the bourgeoisie and the proletariat. To express the same idea in different words, conflicts – and particularly class conflicts – can only be seen as decisively important if the notion of conflict is given a meaning that can be extended indefinitely and all distinctions between the literal and metaphorical uses of the term are rejected.

The second point that must be stressed – even though one hesitates to mention it, as it is so obvious – is that quite major changes can occur without any accompanying conflicts. Epstein's study affords a further very pertinent illustration of this truism. In it, irrigation modified the situation of everyone involved, to which everyone responded in terms of his or her own best interests. The result of this aggregation of individual strategies was profound changes, with the strengthening of traditional structures in some places and transformation in others. Neither change nor the absence of it, however, was in any way the result of conflicts.

The popular interpretation of Weber's work underestimates the importance of conflicts in attempting to explain the influence of Calvinism on the development of capitalism. The popular interpretation of Marx, to which he himself contributed in no small measure, overestimates their importance in the transition from feudalism to capitalism. The fact that there are such interpretations and that they are influential shows clearly that, to use Pareto's language, theories of social change are often derivations clothing residues. That is, they are aimed not so much at accounting for reality as at putting it at the service of sentiments and passions.

Social processes are not necessarily either endogenous, as sociologists so often maintain, or exogenous, as Nisbet seems to claim. Once again, attributing either of these characteristics to a process is a matter of *observation* rather than a *postulate*. Certain processes lend themselves to an endogenous treatment. This is what Smelser does, for example, in his analysis of the development of the English textile industry in the eighteenth century, in which he shows that it was the result of a series of bottlenecks. The appearance of looms, for instance, created a demand for innovations to speed up the supply of yarn. They brought their own consequences, for gradually yarn began to be produced in workshops rather than on the farms, and the mechanization of weaving and subsequently of spinning led to migration, and so on. We should not, of course, conclude from such examples that every process of development is the result of resorbing bottlenecks, or 'dysfunctions' or, to use Marxist terminology, 'contradictions'. Indeed, there are exogenous processes of development, and others can only be described as both endogenous and exogenous, in so far as at a certain stage the way the process is developing produces a reaction in actors who up to then had been passive. It is not hard to imagine examples of these two types. The efforts of the Brazilian government to solve the problem of the North-East provide an illustration of an exogenous process.[2] The appearance of the metal ploughshare in medieval Europe is also an example of an exogenous change that was subsequently to bring about a chain reaction. Mendras's study of the introduction of hybrid maize also provides an illustration of the same phenomenon.[4]

Several examples of processes that are both endogenous and exogenous have already been mentioned. The 'involuntary' racialism that grew up in American trade unions between the two wars created a reaction on the part of 'opinion' and the political apparatus. Once it became visible and it was no longer possible to pretend to be unaware of it or to treat it as an 'internal' union matter, denouncing discriminatory practices that went against the fundamental values of

American society became an exploitable theme for intellectuals claiming to be concerned with safeguarding values and for politicians able to use it as a means of enhancing their reputation and obtaining a following. A process of that kind is certainly both endogenous and exogenous. In its first phase, union practices caused a spiralling endogenous effect that developed within the system and included four categories of actors: heads of firms, white workers, black workers, and union leaders. It was not until a certain threshold had been crossed that the spiral effect triggered off the intervention of actors hitherto outside the system.[5]

Similarly, the development of the agricultural and food industries as a result of the Second World War has meant an increasingly uniform level and perhaps a fall in quality of food products. In such a situation, there is very little that the consumer can do. One reason for this is the fact that he is a member of a large but atomized group. Consequently, the costs of possibly taking part in collective protest are high and its advantages few. What effect could the protest of one individual member of a large 'latent' group have? There is not much to be said for protest as a strategy in that kind of situation. On the other hand, he cannot simply opt out or defect or resort to what Hirschman calls an 'exit'. The state of affairs arises because every producer needs to industrialize his products if the others are doing the same. So there is little point in the consumer trying another producer. So far, the process is strictly endogenous, with producers being encouraged to industrialize their products by a self-maintaining mechanism. That mechanism is very unlikely to bring about any endogenous negative feedback, since to all intents and purposes the structure of the situation the consumers are in deprives them of any possibility of protesting or opting out. As in the preceding case, the *dysfunction* or *contradiction* can be resolved by the appearance of a new group of actors, made up of both consumers and producers, who have so far been outside the system. They must of course exist and have both the ability and the motivation to intervene. Since these three conditions might well not be met, there may in fact be no negative feedback. As was the case in the last example, 'entrepreneurs' might be tempted by the idea of taking advantage of the latent discontent. It is quite likely, of course, that such 'entrepreneurs' would in this case be found amongst quite different categories, since here it is a matter of exploiting dissatisfaction and not of denouncing practices that go against fundamental values.

In short, if we analyse a process

$$(A_t, B_t \ldots P_t) \rightarrow (A'_{t+k}, B'_{t+k} \ldots P'_{t+k})$$

several possibilities might occur. One might be that actors or groups of actors $a_1, a_2 \ldots a_n$ produce at t the results or phenomena A_t, $B_t \ldots P_t$. These would have consequences: they would modify – or in certain cases help to maintain – the situation of certain categories of actors, who would consequently modify their behaviour and produce at $t+k$ the results

$$A'_{t+k}, B'_{t+k} \ldots P'_{t+k}.$$

The process is purely endogenous and of the type to which both the Marxist and functionalist traditions pay the greatest attention.

If the process

$$(A_t, B_t \ldots P_t) \rightarrow (A'_{t+k}, B'_{t+k} \ldots P'_{t+k})$$

has to be explained by the intervention at t of an actor or group of actors not included in the set $a_1, a_2 \ldots a_n$, we are dealing with an exogenous process, or more precisely with an exogenous/endogenous process, or with one that was exogenous *in origin*.

If the process is initially endogenous and the results produced by the groups of actors $a_1, a_2 \ldots a_n$ involve a reaction from a further group (a_p, for instance) outside the interaction system at some specific point between t and k which needs to be taken into account if we are to explain the state of the process at $t+k$, it can also be said to be endogenous/exogenous.

There is a possible objection to these distinctions, which is that since the boundaries of a system are not a natural datum, why should we not define right from the start a system containing the actors a_p as well as $a_1, a_2 \ldots a_n$? The process could then be seen as entirely endogenous. In doing so, however, we should lose an essential distinction. In addition, there would be the danger of seeing the dysfunctions or contradictions produced by the system as the exclusive cause of change. But if there is to be a reaction, there must be actors with a propensity for or interest in bringing it about, which is obviously not always the case.[6] Crozier's study of *Monopole* illustrates a blockage situation in which dysfunctions do not in fact produce a reaction, since no actor either inside or outside the system has both the ability and the motivation to correct them. But there is nothing logically necessary about such a situation, and indeed, as we have seen, it was in this particular case the result of a convergence of data that must be seen as *contingent*. Thus the advantage of keeping a distinction between endogenous and endogenous/exogenous processes is that it avoids making the intervention of actors not originally involved in the system a logical *necessity* arising from the presence of dysfunctions. Dysfunctions (or contradictions) *may* or may not produce corrective reactions, but whether they do or not depends largely on contingent factors, that is, on Cournot effects.

It is interesting that an author like Marx, at least in his esoteric works, was perfectly aware of the relevance of this distinction. Perhaps the reason why chapter 3 of *Capital* was never finished is that he was fully aware of two principles that it is difficult to reconcile. Only endogenous processes are predictable and determined, but an endogenous process can give rise to 'contradictions' for which the 'solution' cannot be seen as automatically proceeding from the contradictions themselves. The law of falling profit rates is put forward as tendential, for Marx had very clearly seen that exogenous factors (the concentration of industry following upon technical advances) and endogenous ones (capitalists were led to slow down falling profit rates by coming to an agreement) could help to make it inoperative, but were not bound to do so. All in all, the law is tendential in the sense that it consists of a mere statement of something that might happen. It follows from a *theoretical* model from which, Marx clearly saw, one could only draw empirical conclusions with caution.

Likewise, one cannot postulate, but merely observe and try to offer an a posteriori explanation of, the form of a process occurring between t and t + k. I shall merely give a very brief example. Following Adam Smith, the division of labour was long seen, as a result of endogenous analysis, as a self-perpetuating process.[7] The consequence, it was assumed, was that undertakings would inevitably tend to combine and concentrate, and that their distribution in terms of size would necessarily be shapeless and shifting. The fact is, however, that in France it has been relatively consistent.[8] Small firms, despite the expectations of theorists of change, will not simply lie down and die. The error in prediction is the result of overstressing certain factors. Constancy of distribution is of course a complex phenomenon and the consequence of both exogenous and endogenous processes. It is harder to account for than the trend towards concentration would have been if it had not in fact been observed. However, certain factors recently working against the 'trend' can be clearly seen. One is simply the growth of the power of trade unions, which in France and Italy has obliged firms to resort to subcontracting and decentralization in order to be able to adapt to the uncertainties of the current economic situation.[9]

So we must accept the obvious: there are not and cannot be any *general* theories of social change. Depending on the circumstances, a process

$$(A_t, B_t \ldots P_t) \rightarrow (A'_t, B'_t \ldots P'_t)$$

will or will not be strictly determined. Whether it is or not depends on its structure. Ideas and values may or may not play a decisive part in terms of the structure of the process. Certain processes are isomorphic with ecological processes that can be observed in the plant world, and we therefore need not think in terms of conflicts when describing them. Others, however, imply strategic interaction between groups of actors. Certain processes have unilinear or cyclical results until their natural pace is upset by some exogenous irruption or a retroactive mechanism is set in motion if the conditions, which are always partly contingent, are ripe.

This position entails accepting that it is always possible to find in the real world an inexhaustible supply of examples of processes capable of supporting any theory of social change.

That is why, as Stark notes,[10] there is an ongoing debate in the history of the social sciences, varying in its precise form from one period to another, between those whose view is mechanistic in nature and those who see change as an organic phenomenon, between 'idealists' and 'materialists', between those whose theory is that of 'conflict' and those who, to talk in the terms Boulding uses, take an 'ecodynamic' view of change. The *words* used change with time, of course: when it is modish to talk of 'culturalism', 'idealism' is no longer valid currency, and yet both reflect ways of seeing the problem that are virtually the same. It would be fascinating to study these linguistic shifts, but all I can do at present is suggest that it should be done.[11]

One thing is certain. They might use different *words*, but theorists of social change are in fact asking themselves the same questions as 'historical sociologists', who, as Schumpeter suggests, are reflecting on the same problems as those raised by the 'philosophy of history'.[12] These questions are always with us because the possible answers to them can all be equally justified by theories which, to use Pareto's turn of phrase, are both based on experience and go beyond it.

That is why the way in which change is represented goes through cycles and variations, alternating between 'culturalist' and 'economicist' and 'conflict' and 'organicist' theories, and so on. However, it is sometimes hard to spot the cycles, because the words used differ from one to another. In one cycle, 'system' will be used instead of 'organism' and 'culturalist' instead of 'idealist', and the like.

DEMARCATIONS

Contrary to what is widely believed, the purpose of scientific activity is not to explain the *real* – which is, as such, unknowable, or at least only knowable metaphysically – but to answer questions about it. As Popper, taking up Kant here, has shown, the form of the question determines whether the answer to it is such that its validity can be verified, or is not certainly true but may be useful and plausible, or indeed whether the question itself might produce irreconcilable answers. The first kind of question is scientific and can be answered *scientifically*. The answers to the second type are *conjectures*. The third type incorporates questions that, following Popper, we can call *metaphysical*.

It is important to make it abundantly clear that there is no reason to *rank* these types of questions and to suppose that, for example, those in the first category are more 'important' than those in the third or vice versa. We do, however, need to pay attention to the demarcations between them. Indeed, it is quite legitimate to maintain that all the ambiguities in theories of social change arise either because such distinctions are not taken into account, or because, although their existence is suspected, they are confused, and some particular *theory* is put under the wrong heading.

I shall not go back over the third type, that of metaphysical questions. I have shown, I think, that many of the questions to which theories of social change address themselves are of this kind.

There are other questions which by virtue of their form entail *conjectural* answers. Most of the 'laws' formulated by theorists of social change seem to me to come into this category. When those reflecting on social and political mobilization say that it occurs particularly when a period of growth is followed by a severe slump, they are not so much expressing a law as stating a possibility. To see the truth of this, we need only note that there are others who maintain the exact opposite, saying that such mobilization appears particularly when a long period of stagnation is followed by sudden growth. Both 'laws' clearly cannot be true at one and the same time, but that does not mean that they are of no interest. Quite the contrary, in fact, since they draw attention to the *possibility* of certain states of affairs. The same is true of the laws of de Tocqueville or Durkheim, for whom a relaxation of constraints could lead to 'anomie' or rebellion. They are important because of the paradox they contain, since they draw attention to the fact that such a relaxation can have quite the opposite effects to those that generally tend to be observed. All these propositions, however, are of the nature of *statements about what may happen* rather than of *laws*.

When a statement of this kind is associated with the feeling that the possible state of affairs is also more likely than its opposite, we like to call them *conjectures*. For example, the proposition that freezing rents in a period of inflation is likely to lead to a deterioration of the housing stock can be seen as a reasonable conjecture. It is very likely that a freeze of that kind would mean that landlords would not maintain their property, and it is certain that in that respect they are free to decide as they wish. Indeed, the conjecture is so convincing that we can talk of a conditional law of the type 'if A, then B'. In such a case, it is easy to anticipate the effects of measure A on the *motivation* of the actors concerned (i.e., they have less reason to maintain their property), and we know that they have the *ability* to act in terms of it. There is thus a logical progression from statements of possibility via conjectures, which may be more or less convincing, to conditional laws.

There is a tendency in the social sciences, as I believe my exposition in the preceding chapters sufficiently shows, to give too high a status to such statements, which are often put forward as conjectures and even as laws, and conjectures are often presented as if they were laws. All the 'laws' of political mobilization are in fact no more than statements of possibility. The same is true of the law of the 'tendential' fall in profits, in which, *ceteris paribus*, the rate of profit must fall. But one cannot state that other things *are* equal, and there are good reasons for believing that the conditions in which the law no longer holds good are very likely not to be constant. This also applies to Parsons's law of the nuclearization of the family. It holds good when we are comparing traditional and modern societies, for family ties are certainly greater in the former than in the latter. That observation is a descriptive proposition that it would be hard to quarrel with, but we cannot blithely deduce from it even a 'tendential' law about the way family structures develop. We should bear in mind that according to Caplow family ties were closer in America in 1970 than at the beginning of the century.

Contrary to the beliefs that emerge from what theorists of social change are trying to do, there are not many laws, even conditional ones. There are *some*, of course, such as those which any prudent government has to take into account. These 'laws' emerge when two conditions are met. These are that the appearance of a state of affairs A produces a readily foreseeable change in the motivation of certain categories of actors and that it is possible to state that the change in question will in fact modify their behaviour. It is not by chance that it is chiefly in the economic field that such laws can be stated, for that is where the preferences of actors can, in certain cases at least, be most easily organized and anticipated.

But although it is generally appropriate to *downgrade* the laws put forward by theorists of social change and to see them for the most part as no more than *statements about what may happen*, we must also accept that other *questions* that they deal with are treated in a rigorously scientific manner. In other words, some of the literature on social change seems to me to include theories as rigorously scientific as the natural scientists aim to make their own. To the same degree that we need to see exactly how fragile certain theories of social change are, we also need to stress that others are established with precisely the same rigour as those in what we call the exact sciences. In my view, these distinctions are essential, since I believe that they enable us to conclude a difficult debate – that is, the argument about whether the social and natural sciences are one and the same or two entirely separate disciplines – that goes back at least to Dilthey and Rickert.[13]

To illustrate this point, I propose to return to one or two of the examples mentioned above. As I suggested in the last chapter, the

Weber-Trevor Roper theory of the relationship between Calvinism and the development of capitalism cannot, from a logical, or more precisely an *epistemological*, point of view, be distinguished from theories in the natural sciences. Weber was struck and surprised by certain facts. In the sixteenth century, too many entrepreneurs were Calvinists for the relationship to be merely fortuitous. Even in Lutheran countries, the bankers were Calvinists. These observations naturally caused him to pay particular attention to the differences between the two faiths and to see the most striking of them, the Calvinist belief in predestination, as a decisive factor. So far, his methods were those associated with the traditional canons of the comparative method as enunciated by John Stuart Mill. He did not stop there, however, since a relationship is only significant if it can be seen as the result of intelligible behaviour. Weber himself in fact never managed to satisfy completely the demands implied in the requirement of *understanding* that he defined, and saying that for the Calvinist success in business was to be the sign of his election in the after life looks rather like an *ad hoc* proposition. In short, he did not succeed in proving that behaviour is explicable in terms of beliefs. In addition, although his theory, in its simplified and popular form given above, 'explains' certain *facts*, there are many others that it does not explain. The Geneva entrepreneurs were all Calvinists, but none of them came originally from that city; the Cologne bankers were Catholics, and many entrepreneurs, as Sombart had noted, were Jews.[14]

Trevor Roper keeps what was valid in Weber's 'intuitions'. The Protestant ethic certainly looked more favourably on commercial and industrial activities than the Catholic ethic, and a Protestant was more likely to embark on them. The chief fact, however, is that an entrepreneur was more likely to be attracted to the ideas of Erasmus and the Calvinist branch of Protestantism. In that form, there is a comprehensible relationship. Trevor Roper, however, has also shown through a study of the effects of the Counter-Reformation on the *situation* of individual members of the commercial elite, that it is possible to account not only for the facts discovered by Weber but also for many others unaccounted for by his theory or apparently incompatible with it. The fact, for example, that the bankers were Calvinists in Lutheran countries is explained as a consequence of migration and seen only very loosely as connected with the belief in predestination. The concentration of Catholic men of affairs in Cologne or their Jewish counterparts in Amsterdam is readily explicable in terms of Trevor Roper's theory.

Weber's theory explains a set of aggregate date (M), but does so by using a microsociological theory mS which is questionable because it is of the nature of an *ad hoc* or *post factum* theory,[15] that is, of one invented to meet the needs of the task in hand, and also because it satisfies the criterion of comprehension only very imperfectly. In chapter 2, we used the term *transposition* to designate the step consisting of an *ad hoc* modelling of a microscopic theory on the aggregate effect that it is supposed to explain. In Trevor Roper, the microsociological statements are entirely satisfactory to the extent that they meet the criterion of comprehension. They also see the behaviour observed as a response to a situation. The man of affairs is likely to be attracted by Erasmian ideology and the Calvinist ethic, which are, however, in opposition on certain basic points, but he is also encouraged to seek out greener pastures and associate himself with international Calvinism - or reconvert - once the Counter-Reformation stifles his activities. All in all, the total number of facts (N) explained by Trevor Roper's theory is much greater than that (M) accounted for by Weber's. In addition, (M) is completely contained in (N). With regard to the relationship mS, it is *comprehensible*. The characteristics of the situation to which the actors are exposed are linked to macrosociological data M' brought to light by the investigation: S(M').

The history of the Weber-Trevor Roper theory is a perfect illustration of the processes of scientific discovery or the 'increase in knowledge' as described by modern philosophers of science from Popper to Lakatos. In the form given it by Trevor Roper, it achieves a high degree of credibility.[16] By combining a small number of propositions, all of which are acceptable, it accounts for a considerable range of observed data, and consequently it is hard to imagine a theory that would both be different and explain the same, or a larger, set of data.

There is no point in giving a multiplicity of examples, but much the same could be said about several of the studies mentioned in earlier chapters. Epstein's work on the effects of irrigation in southern India, for example, accounts for a considerable body of data relating to the development of relationships between subgroups and the two sexes and of symbolic practices and economic activities. These complex patterns are interpreted on the basis of a small number of propositions that completely meets the criterion of comprehension and sees in them aggregation effects arising from the changes brought about in the situation of the actors involved by irrigation. The set of data explained is of such a size that it is hard to imagine a very different theory capable of explaining them, which means that Epstein's explanation is highly credible.

Obviously, this degree of credibility is a great deal higher than that of structuralist and culturalist theories which accept general principles and see any exogenous change occurring in a traditional society as always being bound to cause either a rejection mechanism

$$(A_t, B_t \ldots P_t \rightarrow A_{t+k}, B_{t+k} \ldots P_{t+k})$$

or a chain reaction mechanism

$$(A_t, B_t \ldots P_t \rightarrow A'_{t+k}, B'_{t+k} \ldots P'_{t+k}).$$

Epstein, however, shows that changes can be observed that could, if one so wishes, be described as *incoherent*, but his theory does also explain *why* they are incoherent. A theory like that of Epstein represents an advance on culturalist theories of the same order as that described in the preceding example. A complex range of data $\{M\}$ is explained by a theory $\{M\} = Mm\{[S(M)]\}$ in which all the propositions are readily acceptable. The microsociological theory $m()$ clearly demonstrates the adaptative function of the new behaviour, as the data $\{M\}$ are interpreted as aggregation or composition effects.

We could analyse Hagen's theory in the same way, at least in the form I gave it in chapter 3. It too represents *progress*, in Popper's sense of the term, in relation to more ambitious but less certain theories of development.

It is therefore possible to pick out from amongst theories of social change – a corpus whose limits are very difficult to define – a group that fully meets the criteria which in modern epistemological terms are essential for scientific theories. In certain cases it is possible to observe undeniable cumulative processes, where a theory T' accounts for all the data that an earlier theory included, but also explains others.

The notion of understanding has, of course, no equivalent in the natural sciences. Judgements such as 'X behaves thus because it is to his or her advantage to do so' or 'X sets store by such and such an object because it is a symbol of modernity' are obviously only meaningful if X is a human subject. It is, however, important to accept that judgements of this kind, like judgements about non-subjective states of affairs, can be evaluated critically. I may, for example, feel at one point that someone else is behaving 'irrationally' and subsequently, when I am better informed, realize that his or her actions are comprehensible if I take into account certain facts that I had initially been unaware of.

What really must be understood, however, is that the *form* of the explanation is not affected by the nature of X. A theory is always a set of *acceptable* propositions which, taken together, make it possible to explain a more or less complex set of data. A theory T' will always be preferable to another theory (T) if it either dispenses with doubtful propositions contained in (T) or offers an explanation of a more complete set of data.[17]

So theories of social change *may* and sometimes *do* obey something that we could call the logic of scientific discovery and validation procedures very much akin to those used in testing theories in the natural sciences. Like the latter, they may achieve varying degrees of credibility, and it is sometimes possible to come to a firm decision that one is preferable to another. It would not be hard to give irrefutable examples of progress from one theory to another. The analysis of social change is therefore in no way necessarily an inexact science doomed by the very nature of its object to be condemned to the incommunicable procedures of 'interpretation'. It is true that we can 'understand' the behaviour of an individual, but not that of an atom, but the only way of explaining a social system is the same as that we would use to explain a physical one. The relationship of *comprehension* that Weber was so right to stress is a characteristic of the 'observer/subject' pair but, quite contrary to our occasional distortion of his ideas, totally meaningless in connection with the 'observer/social system' or the 'observer/social process' pair.

Theories of social change can therefore be properly (Popperly?) scientific if the data for which an explanation is being sought constitute a well-defined set, which implies that they can only be *locally* and *partly* valid. We can see this in Trevor Roper's examination of Weber's theory. He explains a more complete set of defined data, but at the same time proposes a more limited theory. He no longer tries to account for the origin of capitalism – a question which is perhaps meaningless[18] – but simply to explain a set of data related to the capitalist entrepreneurs of the sixteenth and seventeenth centuries.

The same applies to Hagen's theory. Although that is what he set out to do, it offers neither a general theory of development nor even a theory of development in twentieth-century Colombia, but it does provide a perfectly convincing explanation of the appearance of a class of entrepreneurs at the time in question and a considerable amount of information about their characteristics. It is also interesting to note that the relative obscurity into which it has lapsed is the result of the fact that by trying to make it *generally* applicable, Hagen was led to interpret his data by means of propositions which, it soon became clear, were rather doubtful. An original and highly credible *partial* theory was thus stifled by a rather unconvincing *general* one.

Notions such as 'modernization', 'political development', 'economic development', 'poverty', 'the development of capitalism' and the like do not designate defined sets of data. Consequently, theories concerning the perpetuation of poverty, modernization and so on cannot belong to the same category as those we have just looked at. Does that mean, as Nisbet suggests, that they are of no interest? I do not believe that we must necessarily come to that conclusion. With regard to this matter, my own position would be *relativistic* and *critical*, while Nisbet's is *sceptical*. It is just as vital to be aware of the different logical nature of Hagen's theory and that of the vicious circle of poverty as it is peremptory to say that the former is meaningful and the latter is not. That the first can be scrutinized using Popper's procedures and the second cannot is a matter of fact, but to see the second as thereby deprived of justification and meaning does not follow from that fact.

That is the distinction that we must now examine.

VARIATIONS ON A THEME OF SIMMEL

In Georg Simmel's view, the social sciences are distinct from history not because their task is to establish *nomothetic* propositions – a task which they clearly cannot have – but because they are *formal* in nature. This distinction is as fundamental as it is generally incorrectly understood. The simplest way of showing this is to illustrate it by an example.

First, however, to introduce the subject, it is useful to recall the long-distance dialogue on the distinction between Durkheim and Simmel. In 1894 a text by Simmel on 'social differentiation' appeared in the *Revue internationale de sociologie*, attacking Durkheim's nomological pretensions and maintaining that 'the mania for being absolutely determined to find "laws" of social life is merely a return to the philosophical credo of the old metaphysicians, in which all knowledge had to be absolutely universal and necessary'. Six years later, in 1900, Durkheim published a tit-for-tat reply in an article in the *Rivista italiana di sociologia* on 'Sociology and its Scientific Field'. The formal sociology Simmel was trying to promote, he maintained, only served to keep the discipline within the metaphysical ideology it felt an irresistible need to escape from. It was therefore Simmel himself who was the metaphysician. At the same time, however – and this is why his text is so important – Durkheim showed that he had completely understood Simmel's aim and the objective summarized in the phrase 'formal sociology', even if he rejected and condemned them for being too abstract. His real criticism of Simmel in fact was that he was trying to follow the example of Adam Smith and Ricardo and use, as we should say nowadays, the method of *models*, a way of proceeding that seemed to Durkheim to belong to a time that had gone for ever. 'The old school of political economy also claimed the right to be abstract . . . ' He was defending his nomological view of sociology against a methodology that seemed to him archaic and reminiscent of the political economy *of former times*. For him the task of sociology was, like that of physics (as he saw it and as it perhaps was then, but no longer is), to attempt to establish the empirical regularities governing social facts considered in their exteriority and their irreducibly and specifically individual nature.

It would be easy to show that a book like *The Philosophy of Money* is in fact a general survey of *models* and that in it Simmel's mode of thought is really comparable with that of the old economists, which is also that of many of their modern counterparts in economics and sociology. Doing so, however, would go beyond what I have set out to do in this book, and in order to illustrate the distinction Simmel makes I prefer to use a more recent example that clearly brings out the enormous epistemological gap between the notions of models and laws.

In 1929, Hotelling published an article that was to enjoy a considerable longevity.[19] In 1970, Hirschman, in a little book that also attracted a great deal of attention, was still drawing his inspiration from it. The article raises a problem which at first sight seems quite artificial and reminiscent of those logical puzzles that certain newspapers offer their readers. Imagine a village made up of houses aligned along a straight road. Since it has no grocer's shop, two propose to set up shop there at the same time. Suppose that they can choose their own spot and that they make their decision independently of each other. If the village is a linear development of which the two extremities are A and B, at what point along the line AB will the two grocers set up shop? It is assumed that both will be of comparable quality, and that the villagers will give their custom to the one nearest their homes. Both grocers want as many customers as possible.

If, of course, the villagers and not the grocers were deciding where the two shops would be, they would have them at one-third (C) and two-thirds (D) of the way along AB. That would also be satisfactory for the grocers, as the customers would be divided equally between them.

In fact, it is not very likely that the *grocers* would choose that solution. One would only settle for C (one-third of the way along line AB) if he was sure that the other would accept D (two-thirds of the way), but the hypothesis rules out such a certainty. All the first grocer knows is that a competitor is also planning to set up in the village. Likewise, the other could only decide to open a shop at D if he or she were sure that the first one would do so at C. As the reader can check, the conclusion would be the same if C and D were respectively a quarter and three-quarters, one-fifth and four-fifths and so on along the line AB. Each of these points gives an equal division of customers, but it is to the advantage of neither grocer to choose them. The only safe spot for either of them is the centre point of the line, since that provides each with the certainty that his or her competitor cannot choose a spot that would deprive him or her of a part of the possible clientele.

We would also get the same result if they were allowed to choose in turn. The first would have to choose the centre point, as any other solution would allow the second to attract more than half the customers. And once the first has made that choice, the second has to do the same unless he or she wants to be put at a disadvantage. There is no advantage in this solution as against the 'one-third/two-thirds' solution, and it has the drawback of being disadvantageous for the villagers as well, since those living on the edges of the village will have twice as far to go as they would if the 'optimal' 'one-quarter/three-quarters' solution had been possible.

Let us now suppose that AB represents not a village but a range of ideological positions extending from the extreme left (A) to the extreme right (B), and that it is theoretically possible to put the voters somewhere along this continuum. Some will have political attitude A, some B, and others will have attitudes somewhere between the extremes. The moderates will occupy a position near the centre of the line. If it were as easy to observe people's political attitudes as it is to note their height, for example, it would be possible to draw up a distribution showing the unequal frequency of the various attitudes. Since that cannot be done, we shall have to be content with supposing that there are more moderate attitudes than any other kind and that an attitude becomes less common as it approaches the extremes.

It is no longer two grocers but two parties who, *ex hypothesi*, are going to try to divide the customers up between themselves or, more precisely, to attract a majority of them. To do that, they draw up an electoral programme that – also *ex hypothesi* – corresponds to one of the points on the AB spectrum. One precisely in the middle would fully satisfy voters whose position is around that point. We have the same question as in the case of the grocers: where is it advantageous for the parties to place their programmes, assuming that the electorate will vote for the one that comes closest to their own position? As also in that case, and for exactly the same reasons, the answer is *in the centre*.

The exercise implies no *empirical* conclusion and hence no prediction, and can only be matched to reality indirectly. At most, it enables us to understand more clearly why, in a two-party system such as obtains in the United States, election results can occasionally be very close and the programmes of the two parties so alike that it seems hard to tell them apart. We know, however, that in the American system the programmes have sometimes been very different and that certain electoral victories, like that of Nixon over McGovern in 1972, have been resounding. It would therefore be quite illegit-imate to deduce from Hotelling's model an *empirical* proposition of the type 'in two-party systems (a) both parties tend to offer similar programmes and (b) election results tend to stay fairly close to a 50/50 division'.[20] Election results are sometimes close, but it would be going too far not only to accept that they *must* be, but even that they *tend* to be. In short, Hotelling's schema provides no *empirical* proposition and can at most be seen as a plausible interpretation of certain real elections of a very specific nature.

As Hirschman has shown, it is, however, possible to extend the theory to enable us to take varying circumstances into account. In doing so, of course, the form it takes must include the facts of every situation and change as they change. We could take Nixon's electoral triumph in 1972 as an example. It certainly contradicts Hotelling's theory if, but only if, we claim that it is empirically valid.[20] If we accept the theory for what it *is* – an ideal or formal model of which the terms must be made precise if it is intended to apply it to the real world – then it does not contradict it.

In its simple form as presented above, it assumes that no voters abstain and that everyone votes for the party whose programme comes closest to his or her own preferences. If both programmes belong near the centre of the political spectrum, the extremists will not be very satisfied, and less satisfied than the middle-of-the-road voters. But suppose that, as happened in 1972, the general climate of political ideas was much more favourable to left-wing than to right-wing notions. In such a case, the left-wing extremists are more likely to protest against the 'centrist' policy of the party they are least separated from than are the right-wing extremists. In that particular set of circumstances, the former will be more likely to show their discontent. That was exactly what happened in 1972, when the left-wing elements of the Democrats actively tried to swing the candidate towards the left. The effect of this, however, was that most votes went to the Republican runner (as Hotelling's schema would suggest) and ultimately an electoral triumph for Nixon.

A symmetrical analysis will explain the rout of the Republican candidate, Senator Goldwater, in 1964, a time when the watchword of law and order was on everyone's lips in Republican circles. What right-wing electors were calling for was a factor in the choice of a candidate who was *too* right wing and this led to a flawless victory for the Democratic candidate.[22] Hotelling's schema also suggests an interpretation of Reagan's victory. The Democrats had been either unable or unwilling to respond to the shift to the right suggested by many surveys, and as a result of this shift, therefore, the party's programme was too 'left'.

These analyses do not, of course, exhaust the topic. My reason for taking Hotelling's theory as an example, however, is that it provides a particularly clear illustration of the logical nature of what I have called *formal theories*. Once again, a theory of this type does not apply, as such, to any real situation, and no forecast can be based on it or empirical conclusion drawn from it. In Popper's sense of the terms, it cannot be *refuted*, since it says nothing about reality, nor is it *scientific*. On the other hand, it is obviously not *metaphysical*. There is thus no place for it in Popper's categories.

If it is properly expressed, it provides a no doubt terse but nevertheless suggestive explanation of a whole series of facts. Appropriately adjusted, the same model accounts, for instance, for both Goldwater's defeat and Nixon's or Reagan's success. I propose to follow Simmel and use the expression 'formal theory' to designate this category of fundamental theories in the social sciences. Hotelling's theory is formal in the sense that it does not apply to any real situation, but is rather a kind of framework that needs to be filled out once we propose to use it to account for observations about the real world. It is *general* not in the sense that it could explain every observable situation, but in the sense that it can be used for very varied situations, provided the appropriate details are fed into it in every specific case. In the same way, the relationship $y = ax + b$ not only does not apply to any particular reality; it is even so *unreal* that as such it cannot be represented. It does, however, give an adequate image of various phenomena once a and b are given precise significance. To use Russell's language, a formal theory in the sense I understand it here is an organized set of 'propositional functions', that is, of propositions that can only be empirically significant when the variables they imply are changed into constants.

Many theories of social change are of this type. Olson's 'logic of collective action' is sometimes seen as a realist theory entailing the disappearance of collective movements in the United States of the 1960s and perhaps in all industrial societies.[23] His main argument is well known: even if it is in the interest of a latent group to act in order to achieve a collective good (i.e., a good that would be of benefit to all if it were achieved) all its members are encouraged to do nothing, both because their individual marginal contributions are very limited and because, since everyone would benefit from the good, everyone is tempted to stand aside and let the others make the effort. As such, however, the theory does not entail any empirical or even any 'tendential' conclusion. It has to do with a deliberately 'idealized' situation which quite clearly is never very likely to come about in such a pure form in reality. It is therefore impossible to say that it is either true or false. It does not meet any of Popper's criteria for validation, but merely provides a formal framework that has to be clarified if we want to use it to interpret real situations.

Olson notes, for instance, that after a long period of stagnation the membership of the American Medical Association began to rise sharply. The upswing came at the very time when, as a result of the increasingly high technical level of medicine and significant growth in medical research, the Association had the idea of offering its members periodical documentation enabling them to keep abreast of new developments. At the same time, the growing volume of court actions against doctors encouraged it to offer to provide not only *collective* benefits, such as the promotion of medicine and the freeing of funds for medical research, of benefit to all and sundry whether they had worked for them or not, but also *individual* benefits for members only. The result was that subscriptions began to flow in and doctors had a powerful organization to look after their interests.

Given the appropriate fine-tuning, the *same* theory can provide, for example, an interesting interpretation of the role of intellectuals in social movements. Since the members of a latent group, particularly if it is large and atomized, may have little inducement to act, attempts to trigger off collective action or to sensitize public opinion may come from those with easy access to the means of communication who as well as favouring its 'cause' may also consider it to be to their own advantage to support the group itself.

These and other applications clearly show that far from leading to the conclusion that collective movements will disappear, the theory may help to explain the ways in which they come into being. In itself, it does not lead to any empirical proposition, but it does provide a framework for explaining anomalous cases of the mobilization and organization of collective action, as well as the absence of collective movements, once the *variables* in the functional propositions of which it is made up are replaced by the appropriate (i.e., adapted to the features of the specific case in question) *constants*.

The two systems above are, to summarize, made up of systems of statements relating not to reality itself but to *principles* that the analyst should observe if he or she wishes to account for certain classes of phenomena, be they electoral results in a two-party system

(Hotelling) or the phenomena of the mobilization and organization of collective action (Olson). The latter, for example, suggests that the analyst should examine the costs and benefits for the individual of taking part in such action. To clarify our ideas, we could say that his 'logic of collective action' is both *formal* and *metatheoretical*, indicating the points that a *theory* aiming at explaining a phenomenon of the mobilization or organization of collective action would benefit from considering, whatever the particular features of the phenomenon may be.

Many theories of social change seem to me to belong to the same epistemological category. In other words, they should be seen as *formal* and *metatheoretical* rather than as *empirical*. We should, I feel, avoid a great deal of confusion if this distinction were always both seen and taken into account.

The models of social *differentiation* Parsons and Smelser have stressed are of this type. When a dysfunction appears in a firm and more generally in an organization or a social system, it *may* be solved by the creation of new roles and, consequently, by role differentiation. As with Olson, the theory does no more than sketch in an empty conceptual framework from which no empirical proposition can be directly drawn but which one can suppose may be useful in analysing certain processes. This differentiation model has indeed been used by Parsons in a celebrated analysis of the differentiation of the functions of authority in firms,[24] by Smelser in his study of the development of the textile industry in England,[25] and in many other instances. It makes it possible to explain various processes, in exactly the same way as Olson's theory makes it possible to explain the spectacular growth of the American Medical Association or the closed shop or the part played by intellectuals in certain mobilization processes. The explanation, however, only emerges when the empty framework of the formal theory is filled out as particular propositions and data relating to particular times and places are taken into consideration.

Differentiation theory thus provides a framework that could be said to be general to the extent that it can be applied to different processes, but the framework is a purely *formal* one. Like Parsons, we can say that differentiation processes are *typical*, provided we realize that the adjective does not imply in any way that they are *frequent*. Parsons is not suggesting that processes of change are *generally*, *very often* or *often* differentiation processes. Such a proposition would be more or less meaningless, since even ideally the frequency in question could not be determined. What he is suggesting is that the model designated by the notion of differentiation can be used when we are analysing *various* processes. A common error, which ought to be avoided but often is not, is to deduce from Parsons's differentiation theory the empirical 'consequence' that is not implied in it, namely that in general processes of social change are differentiation processes.

We could look at another classic example, Merton's 'paradigm of functional analysis', in the same way.[27] The mere fact that he calls it a paradigm rather than a theory is a sufficient indication that in his view functional analysis is not strictly a theory, but a conceptual framework applicable to various processes. His paradigm states that if we are to account for an institution, it is useful to reflect on its *functions*. The Democratic party machine in the United States, for example, assumed around the 1950s certain functions that the social security system could not assume, given its embryonic nature at that time. In return for his allegiance, an unemployed or sick worker out of a job was offered help, and the party also provided subsidies to those too poor to afford decent housing.

As was the case in the preceding example, here too there is a persistent misunderstanding of what is implied. The 'functional analysis paradigm' or, to use the preferred term, the 'functionalist theory' is often wrongly seen as a theory in terms of which society can be represented as an organism, that is, as a system whose elements work together to produce the homeostatic equilibrium of the whole. As the example of one particular application briefly illustrated above shows, the 'theory' entails nothing of the kind. It merely claims to provide an intelligible model that can be applied to various cases, provided the model is adapted to suit the peculiarities of each one.

It must be admitted that not only do theorists of social change not recognize the distinction designated here by the contrast between 'formal' theories and theories in the strict sense of the word. They often play an active part in perpetuating the confusion.

The theory of the 'vicious circle of poverty', to return to a 'theory' of development that I have mentioned at several points, has been put forward by its proponents as a theory *stricto sensu*, that is, as one which describes, in a way that could be interpreted as realist, the mechanism underlying the reproduction of poverty. If it is interpreted in that way, the theory is unacceptable, because it conflicts with many of the observed facts. As it implies that development cannot be exogenous, it cannot, for example, offer a satisfactory account of the development of Japan in the nineteenth century. It conflicts with the fact that even in very poor societies there is always a surplus and savings. The glaring contradictions between it and what is actually observed have been pointed out so often that I need not stress them further. If we interpret it in a realist way, it is quite simply *wrong*. We can, however, also interpret it in a *formal* way, that is, as a theory that has had the merit of isolating an ideal mechanism that we have no chance of observing in a pure state in the real world. In the first case, it is a construct that is not only wrong, but also dangerous, because practical conclusions can be – and indeed have been – drawn from it, with awesome results.

In closing these remarks, it is important to grant the distinction between theories that are purely formal and those that are theories in the strict sense of the term all the importance it merits, by noting that it holds good not only in the social sciences but also in certain areas of the natural sciences. As we know, Popper often wondered whether Darwinism ought to be called scientific or not.[28] If the hallmark of a *scientific* theory is really its *refutability*, as his famous division between metaphysical and scientific theories maintains, the theory of evolution, which is not susceptible to the process of refutation, must be held to be non-scientific. In itself, it does not enable us to draw any empirical conclusions, to state, for example, that a given species with certain characteristics at t will necessarily have certain others at $t + k$. And that proposition holds good whether t and $t + k$ refer to the past or the future. Even when t and $t + k$ refer to past time, it is not possible, in terms of the theory of evolution, to deduce the state of a species at $t + k$ from its state at t. All the theory provides is a model of intelligibility. Between t and $t + k$, mutations have occurred, some of which, because they offer better adaptation, have been 'favoured' and 'retained' by natural selection.

But in order to explain evolution as it is in fact observed between the two points, we should need to be able to fill out the framework provided by the evolutionary model with data of a *historical* kind. And these, as far as the evolution of species is concerned, are often full of gaps. In order to establish that a mutation means improved adapatation, we need to know, for example, the precise characteristics of the environment the species found itself in at t and show that in terms of well-established criteria, the mutation did in fact lead to improved adaptation. What usually happens, however, is that the data needed to prove this are missing. That is why both Darwinist and neo-Darwinist theories of evolution are sometimes seen as being tautologous.[29] Since the relevant data are missing, there is no escape from a vicious circle, and the spread of a characteristic is taken as the result of an ability to adapt for which the only proof is the fact that it *has* spread.

As was the case with theories of social change, the epistemological debate raised by the theory of evolution can, it seems to me, be usefully clarified by considering the fundamental difference between *formal* and *stricto sensu* theories. As such, the theory of evolution entails no empirical consequences, but if the appropriate data are available, it provides a useful framework for constructing *stricto sensu* theories which *do* enable us to explain certain actually observed evolutionary processes.

The same is true of many 'theories' of social change. They are merely formal frameworks which can become proper theories – by which I mean that they can explain actually observed phenomena – only if they are filled out with complementary propositions and appropriate data.

REJECTING DISORDER

We have reached the end of our itinerary. Many of the arguments and debates that theories of social change have provoked are the result of a failure to observe a certain number of distinctions or, if they are observed, of applying them in a questionable way. Many statements about what *may* happen are put forward as or taken for 'laws'. Many theories in the strict sense of the word that are valid in precisely specified sets of circumstances are assumed to be *generally* valid, that is, as holding good whatever the circumstances may be.

It is only possible to construct theories (in Popper's rigorous sense of the word) of social change about partial and local social processes firmly situated in time and particular circumstances. Those which claim to be general in application must at best be considered to be formal theories that are not in themselves directly applicable to reality, but which do offer a mode of discussion or describe ideal examples which may be useful in the analysis of certain processes. At worst – when they claim to produce propositions that are at once empirical and general – they are likely to be disproved by reality.

It is not true to say that the vicious circle of poverty explains underdevelopment in general, or that the division of labour is inevitably bound to increase, that ideas always depend on 'structures', that every institution has a function, that industrialization necessarily entails nuclear families, that development depends on exogenous factors, that growth or a sharp economic recession generally produce mobilization effects or that structures tend to be coherent. Nor is it true that the growth of science and technology has produced or necessarily will produce a fall in religious values, that an extension of political rights generally leads to an extension of social rights, that slow development tends to give rise to centralist states, or that, vice versa, only centralist states can provide the necessary spur for smooth development. It is equally false to claim that the dependence of developing countries on the developed world usually puts them in an unfavourable rather than a favourable position with regard to their own interests. It is also erroneous to maintain that marginalized elites are always likely to be innovative, that a semi-feudal structure will always reproduce itself or, in more general terms, that a given structure implies a given law of development. It is not true to say that institutions form coherent systems and that 'contradictions' between them are a general cause of social change, or that every process is determined, or indeed the opposite, that no process is determined and hence predictable, or that myths or the conditions of production are of absolutely prime importance.

I repeat, the only *scientific* theories of social change are *partial* and *local* ones. Some of them cover situations in which the conditions of production must be seen as fundamental. In others, however, the latter play no part. Some of them consider that, in the appropriate circumstances, values are exogenous, or rightly see innovation as being sometimes endogenous and sometimes exogenous. Others again, with good reasons, use a utilitarian system of axioms , others do not. Both can provide convincing explanations of the processes under investigation, for the appropriateness of a set of axioms can only be established in the light of the process to be explained, and not in any a priori way.

It is because they have not taken cognizance of this handful of propositions and epistemological distinctions that the 'great' theories of social change – those that have inspired positivism, Marxism, functionalism or developmentalism – inhabit a kind of mausoleum.

The problem I set out to solve in this book – why are theories of social change so stubbornly proved wrong by the real world? – seems to entail a solution consisting of one or two simple propositions.

In the sense in which, following Popper, we generally ascribe to the term, a theory of social change can be *scientific* only if it sets out to examine why a defined set of features A_t, B_t ... P_t of a system changes at $t+k$ into another set

$$A'_{t+k}, B'_{t+k} \ldots P_{t+k}$$

To make the question clear, features A, B ... P themselves have to be clearly defined, and the reference periods $t, t+1 \ldots t+k$ must be unambiguously identified. The answer to the question consists of explaining why and how, between t and $t+k$, the situation of the actors changes and gives rise to sets of behaviour which, when aggregated, explain the *result*

$$A'_{t+k}, B'_{t+k} \ldots P'_{t+k}$$

It is my belief that any *real* theory of social change can be reduced to this form.

The whole range of 'theories of social change', however, also contains other classes of theories which cannot be expressed in those terms. Some of them are conjectures, others statements about what may happen, and others again *formal* theories with no direct empirical application, but crucially useful to the extent that they may shape the construction of real theories in a decisive and effective way. Without the 'paradigm of functional analysis' it is difficult to explain a phenomenon peculiar to a particular time and situation, such as the importance of the Democratic party *machine* in the 1950s. Without Olson's paradigm of collective action it is hard to explain the spread of the closed shop in British trade union history. Without the paradigm of differentiation, it is hard to explain the distinction between the function of ownership and those of authority and decision-making in the modern firm.

It can be seen then that all the difficulties and refutations that 'theories of social change' are exposed to come essentially from a confusion of genres. There are scientific theories of change *and* conjectural theories, formal theories *and* real theories, all logically quite distinct from each other. By a kind of upward attraction, however, these distinctions tend to be neglected, and theories whose chief function is to propose formal models of intelligibility are likely to be seen as capable of providing empirical prediction and to be given the status of 'laws' demonstrating a regular empirical pattern when they are in fact merely statements of possibilities.

Theories of social change thus deserve neither the exalted status they are sometimes given nor the accusations of baseness levelled at them by Nisbet. It is not a question of whether they are good or bad, but of what their logical value might be. It might be objected that a critical and relativist attitude of this kind does not lead to any very wonderful results. That may be so, but it does lead to corollaries that it is difficult to imagine being accepted without resistance, since they show, amongst other things, that the notion of a Marxist, functionalist or structuralist theory of social change is meaningless, but also demonstrate that certain theories of change are as rigorously scientific as theories in physics might be.

In this book, I have tried to take up a discussion revived by Popper in his *The Poverty of Historicism* and continued by Nisbet in *History and Social Change*, a discussion which others, and in particular Aron, in his *Introduction to the Philosophy of History*, had already broached. It might therefore be useful to review the differences between my own diagnosis and that of the first two writers. Popper's relativist attitude is based on a distinction between absolute and conditional laws, and he sees establishing the latter as a legitimate aim of both the social and the natural sciences. In his view, however, trying to find absolute laws is a 'metaphysical' activity. The difficulty of this position is due in the first place to the fact that many of the 'absolute' laws proposed by the social sciences follow from conditional laws and in the second to the fact that most of the conditional laws they propose are dubious. Finally, many theories of social change lead on to neither absolute nor conditional laws. In addition, many such theories, whether it be a question of Parsons on differentiation or Olson on collective action, are unclassifiable in terms of Popper's famous dichotomy between 'metaphysical' and 'scientific' theories.

Nisbet's position is a sceptical rather than a relativistic one. In his devotion to the ideal that Ranke expressed in classic form, to describe change as it actually occurred ('wie es eigentlich geschehen ist'), he refuses to accept that an analysis of it can give rise to any nomothetic and general statement. Like the historian in Ranke's or Mommsen's ideal definition, the sociologist, political scientist or economist cannot set him or herself any other aim than the analysis of single processes in all their singularity. In attempting this, he or she must seek neither to discover an explanation for nomological regularities nor to apply *ideal* models.

I have tried to show that Nisbet's position too was untenable in so far as it led to a more or less unacceptable realism: if there are no indubitable nomological or nomothetical statements, there are systems of ideal models and categories which it would be hard to describe as valueless in the analysis of social change and which must be accepted as indispensable if we are to understand it, since they provide frameworks within which real theories are subsequently constructed. Although these systems are not themselves either 'metaphysical' or 'scientific' in the rigorous Popperian sense, they are vital in the construction of theories which do fall within the province of Popper's criteria of verification. In other words, Nisbet ignores the objections that, in their own day, Simmel and Weber had rightly expressed with regard to the realism of a Ranke. In his defence, it has to be said that theorists of social change have rarely been aware of the need to distinguish between the formal and the empirical and have often presented as general empirical theories constructions that for the most part must be seen as ideal models.

A NOTE ON THE NOTION OF VALIDITY

An important and relatively technical question that cannot be discussed in detail in the present context still needs to be raised. We have seen that explaining a process could, in some circumstances, involve such and such a type of axiomatic assumptions at the microscopic level (a cognitive or utilitarian type of psychology, for example), that the nature of the variables involved varied according to the case in question, and that there could be no general rule on that particular matter. In addition, if we follow Simmel and Weber, we must admit, unless we want to be faced with terrible quandaries, that when sociologists, economists or political scientists explain a given phenomenon, they always use *ideal* models, even when they try to adapt them to the portion of reality they are analysing. This means that one basic epistemological question is that of how we can avoid the arbitrary or, to put the question another way, how the validity of a theory can be determined.

As I have discussed this question in detail elsewhere,[30] I shall merely recapitulate my views briefly here. The starting-point of scientific theories always lies in the definition of a finite set of data, {D}. In a theory dealing with social change, these data have the particular feature of being indexed to time. The next stage consists of 'choosing' one or more ideal schemata {S} that seem likely, unless further examination shows otherwise, to provide suitable components for constructing the theory that will explain {D}. From {S}, therefore, a theory T is constructed. It must not contain propositions that are incompatible with Weber's criterion of comprehension, and it must also be quite compatible with {D}. The question of whether it is valid or not can therefore be expressed in the following form: is it possible to imagine a theory, T', which is quite distinct from T and also meets just as fully Weber's criterion of comprehension and Popper's criteria of 'falsification'? If it is possible to do so, we can create 'incommensurable' theories – in Feyerabend's sense of the term – from the single set of data {D}. In that case, we cannot come to any decision about the relative validity of T and T'. In other terms, we cannot make any judgement about the degree of validity of T. If D can be explained by a set of incommensurable theories T, T', T'' . . . containing many elements, T can only be subjectively valid.

Let us imagine the opposite case, in which it is hard to think of a theory T' that would explain {D} just as well as T does. That is what happens, I believe, with certain theories already mentioned, such as Epstein's and the Weber–Trevor Roper theory. In those, T cannot be seen as a *true* theory (since the notion of truth can only be a limited notion) but it is a *highly valid* one. If we create a theory T' that is incommensurable with it, that validity will be impaired. It will also be impaired if we create a theory T'' that is *commensurable* with T and explains the set of data {D''} in such a way that it includes {D}, and in such a case T' can be replaced by T''. Trevor Roper's revision of Weber's theory is a case in point.

The question of the *validity* of theories is thus not unanswerable. Indeed, there is a precise analytical answer to it. Notions like the *validity*, *credibility* or *truth* of a theory can be rigorously defined. However, once the validity of a theory can be determined (ruling out the after all rather rare case of several incommensurable theories all providing an equally acceptable explanation of a set of data), we can make a judgement about the validity of the ideal schemata it uses. These latter can claim to be generally, but not universally, valid, a distinction which, as we have already seen, is very important. This means that they cannot be *ranked*, as theories in the strict sense of the word can. Thus a 'materialist' schema is no better or no worse than an 'idealist' schema, and there are times when neither is applicable. But the fact that it is impossible to ascribe validity to these schemata does not mean that we are in the realm of the arbitrary, since the important question is whether a theory T based on S includes an explanation of {D}, and except when incommensurable theories are involved it is not only defined, but can be answered precisely.

Here, as elsewhere, we must distinguish clearly between two concepts of knowledge, the sceptical on the one hand and the relativist and critical on the other. The former, which can manifest itself in various forms – nothing is certain, 'anything goes' (Feyerabend), 'the world is so complex that everything we can ultimately say about it is as likely to be true as anything else', 'it is true since I believe it', the purity and intensity of feeling as the criterion of truth – begets in fact every kind of dogmatism, since it allows of no distinction between arguments from authority and criteria of truth, and also permits every kind of confusion.

And yet, as Hegel points out, popular wisdom itself admits that it is only in the dark that all cats are black.

KNOWLEDGE, INTERESTS AND INTERPRETATIONS OF
SOCIAL CHANGE

In order to complete my task properly, I should have to deal with one more point. Since, however, that point would need a study to itself, I shall do no more than mention it here. What I am referring to is the influence of what we could vaguely call various kinds of 'social determinism' on theories of social change. How far is the way theories of social change have gone in the last few decades the result of certain social factors?

Taking up an old theme, the German sociologist Habermas sees knowledge, particularly in the social field, as being very much governed by interests.[31] This sociological view of knowledge has had no difficulty in finding an audience, for the intellectual climate has been favourable for it. Historical epistemology, and the work of Kuhn, Lakatos and Feyerabend in particular, has shown that scientific development, in the field of the exact sciences themselves, has been affected by social factors. The image of the disembodied seeker after truth by the application of the highly codified rules for its discovery has been replaced by that of the struggle for life in scientific society.[32] Popper had already put the notion of falsification in the place of that of truth. Lakatos points out that a theory that it is hard to square with the facts can be kept alive for a long time, and that the interests of researchers have something to do with this.[33] Feyerabend stresses that scientific theories can be 'incommensurable', that is, that for a time it may be difficult to decide empirically which is preferable.[34] When these things happen, *interests* – as well, of course, as extra-scientific *beliefs* – may play a decisive part in matters and help to explain why a scientist adheres to this or that theory.

If we cannot erase individual and categorical interests from the history of the natural sciences, should we not assume that they play an even bigger part in the social sciences, both because their rules are less codified and less unanimously accepted, and because the questions they raise have an existential value? I am convinced that we should beware of excessively clear-cut views here. Although interests do undeniably play a part, it is not a large enough one to rule out the notion of *objectivity* in either the natural or the social sciences. The part played by passions and interests in choosing the problems investigators address themselves to is certainly a fundamental one, and ideologies are a factor in their choice of frames of reference from which to construct their theories. Passions and interests may help to ensure that a theory has a wider audience than it deserves, or give it a general validity that it has no right to, or an inflated intellectual status, but *reality* always has the last word as long as the possibility of rational criticism and its rights are preserved.

An example will, I hope, be enough to illustrate my point. The theories of economic development that flourished in the 1950s and 1960s were undeniably linked to the conditions of the post-war 'world order'. The accelerated growth of 'Western' nations meant that they could release a regular surplus, and increased interdependence seemed inevitable. The obvious disparity between nations and the growth of national independence movements helped to establish the notions of the *Third World*, *development* and *underdevelopment* firmly. This meant that economists and sociologists were given, as the result of a demand that was frequently diffuse and sometimes specific, the task of trying to establish the causes of underdevelopment and to cure it. Both the circumstances and the way in which the question was posed encouraged the investigators to produce general theories of development and underdevelopment and to construct exogenous theories stressing, and hence justifying, the part played by foreign aid.

I believe that theories like those of the vicious circle of poverty or the stages of growth put forward by Rostow are not comprehensible if we do not take this context into account. We could go even further and state that the theories produced by economists at the time were largely conditioned by the role that was allotted them and the form of the questions put to them.

However, rational criticism retained its rights. After a time, it was noticed that development theories flew in the face of a certain number of indisputable facts, and their credibility gradually diminished.

In a general way, it is important to see that many conditional laws or tendencies that the social sciences have claimed to discover are in reality based on a bias towards a sociocentric view of events. It was the revolutionary periods in France that suggested to Comte and subsequently to Durkheim that humanity was moving towards a phase in which it would have no further use for the great religions. Weber was more perceptive, noting that in the most developed and 'materialistic' of industrial societies, the United States, a range of factors had in fact helped maintain the vitality of Protestantism. T. H. Marshall, basing his conclusions on the English experience, had thought that the extension of legal rights would inevitably be followed by that of political and social rights, in that order, whereas de Tocqueville, for his part, had clearly felt that extending social rights *could* lead to a 'gentle and protective' despotism, in other words to the *restriction* of political rights. And quite clearly it was his American experience that suggested to Parsons the hypothesis of the disappearance of the extended family. To put it more exactly, his 'law' reflected some impressions that one could have in the 1950s of the likely development of family structures in the United States.

Theories of social change are therefore in fact often *derivations*, in Pareto's sense of the word, and should be seen as a pseudo-scientific reflection of *sentiments*. More precisely, one could say that although they are based on experience, the conclusions they draw from it go too far, and the credibility ascribed to them is not only the result of the intrinsic quality of what they demonstrate, but also of the widespread nature of the feelings they reflect. That is why such derivations have a loose connection with reality and often assume perhaps not the form but certainly the function of rhetorical argument. That is why the same derivations can lead to contradictory conclusions. The vicious circle theory of poverty provides an example. For Nurkse, it was supposed to demonstrate the duty of the developed world to help the Third World by means of foreign aid. In Galbraith's work, the same law is expressed in a form which suggests that any increase in income triggers off forces that cancel it out and re-establish the previous level of deprivation and thus leads to the conclusion that foreign aid serves no purpose. What had happened was that in the intervening period a dominant sentiment had become recessive, and the dogma of exogenous development had been replaced by that of endogenous development.

A *history* of theories of social change would therefore insist that the specific and diffuse demands they have tried to respond to should be expressed in precise terms and that there should be a rigorous assessment of the effect of such demands on the theories.

It would also be necessary to study the influence of the natural sciences, or at least of the images and representations of them that the social sciences have adopted. The importance that in the social sciences is generally ascribed to the postulate of determinism is probably at least partly attributable to such images. The constant refusal to treat social phenomena as the result of the aggregation of individual actions can also probably be seen as the effect of a certain image of 'science' as a discipline in which there is no room for subjective phenomena.

But historical questions of this kind, despite their importance, can only be complementary to the critical questions we have tried to answer here. *Chance* and *subjectivity* are often rejected by the social sciences for reasons that a historical approach can help to illuminate, but it is also important to show that it is only if we give them their proper place that the social sciences can have any claim to objectivity, which implies, as Kant's still very relevant teaching tells us, identifying and rejecting questions to which there is no answer.

It is possible to analyse local and partial processes of development and draw up general but *formal* schemata that can be used in the analysis of real processes of change, modernization or development.

Notions like the (one true) theory of social evolution, development or change, on the other hand, designate composite wholes incorporating elements belonging to one or another of those categories and which cannot be seen as a unity.

This means that the only way of achieving unity is by means of the more often than not implicit addition of value judgements that in themselves cannot be objectively justified, even if they are the object of collective beliefs.

Epilogue:
the Snare of Realism

With Weber, Simmel was perhaps the pioneer of the social sciences with the most uncommitted, that is the least *ideological*, view of social change. He certainly saw that the occurrence of a combination or sequence AB could only be explained as the result of the aggregation of individual actions. If, however, those actions are to produce A and B either simultaneously or consecutively, a set of circumstances K must obtain. If that does not happen, or if it only partly happens, A may occur without B. At the microscopic level, A may be associated with B or with its opposite. In most cases, it is not even possible to say that the AB combination will necessarily occur more often than AB̄. The uncertainty involved in macroscopic combinations is obvious once we realize that they can only be produced by actions and by no means reflect the existence of natural laws. Simmel would certainly not have been surprised to learn that unemployment and inflation can vary in both direct and inverse ratio to each other, and that it does not make much sense to ask which happens most frequently.

On another basic question closely related to this, Simmel and Weber take up a position very different from that of many others, which is explained by their familiarity with Kantian thought. They more than anyone saw the snare of realism and the need for a rigorous distinction between explanatory models created by the observer and reality itself. That is the real meaning of Simmel's notion of formal sociology and Weber's concept of the ideal type. The relationship $y = ax + b$ is a *form* to the extent that until a and b have been given precise values it cannot be applied to any reality. Once they have, however, it can appropriately express certain real relationships.

The same is true of a 'model' like that of Hotelling in chapter 7. In itself, it does not apply to any particular reality, and in that sense

218

it is therefore *formal*. At the same time, it is *general*, since once empirical data have been fed into it – or, to express this in another way, once its parameters have been suitably defined – it can account for very diverse situations. It is also true of other types of explanatory models and in particular of the classical conceptual systems used in the social sciences. Tönnies's distinction between *Gemeinschaft* (community) and *Gesellschaft* (society) is thus a *formal* explanatory model, although of a different type from that of Hotelling.[1] In itself, it does not apply to any particular social reality, but is rather a directing idea enabling the investigator to take cognizance of the differences he may note when comparing both restricted groups and societies. In that sense, its level of generality is therefore high. However, it only becomes really meaningful and properly useable in comparisons between real groups or societies. Like Hotelling's model, its 'parameters' have to be adapted to the objects under consideration for that to happen. If they are not, and it is applied in its raw state, it becomes a vehicle for ideology and utopianism. All this is also true of the 'law' of the *tendential* fall in the rate of profits. Strictly speaking, it is not an empirical law but an explanatory model with parameters that have to be adapted to the situation for which an explanation is sought. If that is done, it shows that the profit rate can fall, rise or remain stable, all according to circumstances. In other words, it provides no grounds for any empirical conclusion or prediction.

The snare of realism, to which Simmel devoted a book,[2] lies in seeing what is a mere explanatory model as properties of real things, in confusing form and reality or, in Hegel's famous phrase, seeing the rational and the real as synonymous. It is not hard to illustrate these shifts. A realist interpretation of Hotelling's model leads to the (false) 'prediction' that in two-party systems, party programmes will necessarily have to be almost indistinguishable from each other and election results very close. A realist interpretation of the distinction Tönnies makes leads to a reification of the contrasts between communities and societies, a utopian view of traditional as distinct from modern societies, and an exaggeration of the harmony of the former and the contradictions of the latter. The notion of community suggested to Hoselitz,[3] for example, that traditional societies form such integrated units that change could only either be rejected (the 'stagnant' community) or cause upheavals that would bring about a loss of identity. A realist interpretation of the tendential fall in profit rates leads to the prophecy of the implosion of the capitalist system. All such interpretations lead then either to prophecies that are contradicted by reality or to utopian representations of change. Generally, the all-inclusive ideologies – such as Marxism, structuralism or functionalism – that the social sciences have produced are the result of the illusion of realism. Structuralism, for example, sees the structural/non-structural division in realist terms, and functionalism tends to take *analogies* (society/system, society/organization, and so on) for *identities*.

In addition, however, it is also important to see, as Simmel clearly suggests in his emphasis on the distinction between the *formal* and the *real*, that such explanatory models are not *in themselves* erroneous. The opposite is the case, and without them it would be impossible to explain social change. The difficulties only appear when they are interpreted in a realist way, as if they described real mechanisms or distinctions, without any perception that they do not apply to any particular object unless they are first adapted and made explicit.

As has been said, the snare of realism is not peculiar to the social sciences. Many of the arguments about Darwinism, for example, have come about because what is in fact an explanatory model has been subject to a realist interpretation. We should not forget that Popper himself had some hesitation as to whether Darwinian theory was 'metaphysical' or 'scientific' and was able to come to a decision only because he did not trouble to distinguish between a theory on the one hand and an explanatory model on the other. All Darwin's theory in fact tells us is what types of mechanism can be seen as operating in the evolution of species. If, however, we wish to explain the process for a given species over a given period, we have to feed the empirical or, if the term is preferred, historical data into the model. In other words, we have to take chance and contingency into account. The fact, for example, that a particular species was protected from competition in some protected ecological backwater may account for some particular development. In itself, however, the theory does not allow of empirical conclusions. There is no need to stress the fact that when it is interpreted in realist terms it may lead to all kinds of airy predictions (such as social Darwinism) and disputable reasoning, as shown by the fact that it is frequently criticized for being tautologous.

The illusion of realism is so deeply rooted in the social sciences (and elsewhere) because it is an essential device in the creation of ideologies.

Properly interpreted – that is, in a formal and not a realist way – the explanatory models provided by the social sciences are indispensable tools for the understanding of reality. Their effectiveness, however, does not come from any rejection of the claims of diversity, contingency and disorder, but from the fact that they *preserve* them. Refusing to recognize them is an essential feature of ideological thought.

There is a third point upon which sociologists who accept the traditional sociologies of action agree, namely that only defined, and consequently partial, processes can be scientifically explained. Here, the Kantian inspiration is once more evident, since the *Prolegomena* maintains that although science has no boundaries (*Grenzen*), it is only possible to engage in it if we recognize its limits (*Schranken*).

It is no doubt largely because it sets very strict limits to the desire to create general theories in the field of social investigation and even to discover empirical regularities of general relevance that the paradigm of the action frame of reference in sociology, although fertile, is permanently opposed to other paradigms.

Lastly, a fundamental point emerges from the methodological enquiry I have endeavoured to conduct. An analysis of the processes of change can only meet the criteria for scientific rigour as defined by Popper and others before him if the ideal model of knowledge with which I have associated Weber's name can be applied. I cannot see how it would be possible to reject such criteria without rejecting any distinction between scientific and other forms of knowledge. And the Weberian model can only be applied to defined and partial processes, in the technical sense I have given to that notion. Once we leave that framework behind, we abandon the area of certainty and enter that of conjecture and plausibility. Conjectural and plausible theories are not necessarily without practical or scientific interest, but we have to be aware of what might be called their *logical status*. It is also important to distinguish between *formal* theories providing ideal schemata that can serve as a basis for constructing *stricto sensu* theories and those theories themselves.

One of the fundamental aims of both the philosophy of knowledge and 'methodology' is to determine what, in processes of knowledge, falls to the knowing subject and what to the object of his knowledge. At one of the poles of the continuum that the two terms enable us to create, there are those theories constructed in such a way as to be capable of unambiguous confirmation, or at least refutation, by reality. At the other, there are those which, like Feyerabend, we could call 'fairy tales'. Between the two extremities, all kinds of intermediate cases are possible. The main aim of the philosophy of knowledge – methodology – is to determine the right place for all these theories. Its importance is more crucial in the analysis of social change than in any other area. This is because of the influence theories of social change exert in practice or, in Pareto's words, because of their 'utility'. It is precisely because of this influence that they are endemically threatened by the snare of realism.

Once that particular trap closes, structures are confused with essences and ideal models with 'tendential' laws; it is forgotten that 'structures' occur only within the context of conjunctural data; local and contingent regularities are seen as universal and necessary; ideal categories and real distinctions are given the same status and no distinctions are made between *general* moels and *universal* laws or empirical and formal consequences. The ability of the social sciences to predict is overestimated, explanation and forecasting are not seen as separate activities, that is, as notions that imply each other only if explanation is defined as a process in which individual facts are subsumed under general laws. Although they have added a great deal to our knowledge of the flow of history, the theories of social change produced in recent decades have largely fallen into the trap of realism because, like nineteenth-century philosophies of history, they failed to take distinctions of this kind into consideration. The doubts that they now arouse perhaps create a favourable setting for a return to a critical reflection on the limits of knowledge in the area of the macroscopic changes affecting societies.

It must of course also be stressed – it is one of the themes of this book – that the only possible basis for a scientific analysis of social change is methodological individualism, the principle that defines sociologies of action. This holds good whether it is small-scale changes, such as those in organizations, or macroscopic changes, that is, those which tendentially affect societies as a whole, that are the object of analysis. It is also true whatever *type* of society is being investigated. As both the examples considered above and many others that could be elaborated show, the principle of methodological individualism can be applied equally effectively to the analysis of social change in modern India, traditional Japan or pre-Revolutionary France or in industrial societies. It is also just as appropriate for the study of, for example, ideological or religious as it is for that of political or economic phenomena.

The last point I wish to stress is that theories of social change often have the status of *models* or *formal theories*. These make up a corpus whose importance for our understanding of the flow of history is so great and whose epistemological specificity is so unimpeachable that they explain why the notion of social change, like that of history, has proved necessary. They also demonstrate why the social sciences are not doomed to be restricted to either the study of one-off phenomena or to a purely nomological role.

The notion of social change is indeed both a familiar and a puzzling one. Why and how has it come to mean a recognized scientific specialism when, in fact, 'social change' is directly or indirectly studied in every branch of every social science? How is it that there is apparently no readily understandable *conceptual* equivalent of an institution that is nowadays generally accepted and recognized? To return to our first question, what distinguishes 'social change' from 'history'?

Basically, there are three possible concepts of the knowledge of 'science' in the social field. The first is the *empiricist* concept. When applied to the analysis of social change, it corresponds to what in late nineteenth-century Germany was called *historicism*. For historicists, the highest form of historical knowledge was the description of past developments or changes as they had actually occurred, *'wie sie eigentlich geschehen sind'*, to use Ranke's famous phrase once more. Historicists do not look for regularities where there are none, and will not say whether there are trends, rhythms or cycles in history. They do not concern themselves with asking whether the great changes in it are brought about by, for example, changes in the conditions of production, as Marx thought, or rather by changes in values, as Weber was to suggest.

The second basic concept that the student of certain historical processes might adopt could be described as *nomological*. The historicist aims above all to describe reality in its concrete complexity. The most he will admit is that one needs to simplify the mass of observational data for the purposes of research and exposition. They need organizing and, in short, fitting into a narrative that cannot but be linear. Those who accept the nomological concept, however, will try to establish trends, regularities, cycles, laws governing which phenomena follow others, covariations between series, causal links between factors, everything, in short, that could be called in general terms *macroscopic* or *structural regularities* within historical reality.

We can, however, also distinguish a third basic type of concept, project or programme which we could call a *formal* or *hypothesizing and deductive concept*, unless the term is too learned. This simply means that here the mode of production of knowledge consists of using *hypotheses* as a basis for *deducing* consequences and using the *model* thus created to explain, illustrate or understand reality. The concept *may*, but need not necessarily, take a mathematical form. Mathematical language is sometimes indispensable if we wish to establish what the consequences of certain systems of hypotheses are, but not always. Mathematical deductions are therefore no more than an example.

This means that a rapid survey of what we call the social sciences will show us that although it is not always easy to distinguish them from history at the *factual* level, they nevertheless deserve the *autonomy* they are generally agreed to have at the *theoretical* or *conceptual* level. The justification for this autonomy lies in the fact that they have identified perspectives (or 'programmes' to use the language of Lakatos, the philosopher of science) which they apply systematically but historians use only occasionally, admitting when they do that they have borrowed them from the social sciences.

A quite fundamental reason for the linguistic fact of the very existence and now customary character of the notion of social change therefore seems to me to lie in such distinctions, for the social sciences have long made frequent use of *concepts* and *modes* of explanation that are not common in history as a traditional discipline. Consequently, when we talk of *social change* rather than of history we mean that we intend to analyse the flow of history in one or another of its aspects in terms of a *perspective* or according to a *programme* proper to the social sciences, namely in terms of either a *nomological* or a *formal* perspective. When de Tocqueville tells us in the first sentence of his *Ancien Régime* that he is not writing a work of *history*, we must take it as an indication of his extreme perspicacity. What he is suggesting is what later writers such as Weber and Simmel were to state more fully and explicitly, namely that a historical object can be apprehended in terms of *programmes* and *perspectives* quite different from those of traditional history, and in particular that it is in such activities that hypothesizing and deductive methods have their place.

The two most characteristic programmes in the social sciences – the *nomological* and the *formal* – are obviously quite distinct from each other. That is clear from the fact that 'law' has a different meaning in each of them. Within a nomological programme, it means a statement about a regular pattern, and in this context we could talk about a law in the sense the word has in, for example, 'Kepler's laws'. On the other hand, Ricardo's famous 'law of comparative advantages' could better be described as a theorem, since it describes a consequence deduced from a hypothesizing and deductive system. Thus, *social change* exists, since there is a considerable body of research following one or other of the programmes I have described.

It must also be noted, however, that as the mention of historicism indicates, there are three doctrines that correspond to the three programmes, once the latter begin to claim monopoly satus for themselves. When the 'experimental' and 'formal' programmes are seen as possessed of neither interest nor justification, we have the classical attitude of historicism. The first instance of this was amongst the classical German historicists, but it is still present in many of our contemporaries. Nisbet's book *Social Change and History* is ultimately no more in both its content and its argument than a fairly traditional historicist manifesto.

When the 'experimental' programme claims to rule out its 'formal' counterpart, we have another doctrine, which could be described as naturalism. The classical representative of it is Durkheim, whose view was, for example, that the models traditionally used in economics and also political philosophy are of the stuff of abstraction, speculation or metaphysics. Despite the differences between their economic theories, Marx, Ricardo and the Austrian marginalists all used hypothesizing and deductive models to analyse economic reality. In so doing, they were applying to economics a method that had been straightforwardly used in political philosophy by both Rousseau and Hobbes. Durkheim's own view was that sociology was a discipline with a great future precisely because – according to the programme he himself intended to establish for it – it would break with the 'speculative' methods of economics. To his mind, the development of sociology was an indication that the social sciences were moving out of their *metaphysical* and into their positive phase. Nor was he joking when he announced that sociology was called upon to relegate 'old-fashioned' economics to the museum, so natural did Comte's evolutionist attitude seem to him.

There is no logical necessity about this view of things, and indeed the classic German sociologists like Max Weber, Simmel and Sombart consider that the model method is just as relevant in sociology as in economics. When he spoke of 'formal sociology' Simmel was indicating that his aim was to do in sociology what had been so successfully achieved in economics. In fact, the view of science that lies behind Durkheim's concept of sociology as a *break* is a very particular one.

There is also, of course, a dogmatic attitude corresponding to the 'formal' programme. We can see it in Marx, for instance, who thought that the consequences his models implied for him were destined to occur in the real world. Just as Durkheim had inherited a certain concept of *science* from Comte, Marx never rid himself of the Hegelian principle that the real is rational. These references to classical examples are indispensable if we are to understand both the interest and the *ambiguities* of modern research connected with 'social change'.

The social sciences have very often thought it necessary, in the attempt to achieve a justification they did not need, to proclaim their ability to *predict*. This was particularly true in the two or three decades after the Second World War, that euphoric period when it was thought that we could control 'social change' in exactly the same way as an engineer can control the way a physical system develops. That particular illusion was very widespread at the time. The 'technical' nature of the models used made them credible and prestigious, and – we thought – all we needed to do to turn them into something else, that is, forecasting instruments, was to interpret them in the realist manner.

When, after a period of regular growth, the world induced in us once more a sense of chaos and social change no longer seemed destined to follow a regular course, this modification of our sentiments brought about a different way of seeing the social sciences. They had assumed that the world was rational, and now it no longer seemed to be. Indeed, reality now seemed impervious to the efforts of reason, and the only discipline capable of describing it was history, what Simiand called 'historicizing history'. In short, we were in a new intellectual situation that brought back the old *historicism* and had no time for all those theories of social change. There was nothing but the flow of history in all its complexity.

The earlier historicism, that of Ranke, had brought about remarkable attempts in the field of epistemological reflection, which led finally to the neo-Kantian perspective adopted by Weber and Simmel that was to send 'historians' and 'Hegelians' off in opposite directions. In our attempts to understand the social field and in particular social change, we must – or at least it is useful to do so – proceed by means of constructing *models*. But it is important that we do not interpret them in the realist manner, that we do not assume that they have a power to predict when the truth is that they have none, for reality is always wider than rationality, especially when it is a question of those particularly complex matters, social phenomena. For it is an illusion to think that we can reach the complexity of the real as such, and that is why the constructs we call models are indispensable tools of knowledge. It is also why reality cannot be contained in them.

Notes

FOREWORD

[1] J. K. Galbraith, *The Nature of Mass Poverty*, Cambridge, Mass., and London, Harvard University Press, 1979, for whom any increase in income triggers off forces which cancel it out and re-establish the previous level of deprivation.
[2] K. Popper, *The Poverty of Historicism*, London, Routledge and Kegan Paul, 1957.

1 THEORIES OF SOCIAL CHANGE

[1] R. Nisbet, *Social Change and History*, New York, Oxford University Press, 1969.
[2] G. Lenski, 'History and Social Change', *American Journal of Sociology*, LXXXII, 3, 1976, 548–64.
[3] H. Spencer, 'Progress: Its Law and Causes' in his *Essays*, vol. I, London, Williams and Norgate, 1868. L. T. Hobhouse, *Social Evolution and Political Theory*, New York, Columbia University Press, 1911; Washington, Kennikat Press, 1968.
[4] M. Sahlins and E. Service (eds), *Evolution and Culture*, Ann Arbor, University of Michigan Press, 1960.
[5] J. Piaget, *Main Trends in Interdisciplinary Research*, London, George Allen and Unwin, 1973, originally published as chapter 1 in *Main Trends of Research in the Social Sciences*, Paris, Unesco, The Hague, Mouton, 1970-8.
[6] R. Nisbet, *The Sociological Tradition*, New York, Basic Books, 1966.
[7] G. Lenski, *Power and Privilege. A Theory of Social Stratification*, New York, McGraw Hill, 1966.
[8] R. Nisbet, *History of the Idea of Progress*, New York, Basic Books, 1980.
[9] J. Schumpeter, *History of Economic Analysis*, Oxford, Oxford University Press, 1954, pp. 135 ff.
[10] G. Simmel, *The Problems of the Philosophy of History*, New York, The Free Press, 1977. R. Aron, *La philosophie critique de l'histoire*, Paris, Vrin, 1950. English translation: *Introduction to the Philosophy of History: An Essay on the Limits of Historical Objectivity*, London, Weidenfeld and Nicholson, 1961.

[11] I. Lakatos, 'Falsification and the Methodology of Scientific Research Programs' in I. Lakatos and A. Musgrave (eds), *Criticism and the Growth of Knowledge*, Cambridge, Cambridge University Press, 1970, pp. 91-196.

[12] K. Popper, *The Poverty of Historicism*, London, Routledge and Kegan Paul, 1957.

[13] W. W. Rostow, *The Stages of Economic Growth*, Cambridge, Cambridge University Press, 2nd edn, 1971.

[14] See for example D. Loschky and W. Wilcox, 'Demographic Transition: a Forcing Model', *Demography*, XI, 1974, 215-25.

[15] R. Dahrendorf, *Class and Class Conflict*, London, Routledge and Kegan Paul, 1959.

[16] S. M. Lipset, 'The Limits of Social Science', *Public Opinion*, October-November 1981, 2-9.

[17] A. de Tocqueville, *L'Ancien Régime et la Révolution*, Paris, Gallimard, 1952, t. II, vol. 1, p. 69. English translation: *The Ancien Régime and the Revolution*, London, Fontana, 1971.

[18] Ibid., 222-3.

[19] J. Davies, 'Towards a Theory of Revolution', *American Sociological Review*, 27, 1962, 5-19.

[20] E. Durkheim, *Suicide*, London, Routledge and Kegan Paul, 1952.

[21] M. Jahoda, P. Lazarsfeld and H. Zeisel, *Marienthal: The Sociography of an Unemployed Community*, Chicago, Aldine, 1971.

[22] P. Feyerabend, *Against Method: Outline of an Anarchistic Theory of Knowledge*, London, JLB, 1975.

[23] T. Parsons, 'Some Considerations on the Theory of Social Change' in S. N. Eisenstadt (ed.), *Readings in Social Evolution and Development*, Oxford, Pergamon, 1970, pp. 95-139.

[24] Cf. chapter 4.

[25] T. Kuhn, *The Structure of Scientific Revolutions*, Chicago, University of Chicago Press, 1970.

[26] M. Crozier, *La société bloquée*, Paris, Le Seuil, 1970. English translation: *The Stalled Society*, New York, Viking Press, 1973.

[27] M. Weber, *The Protestant Ethic and the Spirit of Capitalism*, London, George Allen and Unwin, 1976, especially chapter 5.

[28] D. McClelland, *The Achieving Society*, Princeton, D. van Nostrand Co., 1961; New York, The Free Press, 1967.

[29] G. A. Cohen, *Karl Marx's Theory of Society. A Defence*, Oxford, Clarendon Press, 1978.

[30] L. White, *Medieval Technology and Social Change*, Oxford, Clarendon Press, 1962; *The Science of Culture*, New York, Grove, 1949.

[31] See, for example, the discussion on the 'autonomy' of the state in B. Badie and P. Birnbaum, *Sociologie de l'état*, Paris, Grasset, 1979.

[32] R. Nurkse, *Les problèmes de la formation de capital dans les pays sous-développés*, Paris, Institut pour le Développement Economique, 1963.

[33] M. Piore and S. Berger, *Dualism and Discontinuity in Industrial Societies*, Cambridge, Cambridge University Press, 1980.

[34] T. H. Marshall, *Citizenship and Social Class and other Essays*, Cambridge, Cambridge University Press, 1950.

[35] H. and R. Lynd, *Middletown: A Study in American Culture*, New York, Harcourt Brace, 1930.

[36] R. and H. Lynd, *Middletown in Transition*, New York, Harcourt Brace and World, 1937.

[37] T. Caplow, quoted in *L'Année Sociologique*, 32, 1982, 9–22. Translated by J. C. Whitehouse.

[38] H. Simon, 'The Architecture of Complexity', *General Systems*, I, 1965, 63–76; R. Todd La Porte (ed.), *Organized Social Complexity*, Princeton, Princeton University Press, 1975; E. Morin, *La Méthode*, t. 1, *La nature de la nature*, Paris, Le Seuil, 1977.

[39] R. Boudon, 'Theories, theory and Theory' in *The Crisis in Sociology*, London, Macmillan, 1980, pp. 149–94.

2 INDIVIDUAL ACTION, AGGREGATION EFFECTS AND SOCIAL CHANGE

[1] J. Coleman, E. Katz and H. Menzel, *Medical Innovation. A Diffusion Study*, New York, Bobbs-Merrill, 1966.

[2] This is so as the model is worked out exponentially, with a negative variable in the exposition.

[3] For a more complex example of a case in which the cost of finding information is socially expensive, see the classic study by G. C. Homans, 'Social Behavior as Exchange', *American Journal of Sociology*, LXIII, 6, 1958, 597–606.

[4] The speed of the process at a given point in time tends towards zero when the number of converts is close to the total number involved.

[5] On the decisive part played by interpersonal influence in the credibility an actor allots to impersonal messages, see the classic study by E. Katz and P. Lazarsfeld, *Personal Influence. The Part played by People in the Flow of Mass Communications*, New York, The Free Press and London, Collier Macmillan, 1955 and 1956 respectively.

[6] This is what Popper calls falsification.

[7] See my *The Logic of Sociological Explanation*, Harmondsworth, Penguin, 1974.

[8] W. Sombart, *Why is there no Socialism in the United States?*, London, Macmillan, 1976.

[9] A. de Tocqueville, *L'Ancien Régime et la Révolution*, Paris, Gallimard, 1952, chapter IX, pp. 149–51; chapter XII, pp. 179–80. English translation: *The Ancien Régime and the Revolution*, London, Fontana, 1971.

[10] K. Popper, *Objective Knowledge*, Oxford, Clarendon Press, 1972.

[11] W. Doise, *L'Explication en psychologie sociale*, Paris, Presses Universitaires de France, 1982.

[12] Cf. R. Boudon (ed.), *Unintended Consequences of Social Action*, London, Macmillan, 1982.

[13] H. Simon, 'Rationality and Administrative Decision Making' in *Models of Man*, part IV, pp. 196 to end.

[14] H. Lévy-Garbous, 'L'économique et le rationnel', *L'Année Sociologique*, 31, 1981, 19–47.

[15] In the language of games theory, strategy games with sub-optimal equilibrium.

[16] V. Pareto, *The Mind of Society: a Treatise on General Sociology*, New York, Dover Books, 1973, vol. XXII, §159.

[17] Ibid.

[18] For Pareto, any action falling outside the means/ends system (such as reflex actions) or characterized by an inadequacy of means to ends is non-logical.

[19] See, for example, Y. Barzel and E. Silverberg, 'Is the act of voting rational?', *Public Choice*, XVL, Autumn 1973, 51-8.

[20] A. Downs, *An Economic Theory of Democracy*, New York, Harper, 1957.

[21] M. Weber, *Economy and Society*, part I, chapter I, 'The Definitions of Sociology and Social Action', New York, Bedminster Press, 1968.

[22] S. Epstein, *Economic Development and Social Change in South India*, Manchester, Manchester University Press, 1962.

[23] P. Berger, *Pyramids of Sacrifice: Political Ethics and Social Change*, New York, Doubleday, 1974.

[24] This is the paradox so well described by Hardin, 'The Tragedy of Commons' in G. Hardin and J. Baden (eds), *Managing the Commons*, San Francisco, W. H. Freeman, 1977.

[25] A. Degenne finds in his 'Une méthodologie douce en sociologie', *L'Année sociologique*, 31, 1981, 97-124, that it is helpful to use an interpretation that takes into account the strategic resources determined by the situation of the actor rather than one based on a class *ethos*.

[26] Or to his preferences. Generally speaking, a statement like 'I prefer X to Y' clearly cannot be refuted by an observer.

[27] Letter from M. Weber to R. Liefmann (1920). Since the letter is to a marginalist economist well known at the time, the 'too' refers to economics. It is important to note that methodological individualism did not start with Hayek. Indeed, it had great influence on all the social sciences in Austria and Germany at the end of the nineteenth century. It was perhaps the First World War which, in a way which hardly matched Kuhn's views, pushed this paradigm into the background.

[28] This is the interpretation put forward by G. Le Bon in his *La Psychologie des foules*, Paris, Fayard, 1981, and taken up again by S. Moscovici in *The Age of the Crowd*, Cambridge, Cambridge University Press, 1985.

[29] Letter to R. Liefmann, 1920.

[30] F. Tönnies, *Community and Society*, New York, Harper, 1963.

[31] R. Redfield, 'The Folk Society', *American Journal of Sociology*, LII, 4, 1947, 293-308.

[32] S. Popkin, *The Rational Peasant*, Berkeley, University of California Press, 1979.

[33] J. Buchanan and G. Tullock, *The Calculus of Consent*, Ann Arbor, University of Michigan Press, 1962.

[34] The 'spider's web' theorem. The cyclical effect occurs when the parameters have certain values.

[35] T. Schelling, *Micromotives and Macrobehaviour*, New York, Norton, 1978.

[36] R. Boudon, 'The Logic of Relative Frustration', in *Unintended Consequences of Social Action*, pp. 105-126.

[37] This is Condorcet's paradox. Cf. G. Th. Guilbaud, 'Les théories de l'intérêt général et le problème logique de l'agrégation', *Économie Appliquée*, V, 4, 1952,

501-51. Reprinted in G. Th. Guilbaud, *Eléments de la théorie mathématique des jeux*, Paris, Dunod, 1968, pp. 39-109.

38 R. Boudon, *Education, Opportunity and Social Inequality*, New York, Wiley, 1974.

39 Ibid. This is Anderson's paradox. Cf. C. Thélot, *Tel père, tel fils*, Paris, Dunod, 1982.

40 A. Hirschman, *Exit, Voice and Loyalty: Responses to Decline in Firms, Organizations and States*, Cambridge, Mass., Harvard University Press, 1970.

41 R. Boudon, 'The Freudian-Marxian-Structuralist (FMS) movement in France: variations on a theme by Sherry Turkle', in *Revue Tocqueville*, II, 1, Winter 1980, 5-24; 'L'intellectuel et ses publics: les singularités françaises', in J. D. Reynaud and Y. Grafmeyer, *Français, qui êtes-vous?*, Paris, Documentation française, 1981, pp. 465-80.

42 C. Baudelot, *L'évolution individuelle des salaires, 1970-5*, Collections de l'INSEE, série M, October 1983.

43 Here too it is important to note that old ideas are often disguised in new clothes, which often create a perfect illusion of novelty. Comte used the expression 'retrograde' for what in the 1950s we were calling 'reactionary', and in the 1970s and 1980s we now talk of 'resistance to change'. In the 1950s, we talked of '*conscience reflex*' and now in the 1980s we prefer the term 'habitus', but both expressions contain the essential idea, and both postulate a basic immanent relationship between the individual and society.

44 To remove any risk of confusion, it should be noted that the notion of a 'sociology of action' as used here maintains a simple relationship of form with the same notion as used by Alain Touraine who uses it to indicate the analysis of 'social movements' seen as transmitting 'historicity'.

3 THE LAWS GOVERNING CHANGE: THE NOMOLOGICAL BIAS

1 H. Mendras, *La fin des paysans*, Paris, Sedeis, 1967.

2 As Weber points out. Cf. his essay on some categories of comprehensive sociology in *Economy and Society*, vol. I, Berkeley University of California Press, 1978.

3 On the notion of theory in the social sciences, see R. Boudon, *The Crisis in Sociology*, London, Macmillan, 1980.

4 Cf. G. Simmel, *Grundfragen der Soziologie*, G. J. Göschen, Berlin and Leipzig, 1917. English translation: *Essays on Sociology, Philosophy and Aesthetics*, K. H. Wolff (ed.), Columbus, Ohio, Ohio State University Press, 1958.

5 G. Tarde, *The Laws of Imitation*, Gloucester, Mass., Peter Smith, 1962.

6 D. Snyder and C. Tilly, 'Hardship and Collective Violence in France', *American Sociological Review*, XXXVII, 1972, 520-32.

7 A. Oberschall, *Social Conflict and Social Movements*, Englewood Cliffs, Prentice Hall, 1973.

8 'When a situation is defined as real, it entails real consequences.'

9 Oberschall, *Social Conflict and Social Movements*, p. 221.

10 'Ups and Downs with Ecology, the Issue-attention Cycles', *The Public Interest*, 28, Summer 1972, 38-50.

[11] C. Tilly, *From Mobilization to Revolution*, London, Addison-Wesley, 1978.

[12] J. Davies, 'Towards a Theory of Revolution', *American Sociological Review*, 27, 1962, 5-19.

[13] T. Gurr, *Why Men Rebel*, Princeton, Princeton University Press, 1970.

[14] A. Marchal, *L'action ouvrière et la transformation du régime capitaliste*, Paris, Librairie générale de Droit et de Jurisprudence, 1943.

[15] M. Olson, *The Process of Social Organization*, New York, Holt, Rinehart and Winston, 1968.

[16] A. Hirschman, *Exit, Voice and Loyalty*, Cambridge, Mass., Harvard University Press, 1970.

[17] Cf. Badie, *Le développement politique*, Paris, Economica, 1980. S. N. Eisenstadt (ed.), *Readings in Social Evolution*, Oxford, Pergamon, 1970.

[18] E. Vogel, 'Kinship Structure, Migration to the City, and Modernization' in R. P. Dore (ed.), *Aspects of Social Change in Modern Japan*, Princeton, Princeton University Press, 1967, pp. 91-111.

[19] P. T. Bauer, *Dissent of Development*, London, Fakenham and Reading, 1971, lists and criticizes a considerable number of these laws.

[20] R. Nurkse, *Les problèmes de la formation du capital dans les pays sous-développés*, Paris, Institut pour le Développement Economique, 1963.

[21] E. Hagen, *On the Theory of Social Change*, Homewood, Ill., Dorsey Press, 1962.

[22] The ideology of development by means of foreign aid is discussed by P. T. Bauer, 'Foreign Aid and the Third World' in P. Duignan and A. Rabushka (eds), *The United States in the 1980s*, Stanford, Hoover, 1980.

[23] Hagen, *On the Theory of Social Change*.

[24] Hagen is aware of the difficulty and tries to get round it by using projective tests.

[25] For example I. Kraus, 'Educational aspirations among working-class youth', *American Sociological Review*, XXIX, 1964, 867-79.

[26] L. Feuer, *Einstein et le conflit des générations*, Brussels, Ed. Complexe, 1978.

[27] C. Hempel, *Aspects of Scientific Explanation and other Essays in the Philosophy of Sciences*, New York, The Free Press, 1965.

4 STRUCTURES AND CHANGE: THE STRUCTURALIST BIAS

[1] R. Boudon, *The Uses of Structuralism*, London, Heinemann, 1971.

[2] R. Aron, *D'une sainte famille à l'autre. Essai sur les marxismes imaginaires*, Paris, Gallimard, 1969.

[3] A. Touraine, *Le mouvement de mai ou le communisme utopique*, Paris, Le Seuil, 1968.

[4] To use the terms employed by F. Bourricaud, *Le bricolage idéologique*, Paris, PUF, 1980.

[5] D. Bell, *The Coming of Post-industrial Society*, New York, Basic Books, 1973.

[6] C. Waxman (ed.), *The End of Ideology Debate*, New York, Simon and Schuster, 1968.

[7] D. Bell, *The End of Ideology*, Glencoe, The Free Press, 1960, rev. edn, 1965.

[8] Bourricaud, *Le bricolage idéologique*.

[9] M. Sadoun, 'Les facteurs de la conversion au socialisme collaborateur', *Revue française de science politique*, XXVIII, 3, 459-87; *Les socialistes sous l'occupation*, Paris, Presses de la fondation nationale des sciences politiques, 1982.

[10] S. Epstein, *Economic Development and Social Change in South India*, Manchester, Manchester University Press, 1962.

[11] M. Mead, *Cultural Patterns and Technological Change*, Paris, Unesco, 1953.

[12] B. F. Hoselitz and W. E. Moore, *Industrialization and Society*, Paris, UNESCO and The Hague, Mouton, 1963.

[13] G. Dhoquois, *Pour l'histoire*, Paris, Anthropos, 1971.

[14] A. Bhaduri, 'A Study of Agricultural Backwardness under Semi-feudalism', *Economic Journal*, LXXXIII, 329, 1976, 20-137. In *The Logic of Social Action*, I offered an analysis of this study that I could not elaborate because of the introductory nature of the book. I hope that the present work will answer some of the objections raised in some excellent articles, namely: P. Bénéton, 'Logique et pregnance au social chez Boudon', *Revue Tocqueville*, III, 1, 1980-1, 119-136; D. Swartz, 'Classes, Educational Systems and Labor Markets', *Archives européennes de sociologie*, XXII, 1981, 325-53; P. V. Parijs, 'Sociology as General Economics', ibid., 299-324; P. Favre, 'Nécessaire mais non suffisante: la sociologie des "effets pervers" de Raymond Boudon', *Revue française de science politique*, XXX, 6, 1980, 1229-70.

[15] A. Rapoport and M. Guyer, 'A taxonomy of 2×2 games', *General Systems*, XI, 1966, 205-14.

[16] A minor effect on productivity and a moderate reaction from the tenants is enough to give rise to a non-co-operative game.

[17] Cf. R. D. Juce and H. Raiffa, *Games and Decisions. Introduction and Critical Survey*, New York, Wiley, 1957.

[18] Although it is difficult in this type of situation. Cf. S. Popkin, *The Rational Peasant*, Berkeley, University of California Press, 1979.

5 THE SEARCH FOR THE PRIME MOVER: THE ONTOLOGICAL BIAS

[1] R. Ash Garner, *Social Change*, Chicago, Rand McNally College Publishing Company, 1977.

[2] Cf., for example, K. Boulding, *Ecodynamics*, London, Sage, 1978.

[3] A. Touraine, *The May Movement: Revolt and Reform*, New York, Irvington, 1979; *Production de la société*, Paris, Seuil, 1973.

[4] T. Parsons, 'The Role of Ideas in Social Action' in *Essays in Sociological Theory*, New York, The Free Press, 1954, pp. 19-33.

[5] Garner, *Social Change*.

[6] This is particularly true of Nisbet, who takes up the classical historicist position, despite Simmel's definitive demonstration of its inconsistency.

[7] These propositions do not clash with M. Cherkaoui's interpretation in 'Changement social et anomie; essai de formalisation de la théorie durkheimienne', *Archives européennes de sociologie*, XXIII, 1981, 3-39.

[8] L. Coser, *The Functions of Social Conflict*, London, Routledge and Kegan Paul, 1956.

9 K. Marx, *The Poverty of Philosophy* in K. Marx and F. Engels, *Collected Works*, vol. 6, London, Lawrence and Wishart, 1976, p. 174.

10 R. Nisbet, *The Sociological Tradition*, New York, Basic Books, 1966, clearly demonstrates the importance of the influence of the *Aufklärung* on Marx.

11 Marx, *The Poverty of Philosophy*, p. 162.

12 Ibid., pp. 152-3.

13 Ibid., p. 185.

14 Ibid., p. 174.

15 J. M. Keynes, *A Treatise on Money*. London, Macmillan, 1953.

16 Marx, *The Poverty of Philosophy*, p. 185.

17 D. Legros, 'Chance, Necessity, and Mode Production: a Marxist Critique of Cultural Evolutionism', *American Anthropologist*, LXXIX, 1977, 26-41.

18 G. Hardin, 'The Cybernetics of Competition: a Biologist's View of Society', in P. Shepard and D. McKinley, *The Subversive Science. Essays toward an Ecology of Man*, Boston, Houghton Mifflin, 1969, pp. 275-96.

19 C. Baudelot, R. Establet and J. Malemort, *La petite bourgeoisie en France*, Paris, Maspero, 1975.

20 M. Verret, 'Pour une définition distinctive de la classe ouvrière', *Année sociologique*, 31, 1981, 49-68.

21 J. Karabel and A. H. Halsey (eds), *Power and Ideology in Education*, New York, Oxford University Press, 1977.

22 D. C. McClelland, *The Achieving Society*, Princeton, D. Van Nostrand Co., 1961; New York, The Free Press, 1967.

23 M. Foucault, *The Order of Things*, London, Tavistock Publications, 1970.

24 R. P. Dore, *Land Reform in Japan*, London, Oxford University Press, 1959.

25 A. O. Hirschman, *Journeys toward Progress*, New York, Norton, The Twentieth Century Fund, 1973, chapter 1.

26 T. Kuhn, *The Structure of Scientific Revolutions*, Chicago, University of Chicago Press, 1970.

27 J. Baechler, *The Origins of Capitalism*, Oxford, Basil Blackwell, 1975.

28 E. Durkheim, *Suicide*, London, Routledge and Kegan Paul, 1952.

29 T. Parsons, 'A Revised Analytical Approach to the Theory of Social Stratification' in *Essays in Sociological Theory*, New York, The Free Press, 1954, pp. 386-439.

30 Not only Marxists subscribe to this theory, of course.

31 G. Almond and S. Verba, *The Civic Culture*, Princeton, Princeton University Press, 1963.

32 This is true of E. Hagen, *On the Theory of Social Change*, Homewood, Ill., Dorsey Press, 1962.

33 A. Percheron, 'Les études américaines sur les phénomènes de socialisation politique dans l'impasse?', *Année sociologique*, 31, 1981, 69-96.

34 H. R. Trevor Roper, *Religion, The Reformation and Social Change and other essays*, London, Macmillan, 1967.

35 E. R. Wolf, 'The Study of Evolution' in S. N. Eisenstadt (ed.), *Readings in Social Evolution and Development*, Oxford, Pergamon, 1970, pp. 179-91.

36 R. K. Merton, *Social Theory and Social Structure*, New York, The Free Press, 1968.

6   A WELL-TEMPERED DETERMINISM

[1] R. Thom, 'Halte au hasard, silence au bruit', *Le Débat*, 3, July-August 1980, 119–32. See also the thorough review by J. Largeaut, 'Observations sur l'ordre et le déterminisme', ibid., September 1981, 102–6, which also stresses the complexity of Thom's position.

[2] M. Crozier, *The Bureaucratic Phenomenon*, London, Tavistock Publications, 1964, and J.-L. Peaucelle, 'Théorie des jeux et sociologie des organisations', *Sociologie du travail*, XI, 1969, 22–43.

[3] That is to say, there is another theoretically possible solution that would be unanimously preferred by the participants.

[4] See chapters 4 and 5.

[5] R. Linton, 'Cultural and Personality Factors affecting Economic Growth' in B. Hoselitz (ed.), *The Progress of Underdeveloped Areas*, Chicago, University of Chicago Press, 1952, pp. 73–88.

[6] L. White, *Medieval Technology and Social Change*, Oxford, Clarendon Press, 1962.

[7] N. Smelser, *Social Change in the Industrial Revolution*, London, Routledge and Kegan Paul, 1959.

[8] M. J. Farrell, 'Some Elementary Selection Processes in Economics', *Review of Economic Studies*, XXXVII, 1970, 305–19.

[9] J. Coleman, *Resources for Social Change*, New York, Wiley, 1971.

[10] G. Hernes, 'Structural Change in Social Processes', *American Journal of Sociology*, LXXXII, 3, 1976, 513–47.

[11] G. W. F. Hegel, *Hegel's Science of Logic*, London, George Allen and Unwin, 1969, vol. I, part 2, chapters 1 and 2.

[12] G. Hardin, 'The Cybernetics of Competition' in P. Shepard and D. McKinley, *The Subversive Science*, Boston, Houghton Mifflin, 1969, pp. 275–96.

[13] In 1791, the Le Chapelier law forbade workers to combine in defence of their 'so-called common interests'. In the United States, where the memory of the guilds did not have the same weight as in France, the first trade union was founded in 1792.

[14] T. Parsons, *The Evolution of Societies*, Englewood Cliffs and London, Prentice-Hall, 1962, chapter 2.

[15] D. Colas, *Le Léninisme*, Paris, Presses Universitaires de France, 1982.

[16] R. Brym, *Intellectuals and Politics*, London, George Allen and Unwin, 1980.

[17] A. Gerschenkron, *Economic Backwardness in Historical Perspective*, Cambridge, Mass., Harvard University Press, 1962, p. 44.

[18] In a private communication, Thom furthermore observes that contingency may sometimes be eliminated by an extension of the paradigm. Thus, if psychology were more advanced, we should be in a better position to explain different reactions to similar situations. But it is still true - and I think that is what Cournot meant - that in order to account for the simultaneous nature of certain events, we should have to proceed to a double infinite regress, which will always be impossible, whatever scientific progress there may be.

7 GIVING DISORDER ITS DUE

[1] See chapter 5.
[2] See chapter 4.
[3] See chapter 5.
[4] See chapters 2 and 6.
[5] See chapter 5.
[6] See H. Jamous, *Sociologie de la décision*, Paris, CNR, 1969.
[7] J. Elster, *Explaining Technical Change. A case-study in the Philosophy of Science*, Cambridge, Cambridge University Press, 1983.
[8] M. Didier and E. Malinvaud, 'La concentration de l'industrie s'est-elle accentuée depuis le début du siècle?', *Economie et statistique*, 2, June 1969, 3-10.
[9] M. Piore and S. Berger, *Dualism and Discontinuity in Industrial Societies*, Cambridge, Cambridge University Press, 1980.
[10] W. Stark, *The Fundamental Forms of Social Thought*, London, Routledge and Kegan Paul, 1962.
[11] It could be based on the model of P. Bénéton's study, *Histoire de mots. Culture et civilisation*, Paris, Presses de la Fondation Nationale des sciences politiques, 1975.
[12] J. Schumpeter, *History of Economic Analysis*, London, Oxford University Press, 1954, 1972, pp. 135 ff.
[13] Cf. R. Aron, *Introduction to the Philosophy of History: An Essay on the Limits of Historical Objectivity*, London, Weidenfeld and Nicholson, 1961.
[14] W. Sombart, *Der moderne Kapitalismus*, Leipzig, Duncker und Humblot, 1902-27, 3 volumes; *Die Juden und das Wirtschaftleben*, Leipzig, Duncker und Humblot, 1911.
[15] On this notion, see R. Boudon, 'Theories, theory and Theory', in *The Crisis in Sociology*, London, Macmillan, 1980, pp. 149-94.
[16] For a formal definition, see ibid., pp. 169-83.
[17] Two theories can of course be 'incommensurable' (Feyerabend) if the data set explained in one is not contained in the data set explained by the other.
[18] In his *The Mind and Society*, Pareto notes that research concerning 'origins' is both persistent and non-pertinent. Despite this, there is still active research on the 'origins' of the state.
[19] H. Hotelling, 'Stability in Competition', *The Economic Journal*, XXXIX, 1929, 41-57.
[20] This conclusion has nevertheless been reached, as A. Lancelot shows in his 'Partis politiques' in *Encyclopaedia universalis*, XII, 578-83.
[21] A. O. Hirschman, *Exit, Voice and Loyalty*, Cambridge, Mass., Harvard University Press, 1970, presenting this adaptation of Hotelling's model to the Nixon case, interprets his analysis as a refutation of Hotelling, which it clearly is not.
[22] It also needs to be pointed out that the ideological climate facilitated changes in the laws governing the organization of primaries and conventions, which produced a radicalization effect amongst the Democrats in particular. The effects of Kissinger's success in negotiations on Vietnam also need mention.

[23] M. Olson, *The Logic of Collective Action: Public Goods and the Theory of Involvements, Private Interest and Public Action*, Princeton, Princeton University Press, 1982, A. O. Hirschman interprets Olson's theory empirically and draws this very conclusion. This means that in order to account for the appearance of social movements, he is led to develop a rather shaky theory positing that such movements are partly endogenously determined by the dissatisfaction brought about by 'private' consumption.

[24] T. Parsons and N. Smelser, 'A Model of Institutional Change', in *Economy and Society*, Glencoe, The Free Press, 1956, pp. 255-73.

[25] See chapter 6.

[26] T. Parsons and N. Smelser, op. cit., p. 255. Differentiation is also merely one 'typical' process of change for Parsons. 'De-differentiation' is another.

[27] R. K. Merton, *Social Theory and Social Structure*, Glencoe, The Free Press, 1968, part 1, chapter 3.

[28] See in particular K. Popper, *The Poverty of Historicism*, London, Routledge and Kegan Paul, 1957.

[29] R. Chauvin, 'Sur le néo-darwinisme dans les sciences du comportement', *Année biologique*, XIX, 2, 1980, 203-16.

[30] 'Theories, theory and Theory'.

[31] J. Habermas, *Knowledge and Human Interests*, London, Heinemann, 1972.

[32] G. Lemaine and B. Matalon, 'La lutte pour la vie dans la cité scientifique', *Revue française de sociologie*, X, 2, 1969, 139-65.

[33] I. Lakatos, 'Falsification and the Methodology of Scientific Research Programs'.

[34] P. Feyerabend, *Against Method: Outline of an Anarchistic Theory of Knowledge*, London, NLB. 1975.

EPILOGUE

[1] On the distinctions between the different types of models of intelligibility, see R. Boudon, 'Theories, theory and Theory' in *The Crisis in Sociology*, London, Macmillan, 1980, pp. 149-94.

[2] *The Problems of the Philosophy of History* is presented in the third (1907) German edition as 'a critique of realism in history'.

[3] B. Hoselitz, 'Main Concepts in the Analysis of the Social Implications of Technical Change', in B. Hoselitz and W. Moore (eds) *Industrialization and Society*, Paris, UNESCO, 1963, pp. 11-31.

Index